Walking Gloucestershire with Ivor Gurney

# Walking Gloucestershire with Ivor Gurney

*Poetry & landscape explored through 20 circular walks*

ELEANOR RAWLING

*with maps & drawings by Roger Ellis*

LOGASTON PRESS

First published by Logaston Press, December 2023
The Holme, Church Road, Eardisley, Herefordshire HR3 6NJ
An imprint of Fircone Books Ltd.
www.logastonpress.co.uk

ISBN 978-1-910839-68-3

Designed and typeset by Richard Wheeler in 10.5 on 14 Minion.
Cover design by Richard Wheeler.

Printed and bound in Poland. www.lfbookservices.co.uk

Logaston Press is committed to a sustainable future for our business, our readers and our planet.
This book is made from FSC® certified and other controlled material.

British Library Catalogue in Publishing Data
A CIP catalogue record for this book is available from the British Library

# CONTENTS

# PREFACE

Cooper's Hill is a promontory on the Cotswold Edge in Gloucestershire, overlooking the Severn Vale. I grew up there, and Ivor Gurney, the Gloucestershire musician and poet (1890–1937), wrote about it in his poetry.

*Cooper's Hill – 'high June's Girl's air of untouched purity'*

The Hill has an air of majesty and isolation, and is surrounded by magnificent beech woods in which I roamed as a child. As a teenager, I revelled in the wildness and the opportunities for solitary walking and reflection, but it wasn't until I discovered Ivor Gurney's poetry in my early twenties that I experienced a sudden jolt of recognition. **Cotswold Ways**, **The High Hills** and later **Old Thought** and **That Centre of Old** were some of the first poems I read, in which my home area of the Cotswolds around Cooper's Hill and Cranham was presented in vivid sense impressions.

**That Centre of Old** (*extract*)
And Cooper's Hill showed plain almost as experience.
Soft winter mornings of kind innocence, high June's
Girl's air of untouched purity, and on Cooper's Hill
Or autumn Cranham with its boom of colour …
Not anyway does ever Cotswold's fail …

Gurney's pictures of the *soft winter mornings of kind innocence*, the autumn woodlands with their *boom of colour*, *high June* on Cooper's Hill and the belief that *not anyway does ever Cotswold's fail*, reveal Cooper's Hill as a place of escape and spiritual renewal, and they spoke directly to my own experience. *Yes I've been there. I know that place.* What drew me to this poet was the clarity and distinctiveness of his images of Gloucestershire, and his deep sense of belonging to this place that I knew in a similar way – through walking.

Most writers approach Gurney's poetry from the standpoint of his war experiences and his mental illness. For me, the overwhelming feature of his writing is his sense of knowing and belonging to this one place. **That Centre of Old** (see extract above), usually described as a war poem, is a good example. The remaining lines (Walk 12) refer to *gun-stammer – thud smack, belch of war* and to the *Somme muckage baths*. This is a frightened young man caught up in the First World War, *grateful for silence and body's grace* (still alive and uninjured when the guns stop). Gurney was conjuring up images of Cooper's Hill to save him from the noise and terror of war.

This is why I have written this book – to introduce readers and walkers to those Gloucestershire places that inspired and grounded Gurney's poetry. Ivor Gurney is one of Gloucester's famous sons, whose reputation as a poet and musician is steadily growing as his work becomes more accessible, especially through the work of the Ivor Gurney Society, the BBC4 TV programme in 2014 (*Ivor Gurney, the poet who loved the war*), the recent publication of *The Complete Poetical Works, Volume 1* (edited by Philip Lancaster and Tim Kendall, 2020) and a new biography (Kate Kennedy's *Dweller in Shadows, a Life of Ivor Gurney*, 2021). I will focus on his poetry, although his music undoubtedly also springs from his Gloucestershire roots. In my previous book, *Ivor Gurney's Gloucestershire* (2011) I introduced Gurney's Gloucestershire places; in this book, I follow his steps through the landscape, drawing on his poetry and letters in order to understand more about the entanglement of man and place. As I walked, I rediscovered my own connections with Gloucestershire, finding that the countryside yielded up more secrets and joys when I explored it from Gurney's perspective.

These walks will, I hope, enhance readers' enjoyment and understanding of Gurney, of Gloucestershire and of our own place in the world.

# ACKNOWLEDGEMENTS

This book draws on a huge variety of resources and sources, ranging from geological texts and poetry criticisms to photographs, maps and my own walking expeditions in the Gloucestershire countryside.

Special thanks are due to:

- My colleague, Roger Ellis, who has produced all the distinctive walk maps and beautiful illustrations which bring the walks alive. This project would not have succeeded without him.
- The Ivor Gurney Society for help and support – especially Ian Venables, Chair of the Society and of the Ivor Gurney Trust, and Philip Lancaster, Gurney scholar and joint editor of *The Complete Poetical Works*.
- My 'walk-checkers' who helped with several routes. Thanks for comments on gates, mud and poor signage, and perceptive thoughts about poems and landscape features. Michael Pugh, Caroline Johnson, Craig Blackwell, Sarah Blowen, Valerie Coffin Price, Philip Richardson, Nicholas Mann and Gillian Jeens.
- My family – John, Helen and Richard Rawling for their patience in hearing me 'go on' about Ivor Gurney and in accepting my disappearances off to walk Gloucestershire – and, very importantly, my dog Ceri, an enthusiastic sheepdog who loved all the walks.

Thanks are also due to the following for permission to use the items listed below:

- The Ivor Gurney Trust for items from the Ivor Gurney Collection including: 100 full or part poems (for details, see References & Sources, p. 269); many short extracts from letters and essays; also eight images: Ivor Gurney 1905, Ivor Gurney 1920, Florence Gurney 1915, David Gurney 1915, 19 Barton Street, the sailing boat, Dorothy, Ronald Gurney 1915 and Ivor with Aunt Marie's dog.

- Elaine Jackson, granddaughter of F.W. Harvey, for the use of poems by F.W. (Will) Harvey: an extract from **In Flanders** in Walk 5; the complete poem **To Ivor Gurney** in Walk 5; and an extract from the **Ballade of River Sailing** in Walk 7. Thanks also to the F.W. Harvey Society for their support and approval.
- Gloucestershire Archives for three historic photographs used in Walks 1 and 2: Barton Fair (Mop Fair), Eastgate Street 1882 (SR38/29157.7GS); Gloucester Cattle Market 1936 (SRprints/GL57.30GS); and Gloucester Docks *c*.1872 (GPS/154/93).
- Gloucester Cathedral for the use of a photograph of the first four panels of the Ivor Gurney stained glass window featured in Walk 1. Tom Denny, the artist and creator of these windows has also approved their use.
- Gloucester City Museum and Art Gallery for the reproduction of Charles March Gere's 1947 painting of Gloucester Cathedral, used in Walk 1 and on the front cover (GCM2655565 © Gloucester City Museums/ Bridgeman Images).
- Frances Frith Photographic Publishers for image 45590: Brimscombe, The Bourne from Besbury 1900 used in Walk 10 (© The Francis Frith Collection).
- Fineleaf Editions for diagrams from *Geology Explained in the Severn Vale and Cotswold* by W.J. Dreghorn (Fineleaf, 2005): Figure 28, Severn Terraces in Walk 3; Figure 26, Coalhouse Inn in Walk 17; and Figure 8, Wainlode Cliff in Walk 18.
- Historic England Archives for the aerial photograph of Cleeve Hill (AP 27646-030) used in Walk 15.
- Philip Halling, photographer, for the following photographs: St Peter's Church, Minsterworth; St Lawrence Church, Longney; St Mary's Church, Deerhurst; Odda's chapel, Deerhurst; St Giles Church, Maisemore; Belas Knap; The Banbury Stone and Sundial Farm, on Bredon Hill. (Photographs all on www.geograph.org.uk/of/phil+halling).
- R.K.R. (Kelsey) Thornton, Gurney scholar and a founder member of the Ivor Gurney Society, for the sketches of Ivor Gurney the soldier (Introduction) and Will Harvey (Walk 5).
- The illustration of Uley Bury in Walk 8 is from *The Ancient Entrenchments and Camps of Gloucestershire* by Edward J. Burrow (Ed. J. Burrow & Co. Ltd, 1919, p. 113). It has not been possible to trace the current copyright holder.

- An image of the Leckhampton kilns 1925 in Walk 14 is from *Old Leckhampton, Its Quarries, Railways, Riots and the Devil's Chimney* by D.E. Bick (Runpast Publishing, 1997). It has not been possible to trace the copyright holder. (The Friends of Leckhampton Hill have used the image on their website and are happy for its re-use: www.leckhamptonhill.org.uk/site-description/industrial-archaeology/).

### GLOUCESTERSHIRE WILDLIFE TRUST

A number of walks in this book visit Gloucestershire Wildlife Trust nature reserves, including Coaley Peak, Cooper's Hill, Crickley Hill and Ashleworth.

Gloucestershire Wildlife Trust's mission is a simple one – to value nature. Their ambition is to preserve, recreate and reconnect Gloucestershire's wild places. They want everyone in Gloucestershire to value, enjoy and share wildlife in the county, and for them to believe strongly that nature matters, not only in its own right, but for the huge benefits it brings to the people of Gloucestershire.

Five percent of Gloucestershire households are members of Gloucestershire Wildlife Trust, with over 500 active volunteers who help conserve wildlife, from practical work on one of the Trust's 60 nature reserves to helping with admin in the office.

To find out more about their work or to get involved: visit **www.gloucestershirewildlifetrust.co.uk**

*The Vale of Gloucester from Crickley Hill*

# INTRODUCTION

Minsterworth orchards, Cranham, Crickley and
Framilode reach. They do not merely mean intensely
to me; they are me.

*Letter, Ivor Gurney to Marion Scott, 6 October 1915*

THE GLOUCESTERSHIRE BOY – ABOUT IVOR GURNEY

Ivor Bertie Gurney was born in 1890 in Gloucester,
one of four children of David Gurney, a tailor, and
his wife, Florence. Ivor spent his childhood in that
city, fascinated by its history, roaming the streets and
riverside footpaths along the Severn, and exploring the
nearby hills and woodlands of the Cotswold Edge. He
grew not only to love Gloucestershire but also, as his
talents in music and poetry became apparent, to find it
essential to his well-being and creativity ('they do not
merely mean intensely to me; they are me'), returning
time and again throughout his life to walk the pathways
of Gloucestershire.

As a boy, Gurney sang in the choir of All Saint's
Church, Gloucester where his godfather, Alfred
Cheesman was the curate. Cheesman recognised his
musical talent and helped him gain a choral scholarship to
the King's School Gloucester and an apprenticeship with
Herbert Brewer, the organist at Gloucester Cathedral.
Here, he met his friend and fellow musician, Herbert
Howells. The poetry came later, stimulated particularly
by Gurney's friendship with F.W. (Will) Harvey, another
young Gloucestershire poet of the early twentieth century.

In 1911, Cheesman supported Gurney's application
for a place at the Royal College of Music, London, where
Gurney spent four formative years, with Charles Stanford
as his composition tutor. He also met Marion Scott, the
RCM registrar, who became a lifelong friend. A bout of
severe depression in 1913 resulted in Gurney convalescing
at the lock-keeper's house in Framilode and was probably
a forewarning of his fragile mental health.

*The young Ivor Gurney aged 15 (© Ivor Gurney Trust)*

The onset of the First World War changed Gurney's life irrevocably, as it did for many young men who joined up to serve their country. Gurney enlisted in February 1915 and served in the 5th Gloucester Reserve Battalion on the Western Front. He found that writing poetry was another way to cope with the traumas of war and to express his love for his homeland. As he himself explained much later, the war made him a poet:

**While I Write** (*extract*)
War told me truth, I have Severn's right of maker,
As of Cotswold: war told me: I was elect, I was born fit
To praise the three hundred feet depth of every acre
Between Tewkesbury and Stroudway, Side and Wales
 Gate

(K2004)

*The last four lines of* **While I Write** *from the original manuscript draft (© Ivor Gurney Trust)*

*Gurney the Soldier – a sketch by R.K.R. Thornton*
*(© Kelsey Thornton)*

The final line is significant here, as it defines Gurney's Gloucestershire: *Tewkesbury* (to the north) and *Stroudway* (to the south) are on the Severn; *Side* (Syde) is a village on the Cotswold plateau (to the east) and *Wales Gate* refers to the point where the land rises into the Forest of Dean near Huntley (to the west).

Wounded on the Somme in April 1917 and gassed near Ypres in September 1917, Gurney was eventually sent back to England, though not immediately to Gloucestershire. After several months in hospitals and convalescent homes, he was discharged by the army in October 1918, but without a full pension. He returned to Gloucester but found difficulty in settling back into civilian life, suffering from repeated bouts of mental instability, perhaps exacerbated by his war experiences though not necessarily caused by them.

In the immediate post-war period, Gurney struggled to find a role – he was no longer a soldier but neither was he an accepted musician or poet, despite his early promise. He made several attempts to find work in occupations as different as playing the organ in cinemas, working in a munitions factory, farm labouring and clerking in the local tax office. Between 1918 and 1922, he tried living with his family in Gloucester, experimented with living

*Ivor Gurney in 1920, at the age of 30 (© Ivor Gurney Trust)*

on his own in a cottage on Crickley Hill, and stayed for a while with an aunt at Longford on the outskirts of Gloucester. However, normal life seemed impossible, as eating disorders, depression and mental problems hindered his progress, though did not stop him writing music and poetry. Despite his problems, the period 1917–22 saw the publication of two books of poetry (*Severn and Somme* in 1917 and *War's Embers* in 1919), and the production of many more poems, some of which appeared in publications after Gurney's death and some of which are only now appearing from the archives. He also had some notable successes with his music, including the publication of the five pieces known as *the 'Elizas'* in 1920 and *Five Preludes for Piano* in 1921.

In 1922, after an incident in which Gurney apparently requested a gun and threatened suicide in his brother's house in Gloucester, Gurney was committed to Barnwood House mental asylum, and later that year moved to the City of London Mental Asylum at Dartford, Kent, far away from his native Gloucestershire.

Although he suffered with the instabilities and frustrations of what is now believed to be a bipolar condition, and he chafed under the restrictions of asylum life, Gurney did not stop writing music or poetry. There was an outpouring of poetry during the period 1922–26, supported by his friend and mentor Marion Scott who faithfully visited him in the asylum. After 1926, Gurney's creative output declined and his physical health was failing (he had problems with his digestion and with his teeth). In the 1930s Gurney's condition worsened and, given his restricted life and the delusions that he increasingly suffered, it is not surprising that he gave up writing both music and poetry.

Ironically, even as his faculties declined, Gurney was, at last, beginning to receive more recognition as a poet and musician. The Wigmore Hall had continued to feature his music in the 1920s, Marion Scott had arranged for a special edition of the RCM magazine *Music and Letters* to be focused on Ivor Gurney, and Oxford University Press was to publish 20 of his songs. However, by November 1937, Gurney weighed only seven stone and was found to be suffering from tuberculosis. 'It is too late', Gurney commented when the proofs of *Twenty Songs* were brought to him. He died on 26 December 1937, and only then was he returned to Gloucester. He was buried in Twigworth Church on 31 December, with the music for the service played by Herbert Howells, and with his friend and mentor Alfred Cheesman conducting the service.

**Culpeper** (*extract*)
So walking Gloucestershire, the child or boy learned
  his lessons,
But learned that high on Cooper's in June's scented
  silence,
Wild strawberries grew a host there, and by the
  rippling
Twyver, some fairy made scarlet unmatched cool
  bounties;
Who learned his music under the high sky dappling
The Gloucestershire ploughland with shadows – with
  colour dainties.

(GA)

Although known as a First World War poet, Ivor Gurney wrote vividly and movingly about his native Gloucestershire. Gloucestershire places served as his inspiration and identity when he was away from the area, both in London as a music scholar and in Belgium and France as a First World War soldier. What is most striking about Gurney's poetry is how few poems do *not* refer to Gloucestershire in some way. In the poem **Culpeper**, written in Dartford asylum in 1925, Gurney looks back to his childhood, walking the Gloucestershire countryside, to explain the debt he owes to his upbringing (*learned his lessons*) and the inspiration for his music and poetry. (Nicholas Culpeper is the seventeenth-century botanist, rambler and herbalist, whose work Gurney had read.)

Ivor Gurney wrote some 1,840 poems in all, of which more than 1,000 have never been published (although all will appear eventually in the forthcoming five volumes of the *Complete Poetical Works*). The poems selected for *Walking Gloucestershire with Ivor Gurney* (100 in all) have been taken from many sources – books published in Gurney's lifetime, collections of poetry published after his death and poetry that is still in the archives. They have been chosen to illustrate the landscapes or often the actual places encountered on each walk, and to reveal the full range of Gurney's style and engagement with place.

Gurney's poetry is often difficult to read, sometimes seeming disjointed in thought and structure. This is a feature which some readers see as a compelling way of accessing Gurney's tormented mental state or a sign of his breathless creativity, while others see it as an annoying result of Gurney's failure to perfect the final poem. I have tried to explain some of the difficult poems (for example

**Cotswold Slopes** in Walk 9; **The County's Bastion** in Walk 16), but have still used them where they are essential to relate to a place or an emotion.

Movement through the landscape was essential to Gurney's place experiences and his creativity – particularly, but not only, by walking. His childhood roaming along the riverside was soon followed by explorations of the Cotswold Edge by foot and on his bicycle, by youthful rambles with Will Harvey and Herbert Howells, by sailing experiences on the River Severn and, eventually, to his long and lonely walks on the scarp edge after he returned from Flanders in the 1918–22 period. Listen to his words in a whole range of poems – *Out in the morning for a speed of thought I went* (**Old Times**, Walk 10); *O up in height, O snatcht up, O quickly going, breathing was loving* (**Old Thought**, Walk 14); *my boat moves and I with her delighting* (**March**, Walk 6). His poems often seem not to be *about* the landscape per se, or even *an account* of moving through the landscape – but more like a dialogue between self and place, mind and body moving together through Gloucestershire.

When Gurney was away from Gloucestershire or denied the experience of walking, his poetry reveals a sense of loss. For example, in the 1918–22 period, even though Gurney was in Gloucestershire, his mental illness and depression were beginning to take him 'out of place' and so away from the sources of his creativity. In **The Bronze Sounding**, he talks of the vivid autumn beauty of the woods between Cranham and Birdlip (*a gong of colour*) but fears that his illness means *the body now no longer takes in distance as slow thought* – in other words, he is unable to walk and be inspired by the place.

After 1924, his poetry changed. Gurney's incarceration in the Dartford mental hospital meant the irrevocable loss of opportunities to walk in his known environment in the unrestricted way that he needed. The increasing debilitation and anguish of his untreated bipolar condition must be factored into this as well. Later poems represent distant memories not live events. Instead of the place speaking through Gurney, we begin to see Gurney's fears and anxieties of all kinds speaking through the place memories, as in the poem **The Coppice**, written in Dartford, in which Gurney is *in nine hell-depths, with such memories* (see Walk 13). I have included some of this darker poetry where it is essential in order to understand Ivor Gurney's connection to Gloucestershire.

To avoid providing lengthy details of provenance for each poem in the walk commentaries, I have merely given an indication of where the poem may be found, using a letter code (for example: K2004 or GA), and provided a full list of poems and current sources in the Appendix, including the date of writing, if known. The copyright of all Gurney poems and letters is held by the Ivor Gurney Trust, whose permission and support I acknowledge with thanks.

*The Miles go Sliding by* – about the walks
This book contains 20 walks covering the distinctive landscapes and places that feature in Gurney's walking. He was a keen observer of landscape, often mentioning in his poems the influence of geology and soils. An essay 'On Earth' (see *IGS Journal*, 2009) explains his belief that it is essential to dig deep down into the very soil ('our many textured, coloured, many grained earth stuff') and the rocks beneath in order to appreciate Gloucestershire's beauty. So, it is important to undertake Gurney's walks with a basic knowledge of the threefold nature of Gloucestershire's landscape divisions: the Forest of Dean, the Vale of Gloucester and the Cotswold Hills – and of their underlying geology.

At its simplest level, this landscape is affected by the age and hardness of the underlying rock. To the west, the high ground of the Welsh borderlands, May Hill and the Forest of Dean are formed of older, harder rock (Palaeozoic era: 540–250Ma) while the Malvern Hills that form a backdrop to Gurney's Gloucestershire are even older (Pre-Cambrian: older than 541Ma). The lower-lying Vale is underlain by younger rocks of the Mesozoic era (250–200Ma) consisting of Triassic sandstones and marls to the west of the Severn, and the Liassic clays (about 200–175Ma) to the east of the Severn. Meanwhile, the Cotswold Hills are formed of Jurassic limestones (175–145Ma) with the layers presenting a steep cliff edge ('scarp') to the Vale and a 'dip-slope' sloping south-eastward.

The 20 walks are located on the illustrated map of *Ivor Gurney's Gloucestershire,* originally produced for my previous book. The walks have been grouped into six areas, each comprising a Part, and this allows a broadly chronological approach to be taken to Gurney's life and creative work. Part One begins in Gloucester with Gurney's birthplace and childhood discoveries in the surrounding area (Walks 1–4); Part Two includes Gurney's youthful walking and sailing on the Severn to the south of Gloucester (Walks 5–7); Parts Three, Four and Five move from south to north, illuminating the high Cotswold Edge and the various pre-and post-war

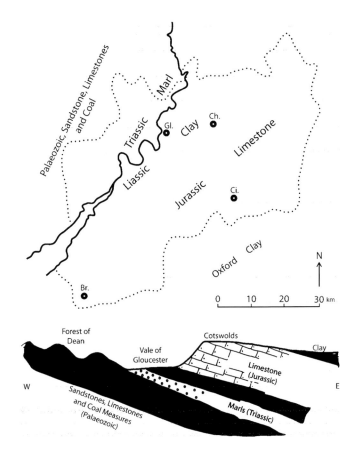

*Simplified landscape and geology of Gloucestershire*

explorations of these landscapes (Walks 8–16); while Part Six returns to the Severn north of Gloucester and presents Gurney's more solitary ramblings and reflections mainly after the war (Walks 17–20). The numbers correspond to the walks listed below and are indicated on the map.

Photographs will help evoke the sense of being in these places, so that even if the reader cannot undertake all the walks, he or she will be able to follow the routes from the comfort of a chair.

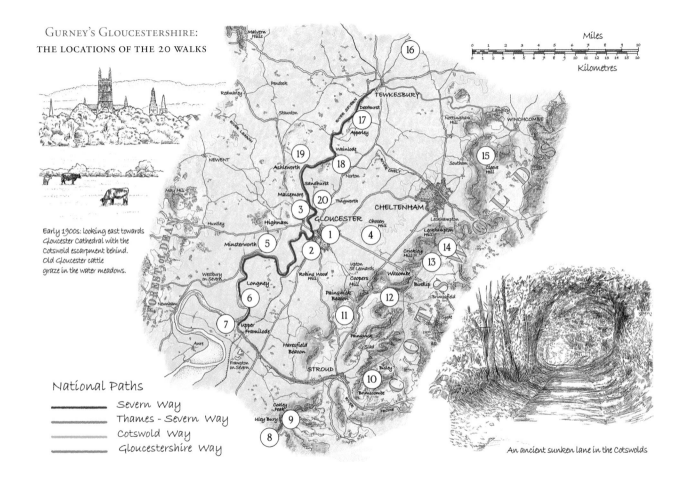

GURNEY'S GLOUCESTERSHIRE:
THE LOCATIONS OF THE 20 WALKS

Early 1900s: looking east towards
Gloucester Cathedral with the
Cotswold escarpment behind.
Old Gloucester cattle
graze in the water meadows.

Miles

Kilometres

National Paths

—— Severn Way
—— Thames - Severn Way
—— Cotswold Way
—— Gloucestershire Way

An ancient sunken lane in the Cotswolds

# THE WALKS

**IMPORTANT POINTS:**

- Each of the 20 walks is provided with a map of the route, a walk commentary, references to Gurney's life, appropriate extracts from poetry and letters, photographs and illustrative drawings.

- For each walk, the route instructions are numbered and in a sans serif type. Information or historical notes are boxed, and the poetry is in a heavier serif typeface.

- The maps are approximately accurate in scale and direction. However, they are for broad locational and illustrative purposes. It is not recommended that you rely solely on them for navigation in the field. The walk introductions list the relevant OS 1:50 000 and 1:25 000 maps to use when walking. Walk times are based on an average speed of 2 miles per hour, plus 30–40 minutes extra for inspecting historic sites and/ or reading poetry.

- Four existing well-established pathways – the Severn Way, the Thames and Severn Way, the Cotswold Way and the Gloucestershire Way – are marked on Ivor Gurney's Gloucestershire map, showing that these can form a 'thread' passing through 'Gurney country', on which to hang the more detailed and distinctive circular walks within each section. If desired, these existing trails could be used to link the 20 walks (135km in total) along a 127km 'Ivor Gurney Trail'.

- Most of the circular walks are attached directly to the national trails and can be walked by leaving from and returning to this route (16 walks). Four walks – Walk 3: Minsterworth; Walk 10: Brimscombe and Bisley; Walk 16: Far Bredon, and Walk 19: Above Ashleworth – are separated from the main route and will need to be visited individually, although they have been included because those places play a significant part in Gurney's life and creative development.

- Refreshment venues have not been given since the existence and opening times of cafés, restaurants and inns are subject to periodic change. Please check suitable refreshment places for yourself before you walk.

*Please note that, whilst every care has been taken to provide up-to-date information, neither the publisher nor the author can be held responsible for any injury to individuals and/ or damage to property as a result of following the walks described in this book.*

# Part One: The Old City

THE City of Gloucester is Gurney's 'Old City', located on the River Severn. In the early twentieth century, it was a relatively compact urban area surrounded by villages and small hills. Today the city's growth has engulfed many former settlements. The walks in this chapter introduce Ivor Gurney's place of birth, and locations connected with his schooling, musical development and his interest in the city's history. Maisemore and Chosen Hill are places where he walked directly from Gloucester with family and friends.

**The Poet Walking**

I saw people
Thronging the streets
Where the Eastway with the old
Roman Wall meets –
But none though of old
Gloucester blood brought,

Loved so the city
As I – the poet unthought.
And I exulted there
To think that but one
Of all that City
Had pride or equity
Enough for the marvelling
At street and stone,
Or the age of Briton,
Dane, Roman, Elizabethan –
One grateful one – true child
Of that dear city – one worthy one.

K2004

*Gloucester City from Robinswood Hill, with the cathedral visible in the centre of the image*

# Gloucester: the Old City

**The Old City** (*extract*)
Who says 'Gloucester' sees a tall
Fair fashioned shape of stone arise,
That changes with the changing skies
From joy to gloom funereal

(K2004)

Ivor Gurney was born in 1890 in Queen Street next to the former East Gate of Roman Gloucester. From his infancy, he was steeped in the historic atmosphere – the Romans, the city gates, the Cross, the market still taking place in the streets since medieval times and, a short walk away, the cathedral. He was fascinated by Gloucester's history, the layers of life lain one on top of the other: *She is a city still and the centuries drape her yet; / there is something in the air or light cannot or will not forget / the past ages of her, and the toil which made her.* (**Time to Come**, K2004).

His poems make continual reference to the city's historic periods (Romans, Normans, Plantagenets, Elizabethans), personalities (William Rufus, Abbot Serlo, Duke Humphrey) and buildings (cathedral, churches, worker's houses). He believed that he was destined to be Gloucester's chronicler – or, as he explained it, *true child of that dear city – one worthy one* chosen to *marvel at street and stone* (**The Poet Walking**). Of particular interest is Gloucester Cathedral, or St Peters Abbey as Gurney called it – the *tall fair fashioned shape of stone.* As a choir boy and later an articled pupil to the cathedral organist, Gurney learned to love and respect the building – its spires, its architecture, its music, its spiritual calm and the way it dominated the countryside around it.

Walk 1 will take in some of the sights and experiences of Gurney's 'Old City', including the streets of his childhood, the original cattle market site, the King's School (to which Gurney won a scholarship in 1900), the cathedral, Southgate Street, and the many churches and historic buildings that crowd into the central area. There is a short extension walk to take in Worcester Street where Ivor Gurney's brother, Ronald, lived and with whom he was staying when eventually committed to Barnwood asylum.

Gloucester was the emotional and creative heart of Gurney's Gloucestershire, a place from which he longed to escape to the countryside but to which he always returned. The walk begins and ends at the former Queen Street, next to the viewing chamber for the old East Gate.

**The Old City** (*extract*)
Who says 'Gloucester' sees a tall
Fair fashioned shape of stone arise,
That changes with the changing skies
From joy to gloom funereal,
Then quick again to joy; and sees
Those four most ancient ways come in
To mix their folk and dust and din
With the keen scent of the sea-breeze.
Here Rome held sway for centuries;
Here Tom Jones slept,
Here Rufus kept
His court, and here was Domesday born,
Here Hooper, Bishop, burned in scorn
While Mary watched his agonies.

Time out of mind these things were dreams,
Mere tales, not touching the quick sense,

Yet walking Gloucester history seems
A living thing and an intense.
For here and now I see the strength
In passing faces, that held at bay
Proud Rupert in an arrogant day
Till Essex' train-bands came at length,
And King's power passed like mist away.
Courage and wisdom that made good
Each tiny freedom, and withstood
The cunning or the strength of great
Unscrupulous Lords; and here, elate,
The spirit that sprang to height again
When Philip would conquer the wide Main
And England, and her tigerish queen.

Here countenances of antique grace
And beautiful smiling comedy-look
That Shakespeare saw in his own place
And loved and fashioned into a book.
Beauty of sweet blood generations
The strength of nations
Hear the passion-list of a fervent lover:
The view from Over,
Westgate street at night, great light, deep shadows,

The Severn meadows,
The surprising, the enormous Severn Plain
So wide, so fair
From Crickley seen or Cooper's, my dear lane
That holds all lane delightfulness there
(O Maisemore's darling way!)
Framilode, Frampton, Dymock, Minsterworth . . .
You are the flower of villages in all earth!

(K2004)

*Gloucester Cathedral from the south*

## Gloucester

The earliest settlement at Gloucester was the Iron Age 'Caer Glow' (favoured place) near to present-day Longford. In Roman times (late AD 40s), the military fort was established at present-day Kingsholm at a strategic Severn crossing; however, the main Roman settlement of Glevum soon moved south-west. After AD 96–98, it became one of only four *colonia* or centres of Roman civilization in Britain and grew into a fine Roman town, boasting baths, walls and gateways (near one of which Ivor Gurney was born), a forum, a basilica and many large houses (*here Rome held sway*).

After the Roman withdrawal in the fourth century, Gloucester's fortunes and its buildings declined. The Anglo-Saxons re-settled the town in the sixth century and it prospered because of its location on the Severn. The first monastery church dedicated to St Peter was built in wood (679/ 681) and Gloucester castle was established sometime after 1066. William the Conqueror ('Rufus') held a great Court in

Gloucester in 1085 when he commissioned the Domesday Book (*here Domesday was born*), and the wooden St Peter's Abbey was replaced with a grand structure using local stone (see Walk 12) in 1089. Many more churches and monastic houses appeared alongside the densely-populated alleyways of the city.

In 1541, Henry VIII granted cathedral status to the abbey (*the tall fair fashioned shape of stone*), so saving it from destruction, and Gloucester flourished under Elizabeth I (*tigerish queen*). In the seventeenth century, Gloucester's role as a market town ensured continued growth, though its role on the Parliamentarian side in the Civil War resulted in a Royalist siege (1643) and large areas of the city were damaged in the fighting and in subsequent destruction by the Royalist victors. Gurney applauded the Parliamentarian side, convinced that he saw signs of Gloucester's strong spirit in present-day faces – *in passing faces, that held at bay / Proud Rupert in an arrogant day.*

In the eighteenth and nineteenth centuries, commercial growth focused on the river and roads, and was boosted by the Gloucester–Sharpness canal (see Walk 2) which opened in 1827, and the coming of the railway in the 1840s. Industries like flax-making, shipbuilding, pin-making and bell-founding flourished and the city expanded across adjacent villages such as Maisemore (see Walk 3), Tuffley, Quedgeley and Longford (see Walk 20) where Gurney's grandparents, aunts and uncles lived and worked. During this period Gloucester was being refashioned in brick and stone. It lost its High Cross at the junction of the four main roads to make way for traffic, but some grand new buildings were constructed, such as the Custom House in 1845, with its classical façade, built to cope with the foreign dock trade (see Walk 2).

In the twentieth century, economic decline before the war and unsympathetic redevelopment during the 1960s and 1970s left the city visually scarred and trailing in popularity behind its more 'upmarket' neighbour, Cheltenham. New developments are in progress which will change the city even more, but it is still possible to trace the bones of Gurney's *old city* and to be surprised by historic vistas and a sense of Gloucester's busy past.

# GLOUCESTER; OLD CITY

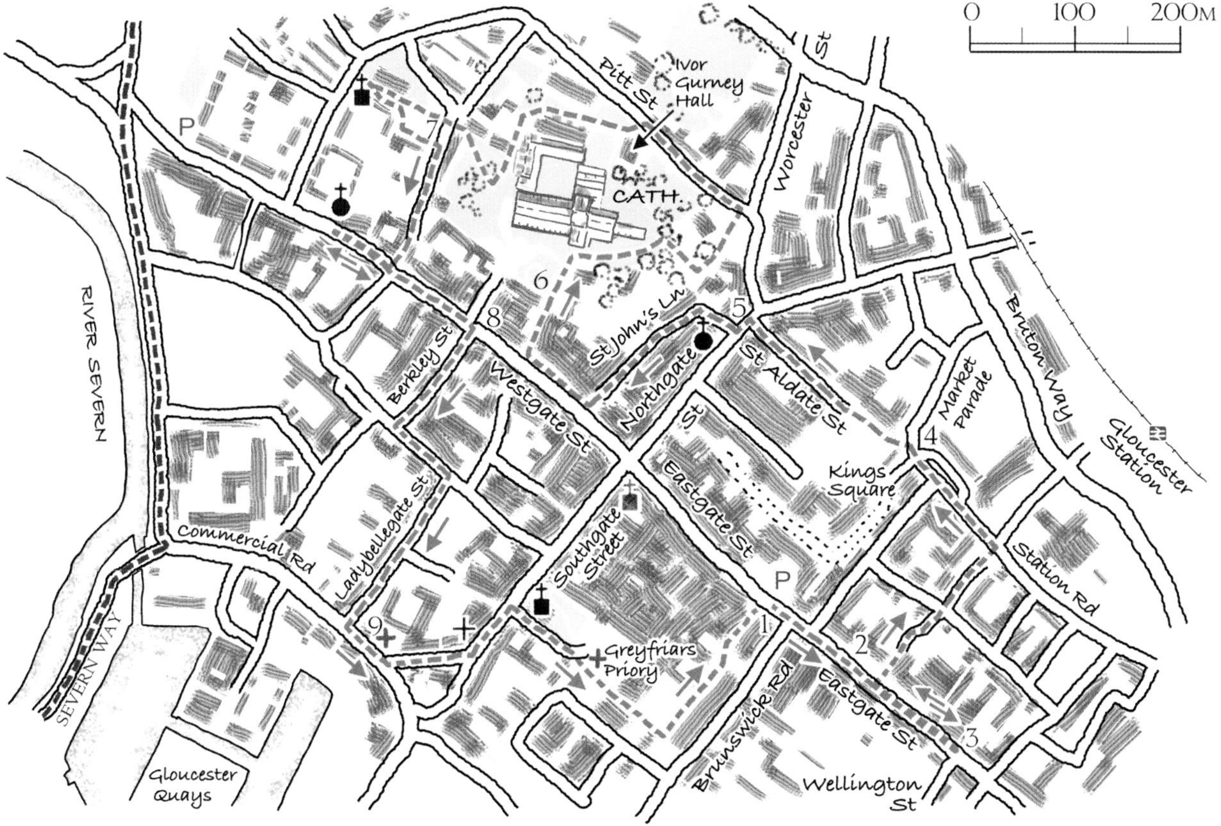

SCALE

0    100    200M

RIVER SEVERN

SEVERN WAY

P

Pitt St

Ivor Gurney Hall

Worcester St

7

CATH.

6

8

St John's Ln

5

Berkley St

Westgate St

Northgate St

St Aldate St

Market Parade

Briton Way

Gloucester Station

Station Rd

4

Kings Square

P

Eastgate St

Commercial Rd

Ladybellegate St

Southgate Street

Greyfriars Priory

1

2

9

Brunswick Rd

Eastgate St

3

Gloucester Quays

Wellington St

## Route Details

DISTANCE/ TIME:

3.2km (1.9 miles)/ 1.5–2 hours (depending on cathedral visit).

MAPS:

OS Explorer 179, 1:25 000, Gloucester, Cheltenham & Stroud
OS Landranger 162, 1:50 000, Gloucester & Forest of Dean

START AND PARKING:

Start at the viewing chamber for the old East Gate of
Gloucester, outside Boots store in Eastgate Street (SO
832184; GL1 1PU). Parking includes King's Walk multistorey,
Gloucester Quays parking, and lower Westgate Street.

## THE WALK

① The walk starts by a commemorative plaque dedicated to
'Ivor Gurney, Composer and Poet of Severn and Somme' on
a pillar outside 'Boots'. In 1890, Gurney's father, mother and
older sister, Winifred, lived in Queen Street (now a narrow
alleyway, Queen's Walk) and Ivor was born in this small

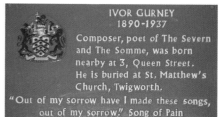

*Ivor Gurney
memorial plaque,
Eastgate Street*

The **Eastgate** viewing chamber is open for visits. The
original Roman gate was part of a fortress built of
wood (AD 68) but subsequently it was extended and
rebuilt. The display here shows one of two towers
that date from c.1230 and a B-shaped gateway. There
was evidently a moat, crossed by a drawbridge, and
a horsepool built c.1550 to wash horses and swell
timber. The tower served at various times as prison,
school and a house. Across Eastgate Street in the
King's Walk Shopping Centre, further remains of the
Roman city wall can be seen at the King's Bastion.
(see the Museum of Gloucester website for more
information: www.museumofgloucester.co.uk/)

*Eastgate Street: the Mop Fair in the late nineteenth century*
*(© Gloucestershire Archives)*

*Number 19, Barton Street*
*(© Ivor Gurney Trust)*

house built directly over the Roman wall. Through the glass floor next to the plaque, a section of the city's medieval walls and the city's Roman East Gate are revealed.

• Look left up Eastgate Street. In the late nineteenth century, this was a busy thoroughfare, full of shops, stalls and trams. Once a year, a street fair caused much bustle and excitement, particularly for children.

• Walk to the right to a place that no longer exists: No. 19 Barton Street. In 1890, the road beyond the Roman wall was Barton Street (now renamed Eastgate Street as far as Bruton Way), and when Ivor was about three years old the family moved here to a bigger premises for his father's tailoring business. Pause outside a modern apartment building with a red post-box outside and you are looking at the site of No. 19.

② No. 19 was a gloomy terraced house with double-fronted shop windows and the ground floor given over to tailoring, apart from a small scullery at the back. Upstairs was one larger room and three small ones including an attic. A brother (Ronald b.1894) and another sister (Dorothy b.1900) were born here, so it was a crowded household.

*Gurney's father (David) and mother (Florence) standing outside*
*No. 19 Barton Street (© Ivor Gurney Trust)*

• Further down the road was All Saints Church (now an Asian cultural centre). Here Ivor's father and mother were married and later, at Ivor's christening, the young curate Alfred Cheesman became his godfather. Cheesman became a lifelong friend and mentor. He persuaded the family to purchase a piano for Ivor in 1896, which had to be hauled in through a window.

• Outside his door, looking east, the young Gurney could see the Cotswold Edge (you might catch a glimpse on a clear day) and he started to roam as a very young boy, up Barton Street towards Portway, the Cranham woods, or the town of Painswick. We know that he often used to leave home *to walk at night on Cotswold* (see Walk 11).

• Walk down to the top of Wellington Street.

③ In the late nineteenth and early twentieth centuries, Wellington Street was part of a genteel area, with the park and Gloucester Spa pump rooms. Number 54 Wellington Street was the home of the Misses Hunt, two sisters who originally came from South Africa where they had been teachers, and who now lived in a spacious house. They were well-educated, musical and sympathetic to the young Gurney's talent, making available to him books, music and the use of their fine Bechstein piano. As a boy, Gurney spent hours here playing music, reading and talking. The poem **First Violets** records the debt he felt he owed, particularly to Margaret Hunt, the younger of the sisters. His creativity was already being awakened by his outdoor walking.

**The First Violets** (*extract*)
She had such love and after my music sent
Me out to woodlands, and to wander by meadow or
    bent
Lanes of Severn – I got them all in my music –
I would wander my soul full of air and return to her
    quick.

Wandering was 4 miles an hour – and caressing stray
    brambles –
With love of earth and God – and sacred friendliest
    grumbles
At God, Who would not grant such great work as to
    Beethoven came –
That felt not such air – nor had such love of clear
    flame.

(BP)

• Walk back up Eastgate Street and turn right down an alleyway next to the bus stop, to follow the route that young Ivor would have taken to the National School, London Road. Cross Russell Street and continue down Whitfield Street to join Market Parade. Ahead is Station Road. In 1900, the station land was on the right (now offices) and on the left was the cattle market (now Gloucester Transport Hub). Gurney walked past it on his way to his school and later wrote about market day in a poem. He mentions the bookstalls that used to set up at the Cross (at one of which he purchased Walt Whitman's *Leaves of Grass*).

*Gloucester Cattle market in 1936 (© Gloucester Archives)*

**Saturday's Comings**

The horses of the day plunge and are restrained,
Dawn broadens to quarter height, and the meadow
  mists
Drift like gauze veilings, the roadway ingrained
With traffic marks shows so, Saturday enters the lists

To show like a panorama – cattle brought in
And dapper farmers bargaining in white spats,
Cross crowded, bookstalls past paupers resisting
And as ever the Cathedral masterfully blessing the
  flats.

(K2004)

• Walk along Market Parade and then past the multistorey car park entrance –

④ – into King's Square

• What would Gurney have made of this? His poem **Time to Come** regrets new building in Gloucester, fearing the gentrification, the *red-brick* and the tidy middle class *smoothing out* of character.

**King's Square**, as Darrell Kirby (*Story of Gloucester*, 2007) writes, 'is probably the most controversial area in Gloucester', a legacy of various attempts at redevelopment. In nineteenth-century Gloucester, this area included some of the worst housing in the city, but it was the 1930s before 'slum redevelopment' was started. Progress was halted by the war, leaving the area first as a big car park and then as a bus station until the Jellicoe plans of 1960s resulted in the brutal brick and concrete buildings of 1974 onwards. By the 1990s, the square was run-down and unpopular, resulting in much discussion over what should happen. Work has started (2021) on a major development of the 'King's Quarter' as it will now be known. Plans include bars, restaurants, a digital hub, office space and apartments with views across to the cathedral.

Read this poem before walking across the square and along St Aldate's Street. The cathedral tower and the spire of St John's Church can be seen over to the left, behind buildings.

**Time to Come** (*extract*)

They will walk there, the sons of our great grandsons and
Will know no reason for the old love of the land.
There will be no tiny bent-browed houses in the
Twilight to watch, nor small shops of multi-
    miscellany.
The respectable and red-brick will rule all,
With green paint railings outside the front door wall,
And children will not play skip games in the gutter,
Nor dust fly furious in hot valour of footer;
Queerness and untidiness will be smoothed out
As with any steamroller tactful, and there'll be no
    doubt
About the dustbins or the colour of curtains,
No talking at the doors, no ten o'clock flirtings,
And Nicholas will look as strange as any
Goddess ungarmented in that staid company,
With lovely attitude of fixed grace
But naked and embarrassed in that red-brick place.

(K2004)

⑤ At the junction of St Aldates and Northgate, turn left to find the main route via St John's Lane, or turn right to visit the home of Ronald Gurney.

---

**Extension walk – Worcester Street and Ronald Gurney**

1. The diversion to Ronald's house will add an extra half-mile to your walk. Start at Point 5 of the main route, which becomes Point 1 of this walk. Walk down Northgate Street until you reach the left turn into Worcester Street and make your way along it under the railway bridge until you are passing some terraced houses on your right.

2. Number 52 is where Gurney's younger brother, Ronald, lived from about 1921. The relationship between Ivor and his younger brother Ronald was a difficult one. From early childhood, Ronald always had to take second place to his older, more talented brother. Ivor was the one who got the scholarship to King's School, who was asked to play at Three Choirs Festival when he was only 13, who was taken on as an articled pupil at the cathedral and eventually took up a scholarship at the Royal College of Music in London.

# WORCESTER STREET
# & RONALD GURNEY

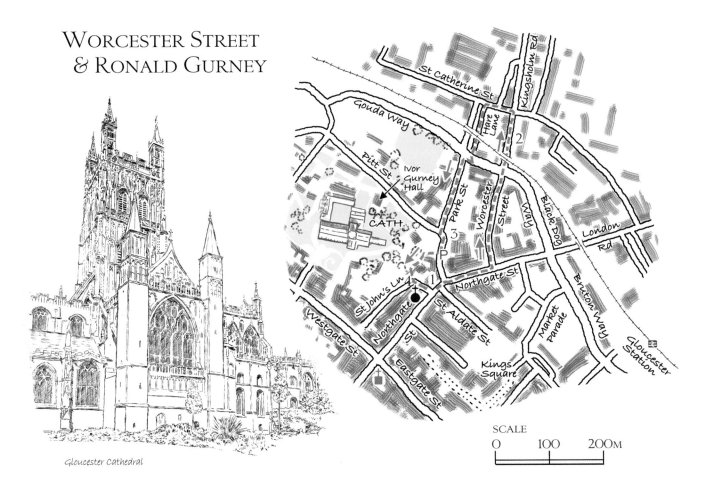

Gloucester Cathedral

SCALE

0    100    200M

Ronald's own ambitions, as he saw it, were put second and he was the one who had to help his father in the tailoring business while Gurney moved in musical and eventually literary circles. Ronald resented this and later, when Gurney began to suffer nervous and mental problems, blamed it on his brother's eccentric and wayward personality and refusal to 'buckle down to real work'.

The climax of all this, and one of the most decisive moments in Gurney's life, occurred at Ronald's house in 1922. After losing one of the many jobs that people had tried to find for him (in this case, at the tax office in Gloucester), Gurney turned up unannounced to stay with his brother. Ronald was newly married and had just settled in a job after wartime service. The last thing he needed was his unstable brother. Apparently, Ivor asked for a gun at one point and announced that he wanted to kill himself, although whether this was a serious statement or a cry for help is not clear. Ronald called the police and Gurney was taken away to Barnwood House mental hospital, and after a few months relocated to Dartford in Kent. This began his long stay (15 years) in an asylum far from his beloved Gloucestershire.

*No. 52 Worcester Street and Ronald Gurney* c.1915 (© *IG Trust*)

• From Number 52, cross the road and take St Catherine's Street opposite. Walk past a café on your left, the Dean's Walk Inn on your right and Hare Lane South car park. Follow Hare Lane back across the inner ring road and along Park Street, to the Pitt Street junction and the back entrance to the King's School.

3. Shortly after the junction, join the path to the cathedral and look for a small alleyway into St John's Lane (4) where you can resume the Gloucester walk.

⑤ (continued) For the main route, join St John's Lane, which is located on an ancient thoroughfare (*Via Sacra*) running just inside the original North Gate of the Roman city. The medieval church of St John, which you see to your left, was structurally unsound by the eighteenth century and a Georgian replacement church was built, leaving only the original medieval tower. More recently, St John's has become a Methodist church.

• As you walk along the lane, notice a solicitor's office on the right. Here Gurney's close friend Will Harvey was apprenticed to Treasures Solicitors after the war. Harvey and Gurney were close friends in the 1908–14 period, walking the riverside together and sharing their love of music and poetry (see Minsterworth, Walk 5). After the war, Will would be working in his office while Gurney was at the cathedral singing or organ-playing, so they often met at lunchtime or after work and, if possible, climbed one of the small hills – Robinswood Hill or Chosen Hill (see Walk 4).

• Walk on down St John's Lane, past the former offices of the *Citizen* newspaper, which merged with *The Gloucester Journal* (for which Gurney wrote a poem in 1922: **On a Two Hundredth Birthday**). On reaching Westgate Street, look left to notice the lines marking where the medieval church of St Mary de Grace once stood. Walk down Westgate Street to the right. Turn right into the little alleyway past the Beatrix Potter shop with its 'Tailor of Gloucester' connections, and under the archway. The cathedral appears magnificently before you.

⑥ The route takes you around to the right of the cathedral, past the Ivor Gurney Hall, back into College Green and then through another archway to Bishop Hooper's monument (Point 7). However, first walk around the precinct, observe the shape and form of the building and visit the interior of the cathedral, a building so significant in Gurney's life.

• After visiting the cathedral, rejoin the route circling the cathedral anticlockwise, to walk alongside a wall and Pitt Street. A gateway in the wall reveals the Ivor Gurney Hall across the tarmac yard. This is a former school room of King's School, one of the rooms in which Gurney studied as a pupil from 1900 to 1906, now creatively renovated as a centre for arts and cultural activities, including meetings of the Ivor Gurney Society.

## Gloucester Cathedral and Ivor Gurney

Gloucester Cathedral is generally acknowledged to be one of the finest cathedrals in England. The original St Peter's Abbey, built of wood, was founded in 681 by Osric, ruler of the Saxon *Hwicce* tribe. Over the centuries, the Abbey's fortunes rose and fell. It was rebuilt and extended in the good times and left to stagnate in the bad times. Notable periods of growth occurred in the eleventh century under the patronage of the Norman Abbot, Serlo, and in the fourteenth century when a major reconstruction followed the burial in the abbey church of the murdered King Edward II. Despite the dissolution of St Peter's Abbey by Henry VIII, the abbey church was made a cathedral in 1541 and prospered to become one of England's finest cathedrals during the seventeenth and eighteenth centuries. New developments took place in Victorian times, including the creation of a Bishop's throne, improvements to the presbytery and choir, and a substantial amount of new glass was installed. By the early twentieth century, the cathedral was the elegant building that Gurney knew, bearing within it the signs of all these eras of growth.

Gloucester Cathedral meant a great deal to Ivor Gurney. In 1900, aged 10, he won a place in the cathedral choir and an associated music scholarship to the King's School. For the next six years, his life revolved round the cathedral and the King's School, where singing and music took precedence over academic learning for the choristers. In 1906, he became an articled pupil of Herbert Brewer, the organist at the cathedral, learning musical appreciation, composition, organ-playing and singing. The cathedral has a commemorative plaque dedicated to Ivor Gurney, describing him as 'composer and poet' and 'chorister of this cathedral church.'

Gurney grew to love the building – the predominantly Norman nave with its massive Norman columns, the fine Perpendicular architecture of the east end with its delicate vaulting, the Lady Chapel, the huge east window and the medieval cloisters. Later he recognised how much his sense of form in poetry and music was influenced by the ecclesiastical architecture all around him. One example is his use of *squaring* or *square-making*, terms which derive from the idea of craftmanship displayed by the builders of the cathedral and churches, but which Gurney thought also reflected the kind of mastery and attention to detail required by a musician and poet, such as himself. In **Compensations** he explains the sequence of creativity: *Spring larch should set the body shaking / In masterless pleasure,* [the inspiration] */ But virtue lies in a square-making* [the craftsmanship] (K2004).

A fragment of poem in one of his notebooks explains that

the squareness of west Gloucester pleases me.
The spires and square places and the supremacy
Peter's Place has above that white-looked stretch,
The river meadows …

(GA)

*Gloucester Cathedral: the choir*

Only five short poems by Gurney are directly about the cathedral. One of these, **The Abbey**, appears in Walk 12. There are possibly more in the archives. However, the shape of the cathedral on the skyline and its role as a symbol of British history and identity appear many times in phrases such as *fair fashioned shape of stone, St Peter's, the abbey, the tower.*

**Ship Over Meadows** (*extract*)
Like any ship over green peaceful seas
But Mightier, more full of peace the Abbey stands.
Segovia they say lifts up ceremonial hands.
This rules the plain, and guards a deeper peace
Than is known on the main.
Whether the centuries shall close that out
With factory chimneys or high railway walls
None knows, but meanwhile the quaker quivers its veils
And the moondaisy boasts, and its pretences found out.

(GA)

*'Gloucester
Cathedral
from the
Meadows' by
Charles March
Gere, 1947
(© The Estate
of Charles
March Gere/
Gloucester
City Museums/
Bridgeman
Images)*

The image of the cathedral as a *ship* in its *sea* of meadows is perfect, as anyone who has glimpsed the cathedral when driving in from the west will know, although the twentieth century did its best to close in the view with railway lines and electricity pylons, as Gurney feared.

Before leaving the cathedral, find the Ivor Gurney stained glass window panels, sited in a chantry on the north side of the Lady Chapel and dedicated in 2014. Tom Denny, the creator, has used eight panels to reflect aspects of Gurney's life and art, and each echoes one or more of Gurney's poems.

Most of the window panels feature local landmarks mentioned in Gurney's poems, such as May Hill in panel 1, the Severn Valley orchards in panel 2 (Walk 6) and the pines above Brimscombe in panel 3 (Walk 10). In panel 4, a man gazes plaintively from behind a hedge at the leafless willows lining the Severn in winter. This could be Gabb Lane at Appleford (Walk 17).

*Ivor Gurney stained glass window by Tom Denny, panels 1–4*

**Dayboys and Choristers** remembers Gurney's school days and was published in *War's Embers* (1919). The jauntiness and the repeated chorus contrast with the more sinister message that many King's School boys would never return.

> **Dayboys and Choristers** (*extract*)
> So here's to the room where the dark beams cross over
> And here's to the cupboard where hides the cane;
> The paddock and fives court, great chestnut, tall tower –
> When Fritz stops his fooling we'll see them again.
>
> (S&S/ WE)

• It is worth a look inside the Hall to see the formerly *dark beams* of the roof, now pastel shades.

• Follow the pathway past Church House, through an archway, past the Monk's Kitchen café entrance and turn right to reach St Mary's Gate.

⑦ Go through St Mary's Gate. and you are confronted with the monument that remembers John Hooper, Bishop of Gloucester in the sixteenth century, who was burnt here in 1555 for his Protestant faith in the time of Queen Mary. As

*The Ivor Gurney Hall, former King's schoolroom, where Gurney studied, with the cathedral beyond*

Gurney describes it in his poem **The Old City** – *Here Hooper, Bishop, burned in scorn / While Mary watched his agonies.* Her representatives watched the event from the room in the archway opposite.

*Memorial to
Bishop Hooper*

de Lode – 'lode' means watercourse – and now beneath the Dukeries flats). As the river silted up and the channel moved west, a new Westgate Bridge was built in 1154–89, with five arches and eventually, in Henry VIII's time, a tower at one end and a gate. By the nineteenth century, work on this bridge and on the causeway across Alney Island was a continuing expense to the city, and after 1806 Westgate became a toll bridge. In 1941, it was replaced by a steel bailey bridge and that was replaced in the early 1970s by a pair of steel and concrete structures as part of a new western approach road. Finally, the present-day separated dual carriageway bridge was built in 1999–2000.

Gurney's poem **The Bridge**, written in the asylum in 1926, was one of the last poems he wrote, and probably refers to the twelfth-century bridge, given its references to Duke Humphrey of Gloucester, who is likely to have been known to Gurney as a soldier and literary patron. The sentiment in this poem is one of sadness because the city's history (ceremonies, buildings, people) – and, one suspects, the poet himself – are being forgotten. The images of *dirty water*, *crampt borders* and the Severn as *the haggard Half-Lady* project Gurney's personal and creative despair.

• Behind the monument is St Mary de Lode Church, reputed to be built on the site of one of the first Christian churches in Britain and one of the *Maries* mentioned in Gurney's poem, **Blessings**. If the church is open, you can see a stained glass window commemorating Ivor Gurney. Walk along St Mary's Street towards Westgate Street.

• Further down Westgate is the site of the original Westgate Bridge called Foreigner's Bridge which crossed the old eastern arm of the Severn (behind St Nicholas and St Mary

**The Bridge**
Ceremony that the boys loved is no more
About those white walls fallen –
Nor will any
At All Hallows' Even cry out Humphrey's ensigns.

At the gate none will praise the well-wrought
Heraldry of the long bridge sun-silver all-honour –
A dirty water drifts between crampt
Borders, lies and goes past the shadow.

In far ravines and on heights love delights in
The trees will pity the haggard Half-Lady
Of crystal-sprung Severn,
The flowers beneath accuse angels betraying.

(K2004)

• Walk back up Westgate Street.

⑧ Turn off into Berkeley Street, then left into Longsmith Road and right into Ladybellegate Street. Ladybellegate House was the birthplace of Robert Raikes, founder of the Sunday School movement. Notice the remains of Blackfriars Priory, situated between Ladybellegate Street, Southgate Street and Commercial Road. This was a Dominican friary, founded 1239, now owned by English Heritage and accessible for guided visits. (See www.english-heritage.org.uk).

⑨ Arrive at Commercial Road which slopes down to the right to the River Severn. Across the road is the entrance to the old Gloucester Docks, now redeveloped with shops, cafés and museums (see Walk 2).

• Follow Commercial Road round to the left to join Southgate Street and walk up as far as Greyfriars Lane. Turn into the lane. On the left is St Mary de Crypt Church, now redundant as a church but used as a cultural centre. The original Tudor Crypt School room (1539) lies behind it. A little further on are the remains of Greyfriars, a Franciscan Monastery (1231) established on land granted by Lord Berkeley, who rebuilt and improved the monastery in 1518, 20 years before its dissolution by Henry VIII. Only the remains of the nave and north aisle exist, and these come as a surprise to walkers making their way through the many redevelopment sites.

• Eventually a left turn takes you into Queens Walk, on the line of the Roman wall. Follow this along to return to Gurney's birthplace and the end of the walk.

# Gloucester Docks and Llanthony Priory

**Down Commercial Road** (*extract*)
But tops'le spars against the blue made fairyland for me;
The snorting tug made surges like the huge Atlantic
 swell.
And Gloucester she's famous in story.

(S&S/ WE)

Ivor Gurney was fascinated by the River Severn, even from an early age. His parents often took him down to the river and across Westgate Bridge to walk the riverside paths to Maisemore, where the children's paternal grandmother lived (see Walk 3). In the poem **Down Commercial Road** his fascination with the docks and the boats is very apparent. Gurney revelled in the busy activity of the dock area and the many ships that could be seen unloading and docking there. As a boy he sailed on the Severn with Will Harvey (see Walks 5, 6 and 7) and, according to a late asylum poem entitled **Dream**, even considered buying a boat in London so that he could sail on the Thames while residing there as a music student:

**Dream** (*extract*)
There had been boat sailing on Severn river,
And when London was reached, it seemed most easy
Of right – to look for such joy as sails quiver
And pull the rudder hard round, against the breezy
Wind out of Essex, or off Kentish shores.

(K2004)

In the post-war period, when Gurney found it difficult to find employment, he walked down to Newport in the hope of being taken on as a sailor on one of the cargo boats, as his sister Dorothy explained to Marion Scott in a letter of October 1918.

Gurney's interest and involvement in the docks is explored in this walk, but the experience will be a strange mix of old and new. The old docks, much-frequented by Gurney, have now been reinvented as two places: the historic docks and the modern designer retail outlet known as Gloucester Quays. This walk will start in the new retail outlet, revealing in its shape and location the bones of the warehouses and docks it replaced, before performing a circular walk around the old docks. At the same time, the opportunity is taken to visit Llanthony Secunda, a twelfth-century priory established by monks fleeing from persecution in the Welsh mountains, and of interest to Gurney as one of the significant historic ruins of the city.

*Gloucester Docks in 1872 (Gloucestershire Archives)*

*Gloucester Docks in 2021*

Route Details

DISTANCE/ TIME:
2.3km (1.5 miles) 1–1.5 hours

MAPS:
OS Explorer 179, 1:25 000, Gloucester, Cheltenham & Stroud
OS Landranger 162, 1:50 000, Gloucester & Forest of Dean

START AND PARKING:
The walk starts at the entrance to the Gloucester Quays shopping centre in St Ann Way (SO 828178; GL1 5SH). Parking includes a multistorey car park for Gloucester Quays shopping, accessed off St Ann Way; also a car park off Southgate Street for the historic dock area.

NOTE:
Numerous dockside cafés, pubs and restaurants exist, and especially relevant to the walk's theme are the Soldiers of Gloucester Museum café and the Gloucester Brewery Bar.

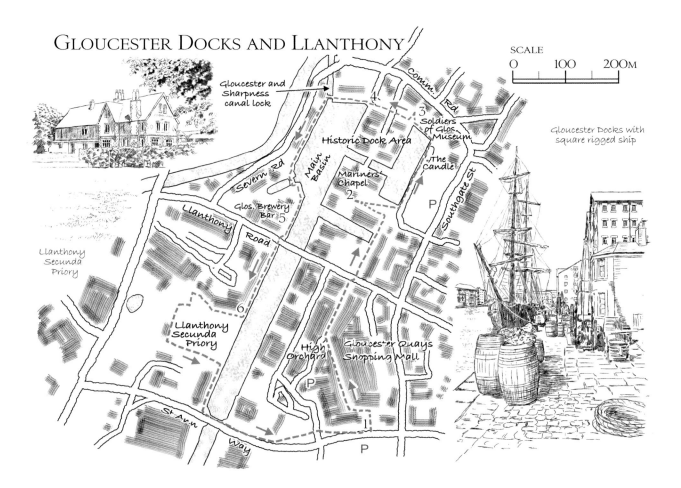

# GLOUCESTER DOCKS AND LLANTHONY

0    100    200M

Gloucester and
Sharpness
canal lock

Comm. Rd

4

3

Soldiers
of Glos.
Museum

Gloucester Docks with
square rigged ship

Historic Dock Area

Severn Rd

Main Basin

Mariners'
Chapel

The
Candle

Southgate St

2

P

Glos. Brewery
Bar

5

Llanthony

Road

Llanthony
Secunda
Priory

6

Llanthony
Secunda
Priory

High
Orchard

Gloucester Quays
Shopping Mall

P

P

1

St Ann

Way

P

26

## The Walk

① The walk begins at the entrance to Gloucester Quays. As you enter the shopping centre, you will see a coffee shop straight ahead with walkways to either side. The map shows the left-hand option but they both take you past gleaming shop fronts and eventually out onto High Orchard Street. This was formerly warehousing and dock-related buildings, a place Gurney knew well, although its present incarnation would have been inconceivable to him. Follow High Orchard Street to reach Llanthony Road. Go right for about 20m and then left into the Historic Dock area. Walk a short distance and look across to the left and to see the former Llanthony Warehouse, now the National Waterways Museum. A visit is well worth while. After another 100m, Reynolds Warehouse appears to the left, and just in front of it is the Mariners Chapel, a small building dwarfed by its neighbours but of significance to Gurney. There is an explanatory plaque.

② The Mariners Chapel was built in 1849 to meet the needs of the sailors and boatmen arriving at the docks from the inland waterways and from around the world. Services could be held on the quayside as ships turned round quickly, and a coffee bar was provided to help combat drunkenness. While the commercial docks have gone, the present church is still serving the area and the chapel is a quiet, spiritual space for those visiting the docks.

*The Mariners Chapel*

After Gurney had left school in 1906 and while he was an articled pupil to Herbert Brewer at the cathedral, he passed professional examinations to become an associate of the Royal College of Music Organists (ARCO). This enabled him to take various piano- or organ-playing jobs at local churches to supplement his income. One such position was at the Mariners Chapel where, according to Alfred Cheesman (Gurney's Godfather), he settled in more easily with the sailors and dockhands than he did playing for the respectable churchgoers of Whitminster and Hempstead. Cheesman described Gurney as being 'wanting in tact' and likely to 'give offence by being too outspoken' (Cheesman to Marion Scott, 19 April 1937, Gloucestershire Archives).

• Look inside the chapel to enjoy the peace. There is a piano there but the organ that Gurney used was removed in the late twentieth century.

• Move away from the chapel towards Victoria Dock basin where pleasure craft are now moored. Turn alongside the far water's edge to reach the iron-red spire known as the Candle. Standing 23m tall, the Candle is a public sculpture prepared by Wolfgang Buttress from Corten steel (which weathers to a rust-red finish), drawing upon the industrial heritage of the area. The Candle is illuminated at night, and etched on the spire is Gurney's poem **Requiem** as well as introductory lines from Gurney's poem **The Old City**.

> **Requiem** (*extract*)
> Pour out your light, O stars, and do not hold
> Your loveliest shining from earth's outworn shell –
> Pure and cold your radiance, pure and cold
> My dead friend's face as well.
>
> (K2004)

• Mention of a *dead friend* is a reminder of the Soldiers of Gloucester Museum, seen across the dock basin. Follow the water's edge and turn up to the right to visit this building.

③ Records of Gloucestershire Soldiers were originally kept in Westgate Street, Gloucester, then in Bristol from 1926, and finally in the old Customs House, Gloucester from 1980. The Museum relaunched in April 2014 after a Heritage Lottery-funded refurbishment. Gurney would have known the old Customs House building fronting onto Commercial Road (see Walk 1), a street often visited by the young Gurney, as the poem **Down Commercial Road** explains, its jaunty rhythm evoking the 'rolling gait' of the sailors.

**Down Commercial Road** (*extract*)

When I was small and packed with tales of desert
    islands far
My mother took me walking in a grey ugly street,
But there the sea-wind met us with a jolly smell of tar,
A sailorman went past to town with slow rolling gait;
And Gloucester she's famous in story.

The trees and shining sky of June were good enough
    to see,
Better than any books or tales the sailormen might
    tell –
But tops'le spars against the blue made fairyland for me;
The snorting tug made surges like the huge Atlantic
    swell.
And Gloucester she's famous in story.

(S&S/ WE)

**The Soldiers of Gloucester Museum** documents the lives of Gloucestershire soldiers from the last 300 years, presenting army uniforms, a model of a First World War trench, information about medals, interactive displays and a small bookshop with café. Of particular interest is a book entitled *The Story of the 2/5th Battalion Gloucestershire Regiment 1914–1918* by A.F. Barnes, available in the shop, which recounts the experiences of Gurney's Battalion. There are many of Gurney's poems that describe his reactions to the war as an ordinary soldier. After the initial patriotic sentiments in early poems, such as **Maisemore** and **To the Poet before Battle**, Gurney's war poetry is much more down-to-earth and often filled with the horrors of war, as in **Pain**, written in February 1917 and sent to Marion Scott in a letter from France.

### Pain

Pain, pain continual; pain unending;
Hard even to the roughest, but to those
Hungry for beauty … Not the wisest knows,

Nor most pitiful-hearted, what the wending
Of one hour's way meant. Grey monotony
   lending
Weight to the grey skies, grey mud where goes
An army of grey bedrenched scarecrows in rows
Careless at last of cruellest Fate-sending.
Seeing the pitiful eyes of men foredone,
Or horses shot, too tired merely to stir,
Dying in shell-holes both, slain by the mud.
Men broken, shrieking even to hear a gun.
Till pain grinds down, or lethargy numbs her,
The amazed heart cries angrily out on God.
(K2004)

Panel 5 of the Ivor Gurney stained glass in
Gloucester Cathedral (see Walk 1) references **Pain**
and shows a nightmare scene from the First World
War trenches, with ghoulish faces of drowned and
drowning soldiers (*dying in shell holes*) in the fetid
waters of No Man's Land.

• Return to the route, to go straight ahead through a gate
and reach the Main Basin. Ignore a left turn back to the
Mariners Chapel.

④ The large expanse of water in the Main Basin is
surrounded by former warehouses. Many are now being
redeveloped, with restaurant frontages on the eastern side
and apartment blocks to the west. Walk around the head of
the Main Basin and cross the bridge at the lock gate. This is
the beginning of the Gloucester and Sharpness Ship Canal.

*The Gloucester
and Sharpness
Ship Canal:
the lock*

The Gloucester and Sharpness Ship Canal was built in 1829 to improve navigation between the Severn at Gloucester and the lower estuary beyond Berkeley. For much of its 26.5km length it runs close to the tidal river, but it cuts off a significant loop at a once-dangerous bend near Arlingham. It was once the broadest and deepest canal in the world and generated large amounts of traffic. At its height in 1905, traffic exceeded one million tons, including oil delivered to the storage depot at Quedgeley. By the mid-1980s, however, commercial traffic had largely come to a halt, with the canal being given over to pleasure cruisers, with the exception of a few passages by grain barges. The oil trade ceased in 1985 with the closure of the Quedgeley petroleum depot.

Standing on the lock bridge on a sunny day, watching walkers alongside the canal and people sitting outside the restaurants, it is difficult to imagine what a noisy, bustling dockside this must have been in Gurney's day. The opening of the canal reinforced Gloucester's already strong role as a trading centre.

Gloucester was at that time the furthest inland of any British port, with a vast array of sailing ships, barges and smaller commercial craft taking goods up into Gloucester markets and down to the sea. Gloucester was a bustling crossroads where town met country and country met sea. As Michael Hurd, Gurney's first biographer (1978), explained, this was hugely significant for Ivor Gurney and for his development as a young poet and musician.

• Once over the lock bridge, turn left and follow the waterside path on towards Alexandra Warehouse. After about 150m, cross the bridge over the dry dock and, if you are lucky, you will see a boat being repaired here, maybe even an historic tall ship. Walking a little further on you will pass (and may wish to stop for refreshment at) the Gloucester Brewery Bar with its own brewed beers.

⑤ The Gloucester Brewery Bar has a beer garden in which you can sit and look across the water at the back of Llanthony

Warehouse. We know that Gurney enjoyed visiting the dockside bars occasionally (though rather different from the Gloucester Brewery Bar!) as much for the atmosphere and characters of the clientele as for the drinking.

**Old Tavern Folk** (*extract*)
Five feet ten and fond of the sea, and glad
To sit the night through drinking, making merry,
Talking infinite sea yarns and widest like-things …
Till dawn stole in and showed masts, ships and wide
Headlands stretching out into gray [sic] mists …
They knew their craft and all such things as English
Might care for, thickets of interest like the masts
And spars of the swaying harbour crew outside.

(K2004)

• Follow the footpath on towards Llanthony Road Bridge and cross it to continue. There are apartments built alongside the canal and beyond them a sign draws attention to Llanthony Secunda Priory.

⑥ Take the right turn off the path as indicated and reach the entrance to the Priory remains. The route of this walk takes you around the area and joins back to the canal-side path about 100m from where you left it.

*Former warehouses at Gloucester Docks, now restaurants and bars*

**Llanthony Secunda Priory** in Gloucester comprises the remains of a once large and important Augustinian priory which was founded outside the city walls in 1136 by Miles of Gloucester. The epithet 'Secunda' refers to the origins of this monkish cell. The original Llanthony Priory (Llanthony Prima) was established in the Welsh borderlands in the Eywas valley near Abergavenny. In his *Journey Through Wales*, Giraldus Cambrensis (1191) recounts that the monks of Llanthony Prima 'suffered so much from the raids of the Welshmen, that under the patronage of Milo of Gloucester, Constable of England, and in 1140 Earl of Hereford, they migrated to Gloucester where a new Llanthony was founded for them in 1136.' Initially, this was a temporary measure but the priory prospered and the monks were reluctant to return to the Black Mountains. By the sixteenth century, the priory owned 50 acres of well-farmed land (the present site is five acres), 60–80 people lived and worked here, and nearby Gloucester (with a population of 40,000) provided a ready market for produce. Llanthony Secunda was known for cheese-making.

*Llanthony Secunda, Gloucester: including the remains of the medieval west range*

In 1502 the Archbishop of Canterbury and the Prior of Llanthony gave presents of 'Llanthony Cheese' to Elizabeth of York, the wife of Henry VII.

The buildings were probably falling into disrepair when Gurney explored them in the early 1900s. Certainly by 1952 the surviving remains of the priory were designated as Grade-I Listed and the wider site as a Scheduled Monument. Major restoration work was completed in August 2018 when the priory reopened to the public. (www.llanthonysecunda.org/).

The two main buildings dating from the fifteenth century (the farm and tithe barn) have been restored and are now back in use. The grounds have been landscaped with new paths, benches, trees and planting, and will include an example of a medieval courtyard garden, the beginnings of which can be seen on the site. Gloucester College has a new building abutting directly onto the Llanthony grounds. If you wish to explore the site fully, there are ample information boards on the site.

*Llanthony Prima near Hay-on-Wye*

Gurney's interest in both Llanthony Priories is revealed by a poem he wrote in the asylum, probably in 1925. It refers to a visit he made to Llanthony Prima in the Black Mountains with John Haines, another Gloucestershire poet and his close friend, who was trying to help Gurney out of his depression. Apparently, Gurney enjoyed the visit – although, in a letter to Marion Scott (August 1919), he feared that his love for Gloucestershire and local knowledge of Llanthony Secunda might prejudice him against the original Llanthony.

The poem **Llanthony** also reveals both his dread that his muse might leave him and his desire to draw on Wordsworth's inspiration. Tintern Abbey, another ruined abbey on the Lower Wye that inspired one of Wordsworth's most famous long poems, is not far from Llanthony. The last few lines of Gurney's poem are difficult, partly because he tends to leave out words. In the poem he is describing aspects of the technical (*shaped to square*) and the creative (*glowed from deep heart out*) processes of writing, and hoping that he can continue to be inspired. The last two lines suggest that, although Gloucester might have been a safer environment, the Black Mountains was a good place for the creative *dreamer*.

**Llanthony**

Llanthony lay in the hill's hollow and dreamed
I who had come from this other Llanthony, there
Sat awhile and drank tea while sunlight gleamed
Above roofless choir of the old Abbey.
Beautiful as peace need ever be it seemed;
Would I might stay to write there, (O that it may be
My place of meditating before long! Here to make song!)
London was a poor sort of companion here;
O for loved Wordsworth and his Tintern manner!
Which glowed from deep heart out and was shaped to
      square
Achieved verse in a few days, for all men to honour…
For raptures, truth and beauty in small space.
Near Gloucester, indeed (might) have been a safer place,
But Mozart or Chaucer might have been dreamer.

(GA)

• Returning to the canal-side walk, pass the Sula Lightship (formerly stationed in the Humber Estuary – see the information board on the canal-side) and some more new development to reach St Ann Bridge. Here, cross over the bridge, turn left and walk back along St Ann Way towards the shopping centre and your starting point.

# Maisemore:
# the Severn and the Salt Box

**Petersburg** (*extract*)
My father looked out on ploughland and willed me.
His was the friendliness of every hill and tree
In all west Gloucestershire, in all west Gloucestershire
Born of that earth, of like love brought to birth.

(GA)

Maisemore is a peaceful village, perched on a low limestone ridge on the western bank of the Severn just over a mile from Gloucester City centre. In Ivor Gurney's mind, the village of Maisemore was forever associated with his father, David, and with the love of countryside that his father tried to instil in all his children. Petersburg is one of several rather rambling poems that Gurney wrote in Dartford asylum as if seeking reminders of his childhood and a recognition of his father's legacy. David Gurney was born in Maisemore and his mother still lived in this riverside village in the late 1890s. As soon as the

Gurney children were old enough, they walked out with their father on a Sunday evening across the Severn water-meadows (Maisemore Ham) to visit their grandmother. Winifred Gurney, Ivor's older sister, remembered that

> When Ivor was in the cathedral choir he was allowed to invite another choirboy, or more, to have tea with us before setting off. In these things, combined with trips up and down the canal or the river, as well as country walks, Mother generally accompanied us, and they were the pleasantest days of our lives.

Later in 1919, when David Gurney was ill with the cancer that would finally kill him, Gurney wrote in a letter to Marion Scott that it was 'Hard to realise that once he took us, the merriest of guides, to Maisemore of Sunday evenings.' (15/16 April 1919).

You can still walk across Maisemore Ham from Gloucester, as Gurney's family did, if you are prepared for the landscape of concrete pillars, pylons, overhead cables, viaducts, and the deafening noise of modern traffic on the A40 and A417. For this walk, however, we will start from Maisemore village and walk along the Severn Meadows, where moments of peace can still be enjoyed. The route climbs up onto the ridge of higher land that connects Maisemore with Woolridge and Ashleworth, before dropping down to the house once lived in by Gurney's grandmother, on Maisemore Old Road. After visiting the site of the former Rising Sun pub, the walk returns alongside a stream to St Giles Church in Maisemore.

*St Giles Church in Maisemore (© copyright Philip Halling geograph. uk/P/7340333)*

## Route Details

DISTANCE/ TIME:
7.9km (4.9 miles) 2.5–3 hours

MAPS:
*OS Explorer 179, 1:25 000, Gloucester, Cheltenham & Stroud*
*OS Landranger 162, 1:50 000, Gloucester & Forest of Dean*

START AND PARKING:
The walk starts in the road next to Maisemore village hall (SO 214814; GL2 8JE). Car parking is available in the village hall car park if not in use for an event. Otherwise find a safe space elsewhere in village.

TRACKS AND PATHS:
A pleasant walk alongside the river and through fields. High Redding Hill and Spring Hill demand about 80m climbing. Two or three low stiles.

# Maisemore; the Severn and the Saltbox

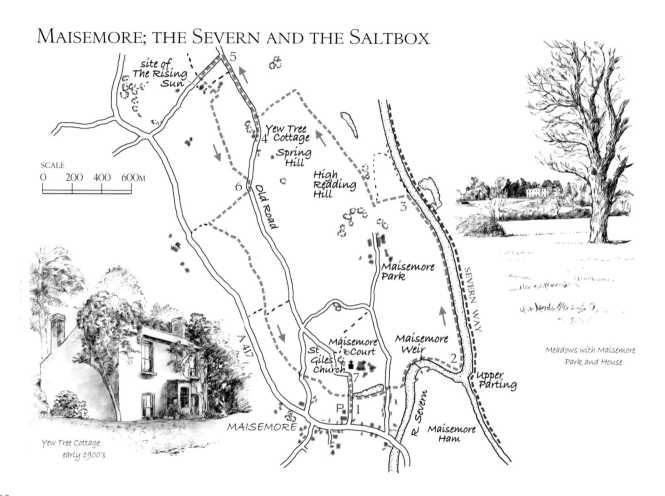

SCALE
0   200   400   600M

site of
The Rising
Sun

5

Yew Tree
Cottage
4

Spring
Hill

High
Redding
Hill

6

Old Road

3

SEVERN WAY

Maisemore
Park

A 417

Maisemore
Court

Maisemore
Weir

Maisemore
Park and House

St
Giles
Church

7

2

Upper
Parting

P  1

R. Severn

MAISEMORE

Maisemore
Ham

Yew Tree Cottage
early 1900's

Meadows with Maisemore
Park and House

# The Walk

① Start from the road outside the village hall and look across the village green to Maisemore Court and St Giles Church sitting at the top of the hill straight ahead of you. In the spring, the green will be covered in daffodils. Read **Petersburg** to gain an insight into Gurney's relationship with his father.

**Petersburg** (*extract*)
My father looked out on ploughland and willed me.
His was the friendliness of every hill and tree
In all the west Gloucestershire, in all west
   Gloucestershire
Born of that earth, of like love brought to birth;
Knowing the flights of birds, and the song of the
   smallest
Bird – the names of flowers, and the likeliest places
Where first spring might bring Her lovely trifles in.
So on a night when Orion ruled with majestic light,
He remembered his past dreams, all broken, and
   hoped for grace
Whereby a son should say what he had never
Been able to say or sing of such beloved Earth.

Walked to Maisemore and made his vows as his father
Had done before – So on the day of one Master
Of us I was born – Leo Count Tolstoi – to be
War Poet, and lover, maker, server of earth, the born
   of Gloucestershire

(GA)

In **Petersburg** Gurney describes his father's love for, and knowledge of, the countryside. He suggests that his father, who had a musical background, would like his son to realise his own ambitions and create the images of Gloucestershire that he, himself, had *never been able to say or sing*. The references to Petersburg and Count Tolstoy are because Gurney shared a birthday with the Russian poet and used the name as a link between poetry and his thoughts about place and identity. (In fact, Petersburg is also the name of an American Civil War battle site, and this poem is part of a group of 'American poems' in which Gurney makes connections between his own life and names that he discovered in an American Civil War atlas that he read in Dartford.)

• Walk down to the dip in the road. Straight ahead is Coronation Avenue bordered by lime trees planted in 1953 to celebrate the coronation of Queen Elizabeth II. At the top of the slope are the cluster of church, graveyard and courthouse joined now by the modern Steadings Business centre, housed in renovated outbuildings.

• Looking to the right, you can see Maisemore Court Lake framed by trees and, to the side of it, the path you should follow.

*Maisemore Court Lake, with Maisemore Court beyond*

• Walk beside the lake and through some trees before dropping down to the lane, the Rudge. Cross this and continue across a meadow to the riverside, following the bank round past Maisemore Weir, the highest point the Severn estuary tides usually reach (although occasional high surges of the Severn Bore have been known to top Maisemore Weir). As you go through a farm gate, the river is on your right and here a track joins from the left. This is a former Roman road which came in from Worcester along the slightly higher ground of Maisemore ridge before fording the Severn here to reach the Kingsholm Fort.

• Through the gate, the riverside meadowlands open out into a wide green space, but stay close to the path along the river bank as there are often sheep or cows grazing.

② After about 200m you reach Upper Parting, the point at which the older (eastern) and newer (western) courses of the Severn part company. The east channel flows past the former tar works, now a reclamation business (Ronson Reclamation), and on to Westgate Bridge; the west channel flows past Maisemore, Over and the confluence of the river Leadon. Between the two courses lies Alney Island and paths across the marshy meadows ('hams') that Gurney used to walk with his father from Gloucester. Looking back, you can see that Maisemore village is on a low ridge (about 20–30m) that runs north to Maisemore Park.

*'Brave carpets' of green, with Maisemore Park House in background*

• From Upper Parting, follow the riverside for about 1.5km through Maisemore Park meadows. The river is glimpsed through hawthorn, willow and ash. Looking across the river you may see walkers on the Severn Way on the opposite bank (Walk 20), whilst to your left are the pasturelands of the river's flood plain – sometimes flooded and at other times a rich green.

### Brave Carpets

Brave carpets had the emperors of old,
Scarlet and gold interwoven, shaken fold on fold
On marble and syenite where their feet should fall
Going down graciously to embassies in High Hall,

Homage and body splendour. But here in meadows
Kine and the errant conies move in shadows
And sleep on mantles emerald of costless stuff –
Where rain falls soft to renew and to assure enough.

(80P)

**Brave Carpets** was perhaps written about these very meadows, revealing Gurney's preference for the glory of the rich grass, *mantles emerald of costless stuff*, here in these meadows rather than any costly scarlet and golden carpets of the Roman emperors. Note that he uses the old countryside words of *kine* (cattle) and *conies* (rabbits).

**Brave Carpets** was one of the poems that Gurney put together in the 1918–22 period, but failed to get published before he was admitted to the asylum. That volume, with Gurney's title of *80 Poems or So*, was finally published in 1997 (edited by George Walter and R.K.R. Thornton). About two-thirds of the poems in this volume are about Gurney's Severn Meadows and are revelatory about Gurney's relationship with this place. He writes about the pastures, the sedges at the water's edge, the wild flowers and trees, and the many different aspects of time and weather that spark his inspiration, from early morning river mists and bitter frosty twilights to sultry midsummer days. Always the reader is struck by how Gurney's music and poetry are an integral part of his enjoyment of this landscape.

### April – Dull Afternoon

The sun for all his pride dims out and dies;
Afternoon sees not one
Of all those flames that lit the primrose lamps;
At Winter's hest; fordone.

Like music eager curving or narrowing
From here to there. Strange how no mist can dull
Wholly the silver edge of April's song
Though the air's a blanket weighing on like wool.

(K2004)

• Ahead the land rises to High Redding Hill, but over to your left a large, white Regency building, Maisemore Park House, will become apparent (seen again from Walk 20). Continue along the riverside and go over a stile to enter the second meadow.

### River Terraces

High Redding Hill, at about 45–50m height, represents the second of a series of 'river terraces', remnants of a former floodplain cut by a wider and more powerful River Severn. At the end of the last Ice Age (c.11,700 years ago) there were alternate periods of advance and retreat of the ice and of fast- and slow-flowing rivers. When the Severn flowed more powerfully or sea levels fell, the river cut into its old valley floor and left remnants of this high and dry on either side of the river. When sea-levels rose or the river flowed more slowly and was filled with debris, there was deposition across the valley plain. This process has happened several times so that a sequence of three sets of river terraces can be seen at 24–31m (80–100 ft), 37–46m (120–150 ft) and 76–80m (250–262 ft). Maisemore village is on the first terrace while to the north is the higher third terrace represented by Woolridge Hill. Each of these terraces will be seen again in Walks 17, 18, 19 and 20, giving rise to features like Apperley Ridge, Wainlode Cliff, Barrow Hill and Sandhurst Hill. The terraces have a core of the underlying hard rock (blue Lias limestone) but with layers of gravel and debris over the top and dominating for the lower terraces.

This landscape is what makes Gurney's Severn Meadows distinctive. The terraces were his *small hills*, mentioned repeatedly in his poetry: *Your hills not only hills but friends of mine and kindly, / Your tiny knolls and orchards hidden beside the river.* (**Strange Service**) and *I will go climb my little hills to see / Severn* (**My County**).

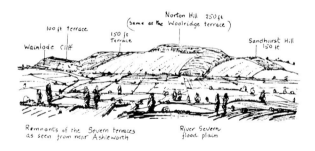

*Sketch diagram of the Severn Terraces*
*(© William Dreghorn)*

③ At the far end of the second meadow, look for a footpath sign pointing away from the river and turn left to follow this footpath along the hedge, the ground rising slightly before it levels out and joins a rough lane (Ragmans Alley). Here, turn left and almost immediately turn right to follow a footpath sign pointing up a steep incline onto High Redding Hill.

• Follow the path along the ridge top, passing a lake in the valley and eventually reaching 57m at the top. There is a good view back to see Robinswood Hill, Gloucester Cathedral and away in the distance the Cotswold Edge from Painswick Beacon southwards to Coaley Peak. The Malverns may be visible ahead. Walk downhill to a field boundary, turn left and walk uphill to join the road (Old Road) from Maisemore. A short detour down the lane to the left, passing Woolridge Cottage and Woodgates farm, will take you to Gurney's grandparents' cottage, Yew Tree Cottage, now a part of the Maisemore Apiaries property.

④ The cottage is red-brick with a date inscription of 1885 and a yew tree still in the garden. Gurney's grandfather, Thomas, grew up here with his grandparents in an agricultural cottage on the site of the existing Yew Tree Cottage.

*Yew Tree Cottage, Maisemore, where Gurney's grandmother lived*

**Gurney's grandfather, Thomas Gurney** 'inherited the tenancy of the cottage after his grandparent's deaths. ... His long-term position as a gardener was probably held at Spring Hill House, a large property owned by the church with landscaped lawns and an impressive kitchen garden, to which the cottage belonged, conveniently tucked away out of view by the lie of the land'. (*The Ivor Gurney Society Journal*, Jordan 2012).

Thomas Gurney and his wife Mary were married in 1865 at St Giles Church, and Gurney's father David, along with six older brothers, was born and raised in the cottage. When Thomas died in 1875, Mary stayed on at the gardener's cottage. By 1881 all her sons had left home, although Mary (at 60) was still working as an agricultural labourer. Several of Mary's sons were in the building trade based in the Barton Road area of Gloucester, so it was not surprising that in the early 1880s Gurney Brothers rebuilt Yew Tree Cottage for their mother. The illustration, drawn from a photograph taken around 1900, shows Mary Gurney, Ivor's grandmother, looking over the gate of her recently built cottage, as the young Ivor Gurney would frequently have seen her during Sunday visits. At Yew Tree Cottage, the children played in the fields. Occasionally David Gurney would visit the Salt Box, a beer house a little way up the hill from the cottage.

**The Salt Box** (*extract*)

There were three poplars there where my
 grandmother lived –
She saw them at first waking – their foliage breathed

Warning or content of all weathers. And on Sundays
My father took us, and we picked up apples, or
 wandered
By anthills or poppies; while the corncrake ground his
 strange cry in the wheat.
Till at half past six time
My father would rise; and say 'Well mother I'm going
Up to the Salt Box' – past meadows of unmatched hay
Now ripening, it lay with thick hawthorn boundaried –
Company was there and perry of true farmers knowing
As worth knowing – Cool perry – And a faraway
Gloucestershire stretched like Heaven for blue and
 golden showing.

(GA)

David Gurney, sometimes with the children accompanying him, would have walked across the fields to the beer house from near Yew Tree Cottage, but we will return the way we came to visit the site of the Salt Box. Notice the reference to the 'corncrake', once a common sight with less intensive agriculture, but no longer seen in Gloucestershire.

• Walk back up Old Road to the point at which you joined it, and carry on up the hill passing a house with a balcony and eventually reaching the road junction.

⑤ Take the left turn and soon a bridleway crosses the road but ignore this and carry on down the road. The Salt Box Beerhouse, more recently known as the Rising Sun Inn, stood in large grounds over to the left. According to the Gloucestershire Pubs Database, in 1891 (just after Ivor Gurney was born) the license was for a beer house, and the landlord was a George Bishop, probably the one that Gurney's father knew in the 1890s. The name 'Salt Box' references the storage of salt on this site before being transported to Gloucester. Gurney refers to the Rising Sun pub again in a poem written in 1917, entitled **The Estaminet** (the name for a French bar or café) when explaining how a small estaminet in Riez Bailleul brought back memories of the pub at Maisemore.

> **The Estaminet** (*extract*)
> And of an inn that Johnson
> Does keep; 'the Rising Sun'.
> His friends him call Jack Johnson,
> He's Gloster's only one.
>
> (S&S/ WE)

When I visited in 2014 the Rising Sun was still open; in 2020 all that remained was a metal bracket that once held the pub sign. All around it new houses were gradually taking shape – detached and semi-detached houses with plenty of windows and balconies, boasting fine views and the appeal of 'rural' life.

*The Rising Sun Inn (Salt Box) just before its demolition in 2019–20*

Gurney would probably have regretted the loss of a Severnside pub – and, judging by some of his writing, he was not happy about changes that seemed insensitive to local surroundings or inaccessible to the poor:

**Changes** (*extract*)
Villas are set up where the sheepfolds were,
And plate glass impudent stares at the sun,
For byres and stackboards, threshing forever is done,
New things are there, shining new-fangled gear.

(K2004)

• Retrace your steps to the public bridleway sign and turn right. For the first 50m or so, the footpath is straight and clearly defined, then it turns sharp right. At the bend in the path, you will see ahead of you a new house with a cattle grid at the entrance. Facing the house with the cattle grid, turn half left and make your way on an ill-defined path through bushes surrounding a small bin compound, onto the gravel drive of a white house. Turn right and walk alongside the drive with the boundary of the property on your right. Take the narrow path continuing straight along the boundary between high hedges, to reach a stile in a wooden fence and cross this into a field.

• **Ignore the sign pointing straight ahead** and follow the fence to the right to a set of double gates. Through the gates, go diagonally downhill across the field tending to the right. The Salt Box would have been up behind you to your right, and Yew Tree Cottage is away down to the left, so these are the fields that Gurney's father would have walked. Go through another double-gated exit and turn slightly right to walk across another field and through another double gate. Go left, following the hedgerow boundary until you reach the road (Old Road) about 0.5km from Yew Tree Cottage.

⑥ Walk down Old Road towards Maisemore village for less than 100m, to find a footpath sign pointing right. Follow this beside a hedge, pausing to take in the wide-ranging view of Gloucester and the Cotswolds beyond. When you reach the stream, the route across the bridge leads to the Hartpury road. **Do not cross the bridge** but instead turn left to walk beside the stream. It is now about one mile back to the village centre. The first part of the walk is a grassy track with willow trees and hawthorn alongside. Eventually, you reach steps to take you down to the Old Road and, after crossing it, there are steps back up to join a grassy meadow with trees. As you walk, notice the church tower peeping above the slope and soon you will be back on the village road.

## Maisemore

O when we swung through Maisemore,
The Maisemore people cheered,
And women ran from farmyards,
And men from ricks, afeared

To lose the sight of soldiers
Who would 'fore Christmas Day
Blow Kaiser William's army
Like mist of breath away!

The war it was but young then!
And we were young unknowing
The path we were to tread,
The way the path was going.

And not a man of all of us,
Marching across the bridge,
Had thought how Home would linger
In our hearts, as Maisemore Ridge.

When the darkness downwards hovers
Making trees like German shadows,

How our souls fly homing, homing
Times and times to Maisemore meadows,

By Aubers Ridge that Maisemore men
Had died in vain to hold …
The burning thought but once desires
Maisemore in morning gold!

O when we marched through Maisemore
Past many a creaking cart,
We little thought we had in us
Love so hot at heart.

(s&s/ we)

⑦ Walk up Coronation Avenue to view St Giles Church. This church has a Norman font shaped in the fifteenth century into an octagon, but was mostly rebuilt in 1869 by the architect Thomas Fulljames (whose Ashleworth house features in Walk 19). In the graveyard, close to the church wall, is the grave of Ivor's grandparents, Thomas and Mary Gurney. Maisemore Court, south-east of the church, is mainly seventeenth-century with later alterations, and behind it is the Steadings Business Centre, occupying renovated outbuildings.

• The First World War memorial is a poignant place to pause. Like many of his generation, Gurney's childhood and adolescence were overshadowed by the call to take up arms. His poem **Maisemore**, with its jaunty rhythm, reflects the innocence and enthusiasm with which young men like him set out to do their duty, but also hints at the heartache and bitterness that would follow for many.

*The War Memorial, Maisemore*

# Chosen Hill

**There was Such Beauty**
There was such beauty in the dappled valley
As hurt the sight, as stabbed the heart to tears.
The gathered loveliness of all the years
Hovered thereover, it seemed, eternally
Set for men's Joy …

(K2004)

Chosen Hill (also known as Churchdown Hill) was of special significance to Ivor Gurney who, with Will Harvey and Herbert Howells, used it as a favourite walking area easily reached from Gloucester. Gurney had come to know Howells through his apprenticeship at Gloucester Cathedral (see Walk 1) and Will Harvey was a local boy studying law with a Gloucester solicitor, whom Gurney met by chance in 1908. Will Harvey and Ivor Gurney shared a love of river sailing (Walks 5, 6 and 7), but all three also enjoyed walking on the nearby hills – Chosen Hill and Robinswood Hill – and did so frequently between 1906 and 1911. They shared ideas and opinions about music and books as they walked. Views from Chosen Hill were the inspiration for some of Gurney's best poems.

Chosen Hill, like its nearby twin Robinswood Hill, is an 'outlier' of the main Cotswold escarpment. A capping of hard Liassic Marlstone rock (a thin sandy limestone) on each hill lies over the softer sands and clays beneath and so protects them from further erosion. These outliers add variety and interest to the flat vale farmlands, and today are treasured as recreational 'lungs' for the towns of Gloucester and Cheltenham. Robinswood Hill boasts a country park and a dry ski slope, whilst Chosen Hill has four nature reserves.

It is difficult to imagine the air of remote rurality that must have characterised Chosen Hill in the 1900s. An extract from H.J. Massingham's book *Cotswold Country* (1937) provides the appropriate flavour:

> High on a steep and isolated tor, so typical of the Lias, I could see from the criss-cross of lanes the 'chosen church' of Churchdown. It was a mild December day, pensive in mist, and, as I climbed, I noticed the white

fleeces of Traveller's Joy, festooned like Christmas decorations upon the trees crowning the conical hills that were grouped about the mount. Many of the trees bore mistletoe. To the west, the silver streak of Severn was paler than the mist; to the east, the scalloped, tossing line of the edge wound in and out in cunning variety of bluff and recess.

Now the hill is boxed in by the A40 and A417 to the north, south and west, and by the M5 passing noisily beneath its slopes to the east. The suburbs of Gloucester move ever closer.

This walk climbs the northern slopes of the subsidiary Tinker's Hill, contours through woodland around the western slopes and then rises to the summit of Chosen Hill at 155m. Here, there are surprisingly wide views. The return path visits the Church of St Bartholomew before rejoining the village.

## Route Details

DISTANCE/ TIME:
3.5km (2.2 miles), 1.5 hours

MAPS:
*OS Explorer 179, 1:25 000, Gloucester, Cheltenham & Stroud*
*OS Landranger 162, 1:50 000, Gloucester & Forest of Dean*

START AND PARKING:
Start at St Andrew's Church Hall (SO 883198; GL3 2JT) in Churchdown, a village a few miles east of Gloucester. A free car park at 3 Church Road (signposted from Station Road) is accessed opposite the Old Elm pub, with a footpath to St Andrew's Church Hall.

TRACKS AND PATHS:
Well-used tracks over the fields and woodlands. It can be muddy and with a steep climb to the summit. Three stiles.

*Chosen Hill – view of the hill from Crickley Hill, showing it as an outlier of the Cotswold Edge (photo by Greig Simms)*

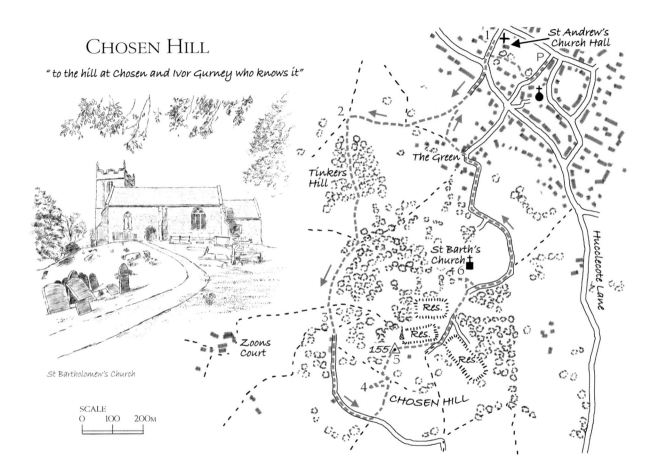

# CHOSEN HILL

*" to the hill at Chosen and Ivor Gurney who knows it"*

St Bartholomew's Church

SCALE
0    100    200M

St Andrew's Church Hall

P

2

Tinkers Hill

The Green

St Barth's Church
6

Zoons Court

3

Res.

Res.
155
5

Res.

4

CHOSEN HILL

Hucclecote Lane

## The Walk

① From St Andrew's Village Hall, walk up Station Road to join Pirton Lane and cross over to find a stile and a footpath sign pointing up the hill. Over the stile, take a short walk to a second gate (usually unlocked) with another stile. Once in the field, follow the footpath diagonally up to the right to a metal gate. Go through and straight across the next field, **not down to the right**. The village of Churchdown lies below you and, if the day is clear, views of the Malverns appear to the right.

② Go through a wooden gate, maybe catching a glimpse of St Bartholomew's Church up to the left, and find a path to your left. Before proceeding, visit the information board ahead of you. This explains that the area is managed for conservation by the Woodland Trust and Gloucestershire Wildlife Trust.

• It is a steep walk uphill, helped by wooden steps which lead you into a wooded area and soon out onto the grassy summit of Tinker's Hill at about 118m. St Bartholomew's Church appears through the trees over to the left, on top of the main Chosen Hill. The paths are confused here but at a path junction, you should turn right to join the path that

*St Bartholomew's Church appearing through the trees*

contours around the hill at about 95m height. Don't take the downhill route, hard right through shrubs, or the steep path with steps uphill, although the latter is another way to reach the summit of Chosen Hill.

• The walk contours along the side of the hill, with traffic noise reminding you that Chosen Hill is now effectively an island, caught between dual carriageways (A40, A417) and the M5. Up to your left is the steep, wooded hillslope. A walk-through fence stile takes you into the next section of woodland, and a few metres beyond are paths crossing to the right and left.

③ Take the right-hand path for a few steps through some shrubs and out onto a field edge. You are looking westward, with Zoon's Court Farm straight ahead followed by warehouse/ industrial buildings, the suburbs of Barnwood, Hucclecote and Longlevens, and eventually central Gloucester with the prominent shape of the cathedral visible. May Hill may be seen in the distance. The main impression is of a large city reaching almost to the edge of the hill, but in the early 1900s, Gloucester was a more compact urban area shaped by the river to the west and the railway to east and north. Barnwood, Longlevens, Tuffley, Hucclecote and Brockworth were only small villages, each with a few houses and a church. A network of paths ran off the hillside, many of which were frequented by Gurney, Howells and Harvey escaping from Gloucester.

• This is an ideal point at which to read Gurney's poem, written as he surveyed the scene from just such a place

*Gurney's 'dappled valley' with the view obscured by modern development*

– maybe even written at this precise location on Chosen Hill (although without the modern industrial buildings now dominating the scene). **There Was Such Beauty** dates from the 1917–19 period when, despite illness and difficulties following his discharge from the army, Gurney was writing prolifically. Writing to Marion Scott in 1919, he described an occasion when he felt such joy at the sight of Gloucester: 'O but you should have seen last Thursday! The whole world seemed to exult and glory in mere being! A Beethoven day by the Lord!' In the same letter he refers to the poem below as existing already, but not yet published.

### There Was Such Beauty

There was such beauty in the dappled valley
As hurt the sight, as stabbed the heart to tears.
The gathered loveliness of all the years
Hovered thereover, it seemed, eternally
Set for Men's Joy. Town, tower, trees, river
Under a royal azure sky for ever
Up-piled with snowy towering bulks of cloud:
A herald day of spring more wonderful
Than her true own. Trumpets cried aloud
In sky, earth, blood: no beast, no clod so dull
But the power felt of the day, and of the giver
Was glad for life, humble at once and proud.
Kyrie Eleison, and Gloria,
Credo, Jubilate, Magnificat:
The whole world gathered strength to praise the day.

(K2004)

It is almost a painterly view of Gloucester that Gurney presents in **There Was Such Beauty**, dominated by St Peter's Abbey (the cathedral) and nestling harmoniously next to the river – *town, tower, trees, river*. One senses the sky and the clouds of a spring or early summer day (*royal azure*) and is aware of the green meadows and pasturelands skirting the city. For me, this poem recalls Wordsworth's sonnet **On Westminster Bridge**, not only in the way the poet is observing a beloved city from a vantage point, but even more directly in the wording and sentiments aroused. Like Wordsworth, Gurney feels the deep sense of contentment and happiness deriving from the sense of place – *Trumpets cried aloud / In sky, earth, blood: no beast no clod so dull / But the power felt of the day and of the giver / Was glad for life, humble at once and proud*, he writes. The sentiments recall Wordsworth's famous lines from **On Westminster Bridge**, beginning *Earth has not* *anything to show more fair: / Dull would be of soul who could pass by / A sight so touching in its majesty* and ending with *Ne'er saw I, never felt a calm so deep.*

We know that Gurney had read Wordsworth and was influenced by his philosophy of reflecting on beautiful scenes in tranquility, after the immediate event that had inspired joy. In October 1915, in a letter to Matilda Chapman, his friend in High Wycombe, Gurney wrote, 'My mind gradually tranquilises itself and more and more I see that splendid teacher Wordworth is for all sorts of men.' He knew the **Westminster Bridge** sonnet very well. In a letter to Marion Scott in November 1917, he adapts a line from Wordsworth's sonnet as an ironic comment on the fact that each year of wartime seems bloodier than the last – 'Dear houses, the very God does seem asleep'.

• Return to the path on the wood's edge and continue contouring round the hill. There are many paths up to the left but keep straight on until you meet a small lane. Follow this past several houses, noticing Robinswood Hill ahead of you through the trees. A footpath sign to the right signals a path joining from Hucclecote. Opposite it, there is a sign pointing steeply uphill through some overgrown shrubbery. Follow this to reach a wooden gate. The way is straight ahead but take a moment to walk to the left onto the summit of a little hilltop.

④ Here you will find an impressive panorama. Starting over to your right (looking north) are the Malverns, Bredon Hill and Cheltenham town beneath, followed to the west by the Severn Vale, the northern suburbs of Gloucester, May Hill, the Forest of Dean and Gloucester city itself in the foreground. Moving on westwards and south, Robinswood Hill appears, and behind it the far-flung edges of the south Cotswolds towards Haresfield. Finally, to the east, the wooded upper slopes of Cooper's Hill come into view, and eventually Crickley Hill, before the panorama is blocked by the woods of Chosen Hill itself.

• It is thought that the curve of woodland on the surrounding hills, as seen from Chosen Hill, inspired Gurney to write the poem entitled **When from the Curve** in the 1917–20 period. It reveals how the experience of viewing such a scene is, for Gurney, closely linked to the kindling of his creative inspiration.

*'When from the Curve of the wood's edge'*
*The mantle of trees on Cooper's Hill seen from Witcombe*

**When from the Curve**
When from the curve of the wood's edge does grow
Power, and that spreads to envelop me –
Wrapped up in sense of meeting tree and plough
I feel tiny song stir tremblingly
And deep; the many birth pangs separate
Taking most full of joy, for soon shall come
The kindling, the beating at Heaven gate
The flood of tide that bears strongly home.
Then under the skies I make my vows
Myself to purify and fit my heart
For the inhabiting of the high House
Of Song, that dwells high and clean apart.
The fire, the flood, the soaring, these the three
That merged are power of Song and prophesy.

(K2004)

• Return to the gate and walk through it along a wooded path for a few metres. At a gap in the fence (where, in 2022, you were advised that there are 'fairies ahead!') take a right turn to climb steeply up some wooden steps and come out underneath the trig point on the summit of Chosen Hill at 155m.

Gurney has helpfully summarised the three stages of his creative process in the last two lines of **When from the Curve**. First is *the fire* which is the initial spark of inspiration, imagination and love invoked by experiencing a place or landscape at first hand (usually by moving through it). In this poem, it is not just the sight of a woodland edge but the whole experience of being where, as Gurney describes it, *tree meets plough* and the *power* of the place *spreads to envelop me*. He is filled with delight and joy and feels *tiny song stir tremblingly*. Then comes the *flood* of emotion – *the kindling, the beating at heaven gate* before the feelings overpower him and *the flood of tide … bears strongly home*. Finally, there is the spiritual ecstasy (*soaring*) which moves him *to purify* his thoughts and so to prepare himself to set them down on a page (*fit my heart for inhabiting the high House of Song*). There is more than a hint of Gerard Manley Hopkins in this poem, although whereas for Hopkins the intrinsic power of the place arose from God, in Gurney there is a more pantheistic Wordsworthian feel about the place being at one with all life. According to the notes in Patrick Kavanagh's *Collected Poems* (2004), Gurney would not let Marion Scott submit this poem for publication in the Royal College of Music magazine (1919/20) because 'it was too intimate'.

⑤ On the summit, another view opens out. Straight ahead, over the topograph on the trig point, Gloucester Cathedral appears, while to the left the distinctive shapes of Cam Long Down and Stinchcombe Hill peep out from behind Robinswood Hill. When I visited the hilltop in 2022, it was a cold, early December day and the bareness of the trees around me accentuated the patchwork view of brown and dull green fields on the lower slopes. Seasonal change triggered Gurney's musical instincts (the *season chord*) as well as his poetry. **The Change** reveals how he enjoyed the spark of inspiration from autumn fields, but also looked forward to settling down in a warm, curtained room to compose and create.

*View from the summit of Chosen Hill: a winter scene with brown fields*

### The Change
Gone bare the fields now, and the starlings gather,
Whirr above stubble and soft changing hedges.
Changed the season chord too, F major or minor,
The gnats sing thin in clouds above the sedges.

And there is nothing proud now, not disconsolate,
Nothing youthful save where dark crocus flings
Summer's last challenge towards Winter's merciless
Cohort, for whom the robin alone sings.

Fields for a while longer then, O soul,
A curtained room close shut against the rime –
Where shall float music, voice or violin's
Denial passionate of the frozen time.

(K2004)

• There is an information board next to the trig point.

• Leaving the summit, walk a short way along the path and take the first right through a wooden gate next to the communications mast (BBC) and follow signs for the reservoirs and St Bartholomew's Church. The path runs between three reservoirs with prominent banks, all constructed during the 1940s and '50s to meet increased demand for water from the growth of Gloucester. Once through a large metal gate you are leaving the reservoir sites. Turn slightly left down a path leading eventually up again to the church.

*St Bartholomew's Church on Chosen Hill*

**St Bartholomew's Church** has connections with several Gloucestershire composers. Herbert Howells used to accompany Gurney on walks on the hill. Howells inscribed the *A minor Piano Quintet* to 'the hill at Chosen and Ivor Gurney who knows it,' and also composed *Chosen Tune* for violin, which he dedicated to Dorothy Dawe whom he married at Twigworth in 1920.

Gerald Finzi spent New Year's Eve 1925 at the Sexton's Cottage, and the ringing in of the new year inspired two works: the orchestral *Nocturne* (New Year Music, 1926) and his choral work *In Terra Pax* (1954).

Showing Ralph Vaughan Williams the hill in 1956, Finzi visited the cottage again, but caught Chickenpox from children living there. Already dying from Hodgkin lymphoma, the illness brought about Finzi's death two weeks later.

⑥ St Bartholomew's Church is on a raised ledge, formed of the Upper Liassic marlstone rock. It is generally agreed that there was an Iron Age camp on Chosen Hill and it may be that the church is built on part of the embankments. It is certainly an impressive site, and from the church door there are wonderful views across to the Cotswold Edge near Crickley and to the north.

• Leaving the church by the left-hand path through the graveyard, go through the metal gate at the bottom. Take the signed bridleway down to the left and this joins the road down to Churchdown village. On the bend, notice views of the north Cotswolds and the Malverns.

• Join the village at the edge of The Green and walk across to find a footpath at the far edge. Cross a stile and walk down the field to join your outward route. Negotiate the two gates and stiles and return to Pirton Lane, Station Road and St Andrew's Church Hall.

# PART TWO: Sailing a Boat on the Severn

THE Severn Valley to the south of Gloucester is characterised by wide flood plains, broad expanses of sand and mud and the sinuous bends of the River Severn. Here Gurney walked and sailed on the Severn with his friend, Will Harvey, before 1914. In 1913, when Gurney suffered a bout of severe depression, he recuperated at the lock-keeper's cottage at Framilode. In later years, he returned again and again to the peace and solitude offered by this landscape.

'On Sailing a Boat on the Severn' is an essay written by Gurney sometime between 1920 and 1922. An extract is presented below and refers to the river south of Gloucester, relevant to Walks 5, 6 and 7.

Walking the Severn Way at the present time, along this very stretch of river, it is possible to experience the sights and sounds of the river very much as it was in the early twentieth century, and to imagine the white sail of the little boat and the glorious feeling of freedom this must have given Gurney. All around him on a fine day, he would have seen the hills of Gloucestershire – the Forest of Dean to the north and west and the curved edge of the Cotswolds to south and east. Beneath him were the ever-changing patterns and flows of moving water. Whereas in the Cotswolds, it was the joy of walking and climbing the hills that heightened the experience, here it was the movement of boat upon water.

*The Severn at Framilode*

# SAILING THE SEVERN

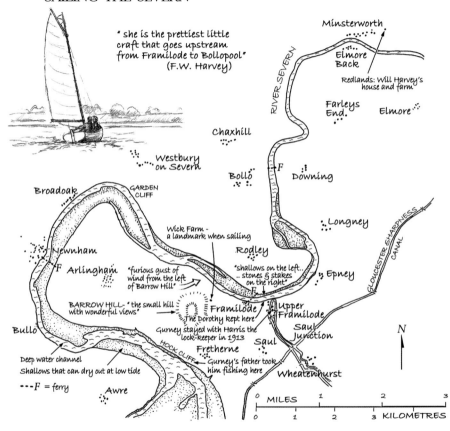

"she is the prettiest little craft that goes upstream from Framilode to Bollopool" (F.W. Harvey)

Minsterworth

RIVER SEVERN

Elmore Back

Redlands: Will Harvey's house and farm

Farleys End.

Elmore

Chaxhill

Westbury on Severn

Bollo

F

Downing

Broadoak

GARDEN CLIFF

Wick Farm – a landmark when sailing

Longney

Rodley

"shallows on the left... .. stones & stakes on the right"

Epney

GLOUCESTER SHARPNESS CANAL

Newnham

F Arlingham

"furious gust of wind from the left of Barrow Hill"

BARROW HILL- "the small hill with wonderful views"

Framilode

The Dorothy kept here

Upper Framilode

Gurney stayed with Harris the lock-keeper in 1913

Saul Junction

Bullo

HOCK CLIFF

Saul

Fretherne

Deep water channel

Shallows that can dry out at low tide

Gurney's father took him fishing here

---F = ferry

Awre

Wheatenhurst

N

0    MILES    1    2    3

0    1    2    3    KILOMETRES

64

When the great tides change a channel twice a week one needs a rough-and-tumble affair, no expensive toy, to get fun out of Severn. If there are shallows on the left hand, stones and stakes on the right, and a sand-bank somewhere, one's pleasure is spiced, and always a furious gust may come down from the left of Barrow Hill.

But there are orchards and spits of pasture, far Cotswold with white scars to look at, the best clouds in England, and a chance of elver fishing at the Equinoxes; to say nothing of eeling in summer.

If one lays lines one may catch flounders also, and mullet, having been trapped by receding water, are also known to have tasted well in that one happy village. The best game, however, is to have gone up river on half-tide as far as impetus went, or on the stillness even of meeting tide and current, and then to return in comparative certainty, with above-Newnham in sight and a headwind of which the return of water makes no account. This is, indeed, worth doing, though the baler be more in use than the rudder almost.

Since there are three o[r] four public-houses within four miles of the river there is no danger of any common thirst being made to suffer, and certainly there are two bakers.

The chief trouble is that this side of the river there are many stones, on the other smooth sand enough, but one does not wish to be ferried across to one's boat – the thing seems absurd – and in big tides the anchor drags; but there is no non-chargeable way of managing the affair. Making friends is not always a cheap arrangement, and beer is a most dangerous equivalent for favours. Cheaper often to purchase an empty barrel and float out to the boat in that.

River-dangers are not serious. River worries not too many to prevent pleasure. Almost always one can sail, save in sultry summer, and the sight of bank objects always delighted myself. One likes to see Wick Farm draw itself out of line of the landing stage. Food and drink are easy to obtain. One can never be becalmed, and there are explorations on the hither shore that one does not get at proper sailing.

(Ivor Gurney, GA, 1920–22)

# Minsterworth: orchards by the river

June-to-Come (*extract*)
When the sun's fire and gold
Sets the bee humming,
I will not write to tell
Him that I'm coming

But ride out unawares
On that old road
Of Minsterworth, of Peace,
Of Framilode

(S&S/ WE)

Minsterworth is a small riverside village to the west of Gloucester and, for Gurney, it was inextricably linked with Will Harvey. These two young men met in 1908 and explored Gloucestershire together, particularly in the 1908–11 period. Will Harvey was already a poet. Gurney was writing music and was soon persuaded by Harvey to

try his hand at poetry. Their creative development was forged outdoors – in walking and talking, in cycling the Severn lanes, in gazing at the stars and humming music, and in sailing their jointly-owned boat on the River Severn between Minsterworth and Framilode (see Walks 6 and 7). The music and poetry of both men reveal how a sense of Gloucestershire, particularly of the Severn Valley, had become part of their friendship and their own identities. In 1917 when June-to-Come was written, Gurney knew that his friend was a prisoner-of-war, and the poem reflects both the joy of their friendship and sadness at not knowing when (or maybe 'if') he would see him again. The poem was included in a letter to Marion Scott from Arras in April 1917. He wrote 'I cannot keep out of my mind what April has meant to me in past years – Minsterworth, Framilode and his companionship. And my sick mind holds on to such memories for beauty's sake and the hope of joy'.

This is a short walk, starting outside St Peter's Church, Minsterworth. It follows the Gloucestershire Way through meadows with the River Severn flowing alongside. The walk is gentle, offering a settled view of low terraces, orchards, riverside trees. In spring there are wild flowers and apple blossom; in autumn browns and golds and probably mud! Away to the east and south the Cotswold Edge can be seen, whilst to the west the hills of the Forest of Dean appear on the skyline. After about 2.4km (1.5 miles), the route turns away from the river over fields to join a lane. From here there is a short extension to visit Redlands, the Harvey family house. The main route takes you back along the lane to Minsterworth Church and Harvey's grave.

*Blossom and the daffodils on the riverside at Minsterworth:*
*'the river flows, the blossom blows'*
*(Will Harvey, Gloucestershire, from abroad)*

## Route Details

### Distance/ Time:
3.8km (2.3 miles)/ 1.5–2 hours

### Maps:
OS Explorer 179, 1:25 000, Gloucester, Cheltenham & Stroud
OS Explorer OL14, 1:25 000 Wye Valley & Forest of Dean
OS Landranger 162, 1:50 000, Gloucester & Forest of Dean

### Start and Parking:
The walk starts next to St Peter's Church, Minsterworth (SO 773170; GL2 8JJ). Parking is available at the village hall, north of the main A48. You can then walk down a lane opposite to reach the church. Parking may be available in the village street or in the church car park (if no service is on).

### Tracks and Paths:
This is an easy, grassy walk alongside the river, with hardly any gain in height. There are several stiles as well as some gates, but the stiles are low and generally well-maintained. The return route is along a small lane.

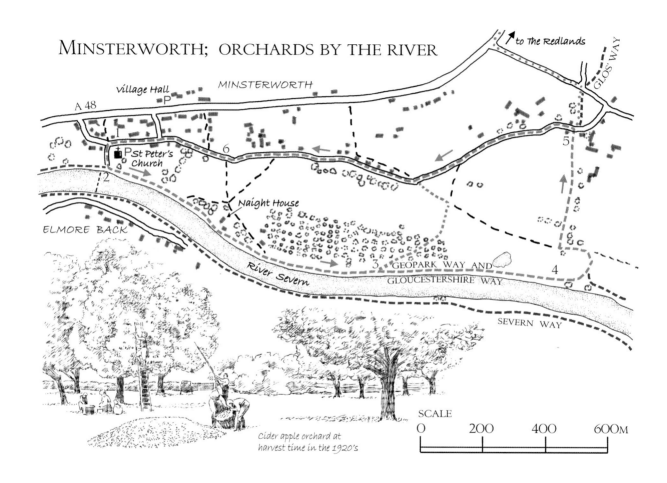

# MINSTERWORTH; ORCHARDS BY THE RIVER

MINSTERWORTH

to The Redlands

GLOS WAY

Village Hall

A 48

P

St Peter's
Church

6

5

2

ELMORE BACK

Naight House

River Severn

3 GEOPARK WAY AND
GLOUCESTERSHIRE WAY

4

SEVERN WAY

Cider apple orchard at
harvest time in the 1920's

SCALE

0        200        400        600M

## The Walk

① Start on the road outside St Peter's Church, where there is an information board about Will Harvey, and read the rest of **June-to-Come**.

**June-to-Come**
When the sun's fire and gold
Sets the bee humming,
I will not write to tell
Him that I'm coming

But ride out unawares
On that old road
Of Minsterworth, of Peace,
Of Framilode

And walk, not looked for, in
That cool dark passage.
Never a single word;
Myself my message.

And then; well … O we'll drift
And stand and gaze,
And wonder how we could
In those Bad Days

Live without Minsterworth;
Or western air
Fanning the hot cheek,
Stirring the hair;

In land where hate of men
God's love did cover;
This land … And here's my dream
Irrevocably over.

(s&s/ we)

• We will return to the churchyard and Harvey's grave at the end of the walk. For now, walk down the path (Church Passage) to reach the river.

**Will Harvey** and Ivor Gurney met by chance on a Gloucester tram in 1908, when Harvey was 20 years old and Gurney was 18. Although Harvey had briefly attended the King's School, Gloucester, they hardly knew each other then due to the age difference, and Harvey was moved away to a Lancashire school in 1902. The 1908 meeting began a new era of friendship, at its most intense and meaningful in the pre-war period and built round their close relationship with Gloucestershire places. They were both at a formative age – no longer children but not yet fully adult; both born in Gloucestershire; both active, outdoor people; both talented, lapping up poetry, music and literary conversation – and their friendship unfolded in this place along the riverside paths and lush meadows of the Severn Valley.

The war separated them when Will Harvey signed up in 1914 to join the 1/5th battalion of the Gloucestershire Regiment and Gurney joined the 2/5th battalion in 1915. Both men used their Gloucestershire experiences as a way of dealing with the terrible ordeals they had to face. In August 1916, Harvey was reported missing, and Gurney believed him dead until October 1916 when news came that he was a prisoner-of-war. The poem **To His Love** (p. 77) refers to his death. Two more poems, **June-to-Come** and **Ypres-Minsterworth**, are dedicated to Harvey in prison. After the war, in 1919/20 the two were able to meet, to walk and even spend Christmas together in 1920 at Redlands, the Harvey family home. Will Harvey recorded in his notebook for Christmas day 1920, 'A memorable evening at home in the music room after 10 miles walking with Ivor Gurney – O joy of that companionship'. But events took them away from each other and from Gloucestershire. For Harvey it was marriage and conversion to Catholicism; for Gurney after December 1922, it was a long-term separation as he was shut away in the asylum. For both men the Severn Meadows would always represent their identification with Gloucestershire, their creative aspirations and their deep friendship.

② Here pause and notice the Severn Bore information board and the river itself. The Minsterworth ferry crossed from this point. It was used by Will Harvey to reach Framilode and the boat he shared with Gurney (see Walk 7), although the ferry service closed in 1941. The river looks serene but can show a wilder side in the spring and autumn months. The Severn Bore is a moving series of waves formed when the rising tide is channelled into the funnel-shaped Bristol Channel and Severn Estuary, and the surging water forces its way upstream as far as Gloucester and beyond.

• After leaving Gloucester, the Severn makes a big loop to the south but generally follows a south-westerly course guided by the geology, picking out the softer clays and flowing between areas of higher ground and harder rock to the west and east.

• Walk on down the Gloucestershire Way, noting that the footpath sign refers to forest, vale and high blue hills, quoting Harvey's poem **A Song of Gloucestershire**. Look to your left at the church in its grounds, with a prominent yew tree under which is Harvey's grave, to which we will return later. In springtime, there will be first snowdrops and then daffodils (or, as Gurney often called them, *dancers*). On the other side of the river is the small hamlet of Elmore Back.

**Gloucester**

Many have praised dancers
As folk of fine pride –
And I have seen foreigners* [*non-native flowers*]
Dance – beauty revealed.

But on sombre ruddy
Lit lands of Gloucester –
Suddenly in March, suddenly
Gold princesses were master

Of lovely and emerald lit fields
Winter saw desolate …
They sang to far hills melodies
Like Easter water in spate.

They were like young children come
To a century-lonely house –
Heralds of glory should soon foam
And glitter beside the hedgerows.

(K2004)

*The salmon hut on the Gloucestershire Way*

• Eventually you will reach a gate. Go through this and walk on the embankment surrounded by trees. To your left, look out for Naight House, a substantial dwelling dating from the Middle Ages, although its looks owe more to Georgian rebuilding. Next to the riverside path is the two-storey, red-brick fisherman's hut, an example of the salmon huts that were used to store equipment (usually upstairs, as the lower level was expected to flood). The huts provided shelter for the fishermen while they waited for the tide, and some had a fireplace to burn driftwood for warmth and to brew tea. Few original salmon huts remain (but see Walk 6).

• Another gateway marks where you leave the Naight House land and return to the riverside fields and the orchards. There were many more acres of orchard trees in the early twentieth century, and both Gurney and Harvey loved *the tangled orchards blowing bright / With clouds of apple blossom* (Harvey, **My Village**). Gurney's poem **Ypres-Minsterworth** is a celebration of this Severnside landscape as well as a heartfelt prayer for his friend incarcerated in a prisoner-of-war camp. The indoor references are to Harvey's home, Redlands.

*The remains of Minsterworth orchards*

## Ypres-Minsterworth

Thick lie in orchards now
Apples the Severn wind
With rough play tore from the tossing
Branches, and left behind
Leaves strewn on pastures, blown in hedges,
And by the roadway lined.

And I lie leagues on leagues afar
To think how that wind made
Great shoutings in the wide chimney,
A noise of cannonade –
Of how the proud elms by the signpost
The tempest's will obeyed.

To think how in some German prison
A boy lies with whom
I might have taken joy full-hearted
Hearing the great boom
Of autumn, watching the fire, talking
Of books in half gloom.

Oh wind of Ypres and of Severn
Riot there also and tell
Of comrades safe returned, home-keeping
Music and autumn smell.
Comfort blow him and friendly greeting,
Hearten him and wish him well!

(K2004)

③ About 1km from the start of the walk, a well-defined path turns away from the river and runs diagonally to the boundary through the orchard trees.

• This can be used as a shortcut to the Minsterworth lane (although it was very overgrown in 2022). If using it, go through the gate and across the next field, also diagonally, to reach a double stile (poorly maintained in 2022) either side of a ditch. Once over the stile, turn left up a farm track to join the road.

• The main path takes you on down the riverside, over two stiles before you reach a pond and reed bed to the left with a bridge straight ahead over the poorly-drained ground. One of the main characteristics of the Severn Valley is the enclosing high land. As you walk, you become aware of the hills – first the line of the Cotswold scarp away to the south-east across the Severn and, looking back to the south-west, you will see May Hill. For both Harvey and Gurney, their enjoyment of the Severn Valley encompassed this long view as well, as in Harvey's famous poem **In Flanders**, that Gurney said would be in anthologies for hundreds of years hence.

> **In Flanders** (*extract*)
> I'm homesick for my hills again,
> My hills again!
> To see above the Severn Plain
> Unscabbarded against the sky
> The blue high blade of Cotswold lie;

④ After crossing another stile (2.4km from the start) your path soon turns away to the left round the edge of the field. Walkers have made a shortcut alongside the fence immediately after the stile, which cuts off a corner. Either way, you reach a copse and a stile into the next field, still on the Gloucestershire Way. Walk straight ahead over two more stiles and a small wooden bridge into a paddock next to a house. The path is a right of way and runs next to the house and yard, and out onto the road.

⑤ At this point, it is possible to do a short extension walk up to Redlands where Will Harvey grew up, and a place much loved by Ivor Gurney. In this case, follow the Gloucestershire Way signs over the edge of a field to reach the road further up. Walk up this road to the site of the former Apple Tree Inn (derelict in 2022). Cross over the main A48 and find Redlands a little to the right on the opposite side of road.

*Redlands – the home of Will Harvey and his family*

## Redlands and Will Harvey

We know from Gurney's later poetry that Will Harvey's family became very dear to him and that he spent a great deal of time in the family home, Redlands, *a creeper-covered house* at Minsterworth near the River Severn. It was a large, comfortable and happy household where Gurney could mingle with the family: three brothers, a sister and their easy-going parents. *Within the house were books, / A piano dear to me / And round the house the rooks / Haunted each tall elm tree* (**The Farm**, *S&S/ WE*).

As Anthony Boden explains in his biography of Will Harvey (*F.W. Harvey: Soldier, Poet*, 2011), the home was always full of laughter, good food and, significantly, books and music. The two boys became virtually inseparable.

As Boden notes,

Whenever possible, the pair would escape together to the welcoming farm at Minsterworth to help in the fields, to walk in the Severn meadows, to pick fruit in the orchard, to play 'ping-pong' on the long dining room table or cricket with Will's brothers and friends, to set off with guns to bag rabbits for the pot, to make music, and always to talk.

Gurney might have found the atmosphere in the Harvey home much more restful than in the sometimes tense and overcrowded conditions of Barton Street. It may have been a natural desire for independence, as well as his increasing sophistication, that led Gurney away from his own family. 'He did not seem to belong to us … he simply called on us briefly and left again without a word', his sister Winifred remembered. While his family felt 'cut out', we do know that it was in this period that his passion for music and poetry, and the connection of both these with walking the Gloucestershire countryside, was greatly enhanced.

The poem **After-Glow** (overleaf), written in 1917 when Harvey was in a prisoner-of-war camp, is a poignant mix of wonder roused by the natural beauty around him and the joys of companionship found at Redlands with Will Harvey.

## After-Glow

Out of the smoke and dust of the little room
With tea-talk loud and laughter of happy boys,
I passed into the dusk. Suddenly the noise
Ceased with a shock, left me alone in the
    gloom,
To wonder at the miracle hanging high
Tangled in twigs, the silver crescent clear –
Time passed from mind. Time died; and then
    we were
Once more at home together, you and I.

The elms with arms of love wrapped us in
    shade
Who watched the ecstatic west with one
    desire,
One soul uprapt; and still another fire
Consumed us, and our joy yet greater made:
That Bach should sing for us, mix us in one
The joy of firelight and the sunken sun.

                                                        (K2004)

• From Point 5, continue along the road towards Minsterworth, enjoying the peace of a rural lane even while the A48 traffic roars a few fields away. Away east is the *blue blade of Cotswold*. About 0.5km along the road, at a layby, you pass the farm track coming in from the left, where the shortcut from river and orchard comes out. In another 0.5km there are signs for Naight House to the left.

⑥ Walk on into the village and back to the church. Go to the church door, noticing steps up to reach it, as a result of the church having been rebuilt at a higher level in 1869/70 after the original one flooded regularly.

• Go round the side of the church to find Harvey's grave on the eastern side under a yew tree. F.W. Harvey is commemorated by a stained-glass window in the church, commissioned by The F.W. Harvey Society, and virtually overlooking his grave.

• Harvey's grave may be a fitting place to read the final two poems, one by Gurney and one by Harvey, both reflecting on the way the war ruined their lives and relationship. Gurney's poem was written in 1917 when he thought that Harvey was dead, but it has since become seen as an elegy for all young soldiers who did not return from the war. Harvey's poem was written later, when Harvey had retreated into domestic and community life in the Forest of Dean. He only visited Gurney in the asylum a few times, seeming to find it too distressing, but his poem shows that he did appreciate the awful sadness of his friend's exclusion – from love and friendship, health and Gloucestershire. Is there, maybe, a hint of an apology there? (*not that I fear to keep the faith*).

*Will Harvey's grave at St Peter's Church, Minsterworth*

**To his love** (*to F.W. Harvey by Ivor Gurney*)
He's gone, and all our plans
Are useless indeed.
We'll walk no more on Cotswold
Where the sheep feed
Quietly and take no heed.

His body that was so quick
Is not as you
Knew it, on Severn river
Under the blue
Driving our small boat through.

You would not know him now …
But still he died
Nobly, so cover him over
With violets of pride
Purple from Severn side.

Cover him, cover him soon!
And with thick-set
Masses of memoried flowers –
Hide that red wet
Thing I must somehow forget.

(K2004)

**To Ivor Gurney** (*by F.W. Harvey*)

Now hawthorn hedges live again;
And all along the banks below
Pale primrose fires have lit the lane
Where oft we wandered long ago
And saw the blossom blow.

And talked and walked till stars pricked out,
And sang brave midnight snatches under
The moon, with never a dread nor doubt,
Nor warning of that devil's wonder
That tore our lives asunder.

And left behind a nightmare trail
Of horrors scattered through the brain,
Of shattered hopes and memories frail
That bloom like flowers in some old lane
And tear the heart in twain.

This hawthorn hedge will bank its snow
Spring after Spring, and never care
What song and dreams of long ago
Within its shade were fashioned fair
Of happy air.

But you within the madhouse wall,
But you and I who went so free,
Never shall keep Spring's festival
Again, though burgeon every tree
With blossom joyously.

Not that I fear to keep the faith;
Not that my heart goes cravenly;
But that some voice within me saith
'The Spring is dead!' yea, dead, since he
Will come no more to me.

It needeth but a tear to quench
The primrose fires: to melt the snow
Of Spring-time hedges, and to drench
With black the blue clear heavens show …
And I have wept for you.

(BODEN AND THORNTON 2011)

# Longney and Bollow Pool

**March** (*extract*)
My boat moves and I with her delighting,
Feeling the water slide past, and watching white fashion
Of water, as she moves faster ever more whitening

(GA)

This walk begins in the village of Longney before joining the Severn Way where wide riverside horizons open out, evoking memories of Ivor Gurney and Will Harvey sailing on the Severn in the 1908–11 period. Their boat, the Dorothy, was kept at Framilode, but much of their sailing took advantage of the tides to go upstream – or, as Harvey's own poem **Ballade of River Sailing** explained it, *see her dancing on the tide, and you'll / Swear she's the prettiest little craft that goes / Up-stream from Framilode to Bollopool.* Gurney would have reached Framilode and Longney by foot or bicycle from Gloucester, while Harvey may have used the former ferry crossing from Minsterworth to Elmore Back and walked down the lanes to meet him.

The Longney walk provides a glimpse of the attractions of this Severnside landscape. Although large housing developments have taken place to the south of Gloucester since the 1960s, the area to the west of the Gloucester-Sharpness canal has managed to avoid major changes, and Elmore Back, Epney, Longney and Framilode would probably still be recognisable to Gurney and Harvey. The route follows the Severn Way upstream, pausing to discover Bollow Pool (Bollopool) and to note the views of the Cotswold Edge, Forest of Dean and May Hill, before reaching riverside orchards, now being revived as part of a Heritage Orchard Project. Returning to the road, the path turns south again to finish at Longney Church.

This walk is closely based on one planned by Phil Richardson. Thanks to him for the route ideas and many insights about the local area.

## Route Details

DISTANCE/ TIME:
5.6km (3.5 miles)/ 2–2.5 hours

MAPS:
OS Explorer OL14, 1:25 000, Wye Valley & Forest of Dean
OS Landranger 162, 1:50 000, Gloucester & Forest of Dean

START AND PARKING:
The walk starts in the road next to St Lawrence Church,
Longney (SO 763 124; GL2 3SL) on the River Severn to the
south of Gloucester. Parking is usually available on the road.
Alternatively, try the layby at Bowlane at Point 5.

TRACKS AND PATHS:
This is an easy walk on footpaths, grassy tracks alongside the
river and quiet lanes, with hardly any gain in height. There
are some gates and one stile (two more stiles if you take the
alternative route at Bowlane).

*Gurney's boat, the Dorothy on the Severn near Longney*
*(© The Ivor Gurney Trust)*

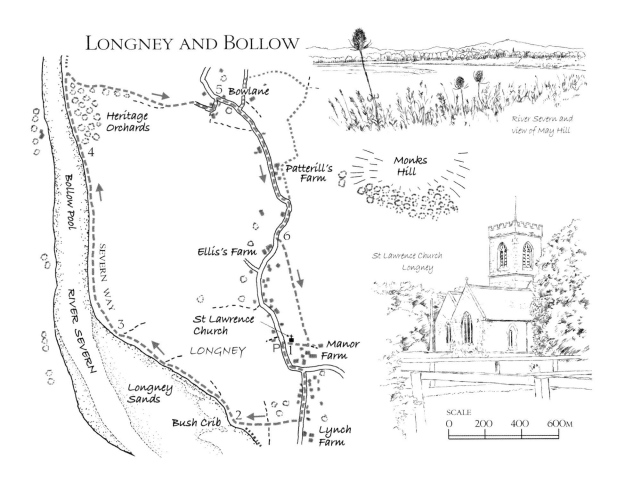

# Longney and Bollow

5 Bowlane

Heritage Orchards

4

Bollow Pool

RIVER SEVERN

SEVERN WAY

Patterill's Farm

Monks Hill

Ellis's Farm

6

St Lawrence Church
Longney

3

St Lawrence Church

LONGNEY

P 1

Manor Farm

Longney Sands

Bush Crib

2

Lynch Farm

River Severn and
view of May Hill

SCALE
0    200    400    600M

## THE WALK

① The walk begins outside St Lawrence's Church in the middle of Longney. Most of the buildings lie on a gravel ridge and there is evidence to suggest that the course of the river once lay to the east. The name, meaning 'long island', seems to hint at this and the present course of the Severn is only two fields away from the houses now. Gurney's poem **Longney** welcomes the peace and sweetness that Longney's situation grants it and, as he frequently does, Gurney compares this with the greater bitterness of town living.

### Longney

These have grown grave-eyed by the smoothy river,
Who gleamed in glance and ran so hard and swift.
Life now has sobered them for ever and ever.

Though in the towns Life's known an evil gift,
And being but a bitterness thrust on,
Here is such sweetness in the wind's light lift.

And such a grace in action from the sun,
This folk is mild of heart; the folk had liever [*rather*]
Keep calm aside from crowds and hot endeavour. (80P)

• Walk south down the road to reach the junction and here take the right turn towards Epney. About 0.5km from the church, notice a white house on the left called Brickmaker's House, a recognition of the many brick kilns present on Severnside. *Severn has kilns set all along her banks / Where the thin reeds grow and rushes in ranks* (**Kilns**).

• Just beyond this house there is a footpath to the right, next to Lynch Cottage. Take this and go through a gate. At a path junction, look ahead, slightly to the right, to see May Hill and to the left the outline of the Forest of Dean. Carry straight on down to the river.

② Standing on slightly higher ground at the edge of the Severn, you are standing on Bush Crib, a reinforced river wall, of which there are many in the Longney area. The Longney Cribs may date from at least the thirteenth century, with eight being recorded in 1569. Their recent strengthening and heightening has allowed the Severn Way to continue all along this stretch of riverside. One main advantage of the height is a much better viewing experience. From the top of Bush Crib there are fine views across Longney Sands, away to the Forest of Dean in the distance. Looking back downstream (left), it is possible to catch sight of the Anchor Inn, Epney.

*Standing on Bush Crib, with May Hill in the distance*

• Follow the Severn Way upstream on a raised embankment, enjoying the open landscape and the views. Depending on weather and visibility, you may see May Hill ahead and behind you a glimpse of the Cotswold Edge near Cam Long Down.

Throughout the twentieth century, this stretch of riverbank has been popular with fishermen, especially during the spring when elvers were plentiful. Gurney's poem **Rainy Midnight** recalls the fishermen with their lights strung out along the banks.

## Rainy Midnight

Long shines the line of wet lamps dark in gleaming,
The trees so still felt yet as strength not used,
February chills April, the cattle are housed,
And night's grief from the higher things comes
  streaming.

The traffic is all gone, the elver fishers gone
To string their lights 'long Severn like a wet Fair.
If it were fine the elvers would swim clear;
Clothes sodden, the out-of-work stay.

(K2004)

Will Harvey also wrote a poem entitled **Elvers** that spoke of the *wormy, squirmy fish that fry for breakfast.*

• Looking to your right as you walk, you should see Longney Church on the horizon. Eventually, you reach a hedgerow and beside it a path running across the field back towards Longney village.

③ From this point, continue along the Severn Way. Alongside you is the stretch of river that Gurney sailed. He needed to avoid the dangerous Longney Sands and to keep in a deep water channel, usually near the far bank. The river is shielded by tall rushes but there are occasional breaks in the vegetation, small pathways down to the muddy shore, and glimpses of the other bank. Eventually the river channel narrows beside you and Bollow Pool, an area of deeper water welcomed by boats of all types, appears below you. This is the stretch of water that Gurney and Harvey would have been waiting for.

*'Over Bollow comes the wind I've been waiting' – the river at Longney*

**March**
My boat moves and I with her delighting,
Feeling the water slide past, and watching white fashion
Of water, as she moves faster ever more whitening;
Till up at the white sail in that great sky heightening
Of fine cloth spread against azure and cloud
  commotion
My face looks, and there is joy in the eyes that asking
Fulfilment of the heart's true and golden passion
(Long dimmed) now gets hold of a truth and an action …
The ears take the sound of Severn water dashing.
The great spirit remembers Ulysses with his courage
  lighting
Before the danger of sea water, in a rocky passion
Of surges – and over Bollow comes the wind I've been
  waiting.

(GA)

As Gurney explains in **March**, *My boat moves and I with her delighting, / Feeling the water slide past, and watching white fashion / Of water, as she moves ever whitening.* The reader appreciates the same hypnotic effect produced by watching the water; hears with the poet the *sound of Severn water dashing* and even raises one's head to glimpse the azure sky. **March** expresses delight and wonder in the place, as produced through the activity of sailing. The place is speaking through the poet and the movement is crucial to all this.

• After 1km of walking from Point 3 you will reach a gate. Go through it to find an information board about the Gloucestershire Orchard Trust and the work being done to celebrate and preserve traditional 'heritage' orchards. The next four fields represent a key feature of its work.

④ The first field is Lower Orchard and the route then passes through Middle Orchard, where you may see plum trees as well as apple. (Take care as there may be sheep grazing between the trees. Please leave all gates as you find them – open or shut.) Immediately after entering Bollow Orchard (the third field), look ahead to see a huge patch of brambles covering an old building with fences around it. This is a ruined fish hut, dating originally from the eighteenth century and due for renovation as an historic building (see also Walk 5). Your path now lies this side of the fish hut and to the right into Long Tyning Orchard.

*Bollow Orchard in autumn*

### The Longney Orchards

In 2015, generous donations allowed Gloucestershire Orchard Trust to buy 18 acres of Severnside land near Longney, which included two fully productive but ancient orchards and an area of old orchard that can be replanted. The old orchards of Bollow and Long Tyning contain hundreds of fruit trees representing over 35 varieties of apple, perry pears and plum. The priority in Long Tyning and Bollow Orchards is to rejuvenate the trees and grassland whilst protecting and enhancing their high ecological value. Sheep-grazing has been reintroduced now that fencing is completed. The field known as Middle Orchard was a remnant orchard with just a handful of trees remaining. Together with an adjacent field, now renamed Lower Orchard, it has been planted up with new fruit trees, including plums and the Gloucestershire Apple Collection.

All activities at the Longney site are being undertaken in partnership with local community groups and with help from the Three Counties Traditional Orchard Project. The nineteenth-century field barn between Long Tyning and Bollow has been repaired to use as a base for work in the orchards and educational visits. There are plans to restore the other building on the site – notably one of the last remaining Severn Fish Houses, dating back to the mid/ late 1700s. (Edited extract from Gloucestershire Orchards Trust website: www.glosorchards.org/home/got-orchards/).

*The ruined and fenced-off Old Fish House, awaiting restoration*

• Make your way through the orchard trees, passing and maybe stopping to inspect the Orchard Centre in a repaired barn to the right of the path. There are usually posters and information boards to read. During autumn, you may see the Longney Russet apple growing, with its distinctive browny-gold skin and musky smell. This type of apple originated here and was particularly prized as a cider apple.

• Gurney relished all the seasons and the orchards must have been a beautiful sight in spring. A poem entitled **April Mist** expresses his feelings.

**April Mist**
Dampness clings about me as I walk
And the sun but filters through
High clouds unmoving, threatening rain.
Leaf mould clings, and the leafy drift below.

But how the green has sprung in a single night;
What sudden flood bears high the foam of May!
Pear trees and apple trees grown twice as bright
And pinpoints grown to buds between day and day!

(80P)

• The footpath leads onto a track heading out of the orchard area, over a stile, around a field edge and a house and out onto the Elmore-Longney Road. In Gurney's day, there was a beerhouse called the Bowlane Inn, run by David Matthews, at this roadside. There is still a Bow Lane House and Bow Lane Cottage here, and according to the Gloucestershire Pubs Database (October 2022), 'presumably one of these properties was once the Bow Lane Inn. Bow Lane Cottage is a sixteenth-century, timber-framed thatched property with cruck frames. The low rateable value of just £6 in 1903 suggests that the pub was a very small cottage style beer house.' The pub closed in 1924. In his essay 'Sailing', Gurney commented that there were plenty of public houses in this Severnside area: 'there is no danger of common thirst being made to suffer'. Unfortunately, he would find the situation very different now!

⑤ At the road, turn right (back towards Longney) walking past Bowlane Farm on the left and Peglass Cottage and Glamping Orchard to the right. You now have a choice. The most straightforward route is to walk on the road about 0.7km to Ellis's Farm. Alternatively, at the entrance to Briery Hall, take the footpath sign to the left and follow the field paths (this can be slightly overgrown in places and has several stiles).

**Alternative route by field paths**

Ignore the first path to the right, which passes through the grounds of Briery Hall (this can be difficult to access), and walk further on a gravel track, eventually bearing right, and walk along the edge of a long, grassy field. At a path junction turn right and over a little wooden bridge. The path is sometimes overgrown. You will come out in an area planted with vines.

The original path ran diagonally across the field, but you will need to go round the left edge of the field to reach a stile. Cross this and walk along the field edge to find another stile. Now pass a pond to your left and make your way all along behind Patterill's Farm buildings and a couple of houses to reach a final field of rough grazing with a gate diagonally down to your left. The path is only faintly marked in this last section. You are now back on the Longney road not far from Ellis's farm.

• Eventually, there is a faint footpath across the field behind the church leading to a gate in the church wall. Take this into the churchyard and return to the village street.

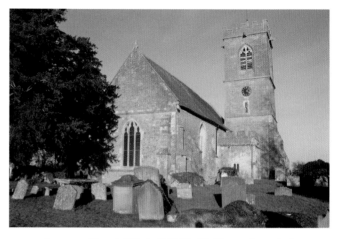

*Longney Church (Photo © Philip Halling cc-by-sa/2.0)*

⑥ Just before Ellis's Farm, cross a footbridge on your left, turn right and then follow the path round to the left before walking the grassy footpaths that run south, parallel to the road. Most of the paddocks around you are occupied by horses from the Manor Farm Stables.

# Framilode:
# a blowy Severn tided place

### First Framilode

When I saw Framilode first she was a blowy
Severn tided place under azure sky
Able to take care of Herself, less girl than boy.
But since that time passed, many times the extreme
Of mystery of beauty and last possibility
Of colour, sea-breathed romance far past any may dream.

(GA)

This walk introduces Framilode, a place that Gurney loved and viewed as a second home. It was at Framilode that Gurney learned to sail and it was from James Harris the lock-keeper (or with his help) that he and Will Harvey probably purchased the small boat, the *Dorothy*, in 1908. Gurney often visited this area and sailed on the river with Will in the 1908–11 period. He also stayed with Harris at Lock House in 1913 when he was recovering from a breakdown, and the restorative effect of his stay can be judged from the letters he sent to Marion Scott in that year: 'Why stay in Bridgewater? Come to Framilode, Fretherne, Elmore, Arlingham, Saul!' (June 1913) – all places on this stretch of the lower Severn. Here, the Severn is wide and expansive, occupying the foreground with its long gleaming stretches of water and yellowy-grey sandbanks (*extreme of mystery, of beauty and last possibility / of colour*), while the Cotswold Edge to the east and the Forest of Dean to the west provide a permanent backdrop of hill shapes. Framilode also meant the companionship of Will Harvey, with whom Gurney spent many a happy hour sailing or watching the elver fishermen, *when elver-lights made the river like a stall-road to see*, as Gurney explains later in **First Framilode**.

This walk begins at St Peter's Church, Upper Framilode, before heading downstream alongside the Severn. In Gurney's day the Stroudwater Canal, now disused, met the Severn just upstream of this point and the lock-keeper's house (Lock House) is situated a few metres up the village street (to be viewed later). The walk follows the riverside past the former ferry crossing point, through the hamlet of Priding and alongside river meadows. It leaves the riverside to walk up Overton Lane and ascend the second Barrow Hill (another Barrow Hill will be encountered in Walk 19). From this 'small hill not a mile away from where I stayed' (June 1913), there is a wonderful view of the river and all the surrounding hills of the Forest of Dean and the Cotswolds. The descent of the hill takes you through the copse where Gurney heard the nightingales sing. Field paths take you back via Wick Court, an old, moated farmhouse, returning to the riverside to regain the church.

*'A Blowy Severn tided place' – the Severn at Framilode*

## Route Details

DISTANCE/ TIME:
4.7km (2.9 miles)/ 1.5–2 hours

MAPS:
*OS Explorer OL14, 1:25 000, Wye Valley & Forest of Dean*
*OS Landranger 162, 1:50 000, Gloucester & Forest of Dean*

START AND PARKING:
The walk starts by the river next to St Peter's Church, Upper Framilode (SO 750105; GL2 7LJ). Parking is available on the track outside the church.

TRACKS AND PATHS:
This is an easy walk on footpaths and lanes alongside the river but with about 50m gain in height to climb Barrow Hill (two stiles if you use the field route between Points 1 and 2).

# A Blowy Severn-Tided Place; Framilode

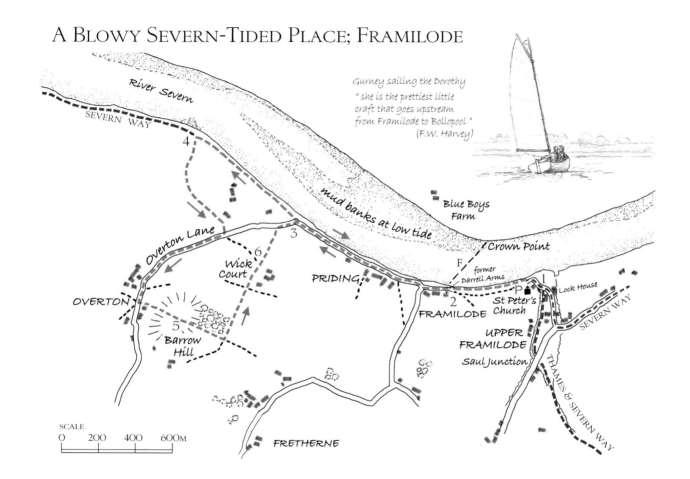

River Severn

SEVERN WAY

*Gurney sailing the Dorothy*
*" she is the prettiest little*
*craft that goes upstream*
*from Framilode to Bollopool "*
*(F.W. Harvey)*

mud banks at low tide

Blue Boys Farm

Crown Point

Overton Lane

Wick Court

PRIDING

former Darrell Arms

OVERTON

FRAMILODE

St Peter's Church

Lock House

Barrow Hill

UPPER FRAMILODE

SEVERN WAY

Saul Junction

THAMES & SEVERN WAY

FRETHERNE

SCALE
0   200   400   600M

## The Walk

① Start at St Peter's Church.

> 'In 1846 the inhabitants of Framilode were described
> as "watermen and their families in a most demoralised
> and unenlightened state." It is tempting to link this
> statement to the building of the church, designed by
> Francis Niblett, which was consecrated in 1854. St
> Peter's is a fine example of early Victorian design,
> simple and economic with a hint of the exotic in
> its Italianate bell tower. As befits a riverside church
> the decoration incorporates nautical motifs, such as
> anchors and representations of the tinplate workings
> that took place in the village.' (Extract from:
> www.stroudwaterchurches.org.uk/)

• Before you start walking, look up- and downstream to see
the main stretch of river along which Gurney and Harvey
sailed the Dorothy. Gurney's poem, **Framilode the Queen**
and Harvey's poem **The Ballade of River Sailing** both express
delight and wonder in this place, as produced through the
activity of sailing. The companionship, movement and sense
of adventure involved in sailing strengthened the bond
between them as well as developing their work in their own
distinctive ways.

**Framilode the Queen** (*extract*)
The tanned faced Vikings venturing the open Sea
Were not so full of glory as was I
When the wind played treacherous boisterous tricks
　on me
Hot faced with rudder hauling, nowhere dry
(Shaving the sandbanks barely
By God – right over – nearly)
Filled with the noise of water, sight of the sky.
I loved it all, despite wise folks warning
That they'd wake up some morning,
And find my body over there on the mud.
The song of waters rushing sang in my blood,
Prudence and the tattle of gossips scorning
Since danger was so high and jolly
Why Prudence might go hang with melancholy.

(CPW)

**Ballade of River Sailing** (*extract, by F.W. Harvey*)
The Dorothy was very small: a boat
Scarce any bigger than the sort one rows
With oars! We got her for a five-pound note
At second-hand. Yet when the river flows
Strong to the sea, and the wind lightly blows,
Then see her dancing on the tide, and you'll
Swear she's the prettiest little craft that goes
Up-stream from Framilode to Bollopool.

Bare-footed, push her from the bank afloat,
(The soft warm mud comes squelching through your
    toes!)
Scramble aboard: then find an antidote
For every care a jaded spirit knows:
While round the boat the broken water crows
With laughter, casting pretty ridicule
On human life and all its little woes,
Up-stream from Framilode to Bollopool.
                    (BODEN AND THORNTON 2011)

*'Up-stream from Framilode to Bollopool'*

• From the church, follow the Severn Way signs westwards besides the river. You can walk inside the field (with stiles to cross) or directly along the riverbank if the river is not too high, peering through waterside rushes to see the wide muddy riverscapes.

② In less than 1km you go through a gate and reach lower Framilode. The first large timber-framed house on the left is the former Darrell Arms, an inn which flourished in the nineteenth and early twentieth centuries as the servicing point for ferry passengers from Rodley. The Darrell Arms closed in the 1980s but the private house still has the iron balcony designed for spectators to view the river crossings as they drank their beer. Walk on through Framilode, take the right turn and proceed on down the road, passing the long line of houses known as Priding. The views of the Cotswold Edge are always changing behind you.

*The former Darrell Arms at the ferry crossing point*

**Near Midsummer** (*extract*)
Severn's most fair today!
See what a tide of blue
She pours, and flecked alway
With gold, and what a crew
Of seagulls snowy white
Float round her to delight
Villagers, travellers.
A brown thick flood is hers
In winter when the rains
Wash down from Midland plains,
Halting wayfarers,
Low meadows flooding deep
With torrents from the steep
Mountains of Wales and small
Hillocks of no degree –
Streams jostling to the sea;
(Wrangling yet brotherly).
Blue June has altered all –
The river makes its fall
With murmurous still sound,
Past Pridings faery ground,
And steep – down Newnham cliff …
O Boys in trenches, if

You could see what any may
(Escaping town for the day),
Strong Severn all aglow,
But tideless running slow:
Far Cotswolds all a-shimmer,
Blue Bredon leagues away –
Huge Malverns, farther, dimmer …
Then you would feel the fire
Of the First Days inspire
You, when, despising all
Save England's honour's call,
You dared the worst for her …

(S&S/ WE)

In this poem, written after Gurney's return to England, he explains how Gloucestershire is seen as a home worth fighting for: *my county Gloucester, that whether I die or live stays always with me, being in itself so beautiful, so full of memories …* (Preface to *Severn and Somme*, 1917)

③ Where the road turns sharp left after Priding's House, take the Severn Way footpath straight on across fields. Cross two fields, a coppice and join a third field (note that it is difficult to be exact about the number of fields as they are often merged and temporary fences moved). Ahead of you, the Forest of Dean is often visible and May Hill to the north-west; behind you Painswick Beacon and the Cotswold Edge appears. After the third field, there is a small bridge over a drainage ditch. Our route turns left here.

• If you wish to extend the walk via Arlingham (something which Gurney often did, enjoying the Roman connections and the Severn landscapes), go straight on, though note that this will add about 4km to the walk. One of Gurney's favourite pubs, the Red Lion, is in the village of Arlingham.

④ For this walk, take the left turn going uphill alongside the field edge. The path narrows as it crosses another field (sometimes divided up and with fencing, depending on the livestock arrangements). Go through a gate to reach the road, with the entrance to Wick Farm opposite (as this is a public right of way, the way to the road should remain accessible).

• Turn right to walk along Overton Lane to the village. Pass a barn and Oldbury Farm and then Saltway House. At a cross-path junction, turn off the road left and uphill to climb through pasture to the top of Barrow Hill. The trig point, at 62m, is slightly off the path to the right next to an old oak tree.

⑤ Pause at the top of the hill to enjoy the view on all sides, including of the river (on three sides), the Forest of Dean, May Hill, the Cotswolds, the Malvern Hills and, if you are lucky, a glimpse of Gloucester Cathedral. Gurney loved this hill and its view – 'Oh what a place! Blue river and golden sand, and blue-black hills – in fine weather, of course.' (Letter to Marion Scott, June 1913).

*The view from Barrow Hill looking south-east, with the Cotswold Edge in distance*

• From the top, retrace your steps to the path before descending the hill to the right, first to a gate out of the pasture then alongside a wood to a second gate. Do not follow the path straight on but turn left through another gate into the woods. Take this path and you are now in the copse, written about by Ivor Gurney in the poem **The Nightingales**. Imagine the darkening woods *with a slip of moon, in a sort of dusk* as he heard not one, but three nightingales sing. This is not a sentimental poem – *should I lie because at midnight one had nightingales?* Gurney seems to prefer the song of the linnet he had heard in Fretherne Lane!

### The Nightingales

Three I heard once together in Barrow Hill copse –
At midnight, with a slip of moon, in a sort of dusk.
They were not shy, heard us, and continued uttering
   their notes.

But after 'Adelaide'* and the poets' ages of praise
How could I think such beautiful; or utter false the lies
Fit for verse? It was only bird song, a midnight strange
   new noise.

\* Adelaide – A song by Beethoven

But a month before a laughing linnet in the gold had
   sung,
(And green) as if poet or musician had never before
   true tongue
To tell out nature's magic with any truth kept for long …

By Fretherne Lane the linnet (in the green) I shall not
   forget
(Nor gold) the start of wonder – the joy to be so in debt
To beauty – to the hidden bird there in spring elms elate.

Should I lie then, because at midnight one had
   nightingales,
Singing a mile off in the young oaks that wake to look
   to Wales,
Dream and watch Severn – like me, will tell no false
   adoration in tales?

(K2004)

• At the end of the wood, continue straight ahead through
a wooden gate and walk across a meadow by the hedgerow
and reach another gate. Ignore the cross-path halfway
through the next field and carry straight on down a narrow
strip of land to Wick Court.

⑥ Stand in front of Wick Court gate and look at the section
of moat in front of you and the house behind.

*Wick Court with the moat in the foreground*

**Wick Court** is a Grade-II Listed late sixteenth- / early seventeenth-century timber-framed manor house standing on the site of a former medieval house dating back to the thirteenth century. The house has an intact, square-shaped moat, part of which may be seen from the gateway. The farm is in the Countryside Stewardship Scheme and is farmed directly by the Farms for Children Charity, using low impact, traditional methods. There are a total of 140 acres, 80 of which are grazed by neighbouring farmers. The charity farms 60 acres as a small-scale traditional livestock farm, with sheep, beef cattle, pigs and poultry. Wick Court also has a busy stable yard, where the children help care for ponies and horses.

• Walk across in front of the house and find another gate leading to a grassy track and footpath sign. Follow this down through two more gates and eventually walking through orchards to reach the road at Priding. Walk downhill to join the road where you left it at Point 3, next to Priding House.

• Retrace your steps (Points 3, 2 1) via the Priding Lane, Framilode, the Darrell Arms, and the river bank to St Peter's Church at Point 1.

• Before leaving Upper Framilode, it is worth walking up the village lane to find Lock House, a handsome red-brick house that you may be able to catch a glimpse of, behind tall hedges on the left-hand side of the road.

### Lock House

James Harris the lock-keeper lived at Lock House from 1911. As explained in the walk introduction, he was good friends with Gurney and had allowed him to convalesce here in 1913 when he was recovering from a breakdown. A poem entitled **The Lock Keeper** (dedicated to Edward Thomas) shows the deep respect and love he felt for this man who died before Gurney was able to see him again after the war. There are two versions of the poem. The shorter one printed in *War's Embers* (1919) is given below.

*Lock House, Upper Framilode*

### The Lock Keeper

A tall lean man he was, proud of his gun,
Of his garden, and small fruit trees every one
Knowing all weather signs, the flight of birds,
Farther than I could hear the falling thirds
Of the first cuckoo. Able at digging, he
Smoked his pipe ever, furiously, contentedly.
Full of old tales his memory was;
Yarns of both sea and land, full of wise saws

In rough fine speech; sayings his father had,
That worked a twelve hour day when but a lad.
Handy with timber, nothing come amiss
To his quick skill; and all the mysteries
Of sail-making, net-making, boat-building were his.
That dark face lit with bright bird eyes, his stride
Manner most friendly, courteous, stubborn pride,
I shall not forget, not yet his patience
With me, unapt, though many a far league hence
I'll travel for many a year, nor ever find
A winter night companion more to my mind,
Nor one more wise in ways of Severn river,
Though her villages I search for ever and ever.

(S&S/ WE)

• From the lock-keeper's house, you can walk back to the disused Stroudwater canal and follow the path alongside it, with small cottage doors to your left and the overgrown, reedy canal to your right. In a short while you will reach the Ship Inn, a place for refreshment before you leave Framilode.

'Sheer Falls of Green Slope' – looking out from Coaley Wood

# Part Three: Sheer Falls of Green Slope

The Cotswold Edge to the south of Gloucester is not so much a straight edge as a sinuous curving mosaic of hillsides dissected by valleys and combes with their *sheer falls of green slope*. The walks here introduce Gurney's explorations, mainly on his own, taking in high hilltops (such as Cam Long Down and Coaley Peak), prehistoric barrows and earthworks (Nympsfield Long Barrow, Uley Bury) and glimpses of the industrial heritage of the Stroud Valleys (at Brimscombe).

**Sheer Falls of Green Slope**  (*extract*)
Sheer falls of green slope against setting sun
And ruled by high majestic Severn vapour –
These are not easily known, when talking is done;
Life's truths fade awfully set down on plain paper
When Cotswold or the Severn-land's in question
And the maker must do – before the poem is done or
  known.

Here, as of Aeschylus or Sophocles the reading
Square Greek things thrust from thought and brought
  to that height
By happy or strong men wrought to a known master thing
Rough with no thought of small pains, wrestling not
  minding of bleeding.

(RW)

Gurney is explaining how difficult it is to sum up in words the beauty and transcendence of this landscape when the poet (*maker*) tries to set it down on paper. The poem also presents the reader with Aeschylus, Sophocles and Homer alongside the Cotswold slopes. 'Gurney holds up "the strong Greek things" as examples of the kind of aesthetic control to which he aspires' (George Walter, *Rewards of Wonder*, 2000). He looks for what he calls *squareness* or craftmanship in Cotswold buildings and landscapes, just as it exists in the work of Greek and Roman writers.

# Cam Long Down and Uley Bury

**Passionate Earth**
Where the new turned ploughland runs to clean
Edges of sudden grass-land, lovely, green –
Music, Music clings, Music exhales,
And inmost fragrance of a thousand tales.
There the heart lifts, the soul takes flight to sing
High at Heavens-gate; but loth for entering
Lest there such brown and green it never find;
Nor feel the sting
Of such a beauty left so far behind.

(CPW)

This walk is located at the southern edge of Gurney's Gloucestershire, which is recognisable by the rounded slopes of Cam Long Down, an outlier of the main Cotswold Edge, that Gurney saw like a sentinel on the skyline when he sailed on the Severn and walked the riverside footpaths.

Gurney knew the Stroud area from his boyhood. One poem written in the asylum (**Stroud**, BP) remembers exchanging stories with army comrades about games of football in Dursley and market days in Stroud. In the immediate post-war years, Gurney roamed on his own on the Cotswold Edge, often struggling with his mental and physical health, as we know from his writing and the letters of friends. In July 1921, Marion Scott's letter sympathised: 'these days have been dreadfully trying for you and the difficulties of finding work such a constant worry', she wrote, 'How are you feeling as to health? Are you better?' Gurney's replies ranged from the upbeat to the depressed, sometimes talking of the latest temporary job he had found (farm labourer, cinema pianist) or his attempt to return to the Royal College of Music, but always referencing the Cotswold and Severnside landscapes – 'one sight of Cooper's Hill beats all' (letter to Marion Scott, May 1922).

Gurney's poetry suggests that he visited the hills and villages around Stroud including Cam, Stinchcombe Hill, Dursley and Coaley Peak. There are frequent hints in his writing that Elizabethan players knew Cotswold places: a long, discursive poem of 1925 entitled **Twelfth Night** begins with the lines *For three weeks to Cotswold the*

*Southwark men went / Expecting to find the old goodness and the old kindness – / And found (as ever) the people of more sweet intent ….* In a poem about Dursley presented on this walk, Gurney considered the suggestion that the young Shakespeare may have briefly worked as a schoolmaster in Dursley school, and wondered about the impact of the Cotswold scenery on Shakespeare's writing.

   This walk begins at Uley Bury, one of the finest Iron Age hillforts along the Edge. It then drops down the Edge before rising to climb Cam Long Down, offering a fine view over the Severn Vale and the small town of Dursley. Finally, the route crosses the farmland under the Cotswold Edge and climbs back up through beech woodlands to complete a circuit of the Uley Bury Iron Age Camp.

*Ploughland edge on Cam Long Down*

## Route Details

DISTANCE/ TIME:

6km (3.7 miles)/ 2.5–3 hours

MAPS:

OS Explorer 167, 1:25 000, Thornbury, Dursley & Yate
OS Landranger 162, 1:50 000, Gloucester & Forest of Dean

START AND PARKING:

The walk starts in the Coaley Woods layby next to the
Cotswold Way beside Uley Bury (SO 787993; GL11 5AN)
to the west of Stroud. Park here or an alternative parking
place is at Nympsfield Long Barrow (GL11 5AU) on the
B4066, or the car park below Cam Peak (GL11 5HH).

TRACKS AND PATHS:

Well-used paths and grassy tracks, some very steep. This is a
challenging walk, with 262m of height gain. One stile on Cam
Long Down.

## THE WALK

① At the layby, ignore the footpath to the left signed to
the Iron Age camp; we will visit it on our return. Instead, go
through a gate looking down the slope to join the Cotswold
Way. Your route lies down to the left but, before you start,
find the seat from which to view Cam Long Down, the broad
curves of the River Severn and Dursley peeping out to the left.

• Follow the Cotswold Way signs leading down steeply to
the left, following a long-established and deeply-sunken track
through the woods. Such sunken tracks are typical of the
Cotswold landscape, representing lines of movement for
people, animals and goods, and often bearing names that
reflect their origins ('Salt Way', 'Drovers' Road'). Although
some have been surfaced and have taken their place in the
modern road system, others have been left as bridleways
and footpaths, retaining memories of earlier times. Gurney
noticed and celebrated tracks and small roads.

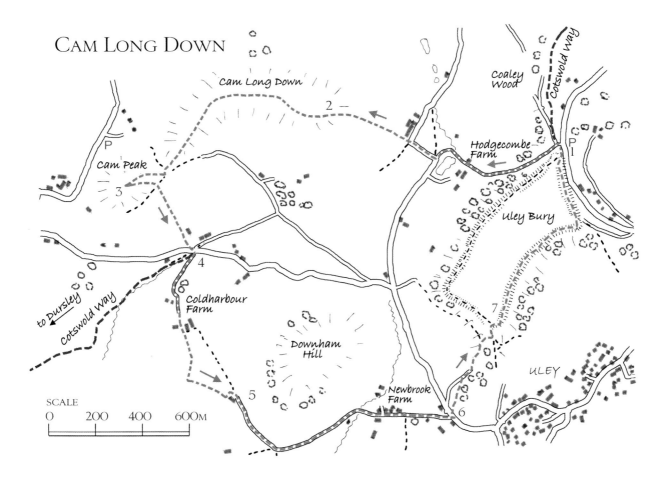

# CAM LONG DOWN

Cam Long Down

2

Cam Peak

3

P

Coaley Wood

Cotswold Way

Hodgecombe Farm

P 1

Uley Bury

to Dursley

Cotswold Way

4

Coldharbour Farm

Downham Hill

7

5

Newbrook Farm

6

ULEY

SCALE

0    200    400    600M

**Roads**

Roads are sometimes the true symbolical
Representation of movement in the fate of man.
One goes from Severn of tales and sees Wales
A wall against England as since time began.

Hawthorn and poplar call to mind the different people
That ruled and had shaping of this land at their periods.
One goes from the Abbey to the smaller steeples,
There made worthy, and by tithe barns, and all by roads.

Daylight colours gray [sic] them, they are stained blue
   by the April
Skies on their pools and Summer makes carpets of dust
Fit for the royal: Autumn smothers all with colour
Blown clean away by the withering cruel of Winter's gust.

Roads are home-coming and a hope of desire reached,
(There is the orange window at the curve of the dark way)
Whether by Winter white frozen or by Summer bleached,
Roads are the right pride of man and his anxiety.

(K2004)

• At the bottom of the track, pass Hodgecombe Farm, gain the road and turn right to pick up the Cotswold Way signs. Walk alongside a field and climb up the rough pastureland sloping up to the nose of Cam Long Down. Looking back, you can see the flat-topped plateau of Uley Bury and over to your left, the outlier of Downham Hill. On a clear sunlit day, you may well feel a sense of the wonder and joy expressed by Gurney in the poem, **Passionate Earth**. For him, such visions inspired creativity in music and words – *the soul takes flight to sing / High at Heaven-gate* (the same thought expressed in **When from the wood's edge** – see Walk 4).

② Reaching the trees, climb the stile into the woodland, mainly beech and full of bluebells in the spring. A steep climb brings you out on the ridge and the views open up, offering a full panorama of Coaley Peak and Frocester Hill over to the right and, if the weather is clear, the long blue line of the Cotswold scarp stretching beyond and to the north. Straight ahead and slightly left, Dursley will be seen, with the outlying Stinchcombe Hill behind it and, further left, a much clearer view of Downham Hill. As you walk you will also pick up glimpses of the meandering bends of the lower Severn.

*Cam Long Down with Dursley and Stinchcombe Hill behind*

### The Dursley Schoolmaster

With Dursley below you, consider the often-repeated suggestion that Shakespeare acted as a schoolmaster at the local school for the period 1579/80–82. This period is sometimes referred to as the 'lost years' – the time between Shakespeare leaving school and

Stratford and marrying Anne Hathaway in late 1582. There is a story explaining that the young poet fled the consequences of being caught illegally in the park of Sir Thomas Lucy in Warwickshire. It is surmised that he sought shelter in Dursley, a small town seated on the edge of a wild woodland tract. The seventeenth-century diarist, John Aubrey claimed that the bard was at some time a schoolmaster 'in the countrey', and although he did not suggest a location, others have done so. It has been claimed (by local historian Nora Barnes) that not only do some passages in Shakespeare – especially in *Henry IV* – show an intimate acquaintance with Dursley and its inhabitants, but there has long been a family of Shakespeares living in the Dursley area. Others (for example, Robert Beckinsale in 1948) have confirmed this idea. Whatever the truth, Ivor Gurney, whose fascination with Shakespeare is seen in other poems – such as **By Severn** (Walk 18), **Shakespeare's Day** and **April 23, 1922** – had clearly also heard this rumour of Dursley connections.

### The Dursley School-Master

If he taught children, as 'tis said
And with vast patience earned a board and bed,
How must the Severn Plain have entered in
His walking thoughts when school door was in pin.
Vast Egypt with her sandy spaces lay
Circont by Malvern and Wales up to the Hay,
And Nilus brought the elvers up on flood
(Framilode sent a many; they were good.)
Plain country talk all salted of the soil,
And Shallow, and young Hotspur (won the mile
In May Day races) Perdita, Viola; avoided;
With folk against one Coriolanus crowded
And all the clowns, with all the jests of men,
Feste, Touchstone, Bottom, Edgar and Lancelot,
Their lucky phrases stuck, and not forgot,
The hardship brought the best of them to pen.
O dreams! O bright ambition, how was that?
Fulfil where Dursley Hill falls to the flat:
Was it not easier to trust to memories
In London town, with Court and stage to please.          (80P)

Gurney's contention in this poem is that Shakespeare would have been influenced by walking the landscape (the Severn Plain, the river with elvers, the high Dursley hills) and meeting the local characters around him in Gloucestershire. Local Cotswold May Day races were common and he would have undoubtedly seen local people competing on temporary racetracks laid out on the hilltops. As Gurney sees it, these memories would have formed the basis for character descriptions (Shallow, Hotspur, Perdita Viola) and scenes written later in *London town*.

In another nameless poem written in 1917, Gurney makes this same point when recalling his time at the Front and listening to a Gloucestershire voice.

#### Untitled (*extract*)

How strange it was to hear under the guns
That slow sweet Cotswold voice go droning through
His tales of flowers and trees, his little ones,
All that in years he hoped to do …
The things he'd plant, the sheds he'd build,
   contraptions

Cunningly plotted, curious adaptions …
And all the while, under the sullen guns
I heard the sound of lovely words I'd read
Secretly reading, long ago, in bed.
O surely, Shakespeare knew such men as these
And chose to shape out of their artless talk
The mellow wonder of his comedies
Though made in London where the vulgar walk
Nor ever speak of flowers or good grey stone
But stumble in an evil dark alone …　　(CPW)

*Bluebells on Cam Peak*

thought of Cam Long Down and Cam Peak as the sentinels marking the southern edge of his Gloucestershire. The glinting waters of the River Severn should be seen below you, and behind them the hazy outlines of the Forest of Dean, whilst to north-west and north the Cotswold Edge can be traced to Haresfield Beacon and possibly beyond it. Return to the main path. Follow the Cotswold Way downhill through a field to join the road.

• At the end of the main ridge walk, follow the Cotswold Way signs down to the left to reach a major path junction. If you wish to finish your ridge walk by seeing the view from Cam Peak, take the middle path for about 500m uphill through grassy common land, awash with bluebells in the spring.

③ From the summit of Cam Peak the view is even more inspirational than from the main ridge since the ground falls away steeply on all sides. It is easy to see why Gurney

④ Here you leave the Cotswold Way and take a bridleway which heads off through a farm gateway to the left of it. The bridle path almost immediately leaves the farm track and

*The view from Cam Peak with Dursley and Stinchcombe Hill*

runs parallel to it behind a fence. Go through Coldharbour farmyard and, where the path leaves the farm track, notice a small gate and a bridleway running to the left. Take this path and walk along first through fields (often grazed by sheep), and then into a rough lane between fields.

⑤ Up to your left is Downham Hill, once known as Smallpox Hill because of the isolation hospital located there in the eighteenth century. It was, apparently, one of the earliest of such hospitals, and may have had a link with Dr Edward Jenner, who discovered the vaccination for the disease, and who lived at nearby Berkeley. On the top of the hill there are remains of an older tower-like cottage put up during the reign of Edward III at the time of the Black Death.

• Keep following this bridleway as it makes its way around the base of Downham Hill, passing houses, smallholdings, Wresden Farm and Newbrook Farm equestrian centre. Finally come out on the Dursley–Coaley road.

⑥ Cross the road and find a footpath continuation just to the left. Follow it up steeply zigzagging into the woods. Eventually it joins a wider bridleway and rises to reach a gate at the base of the Uley Bury embankments. Once through the gate, scramble up the small, steep path onto the edge of Uley Bury and contemplate the sheer size and impressive location of this Iron Age hillfort. Join the footpath running clockwise around Uley Bury ramparts to gain views across Dursley and Cam Long Down, or anticlockwise for a better impression of the huge open space (32 acres/ 13 hectares) encompassed by the ramparts. Uley Bury hillfort is a very large Iron Age settlement with evidence of occupation from approximately 300BC to AD 100. It is similar to the hillforts at Painswick Beacon and Crickley Hill (Walks 11 and 13).

**The Unfamiliar Camp** is one of Gurney's poems which was published in *The Book of Five Makings* (edited by R.K.R. Thornton and George Walter, 1995). As the editors explain, the book comprises a collection of manuscripts in various stages of completion and is best seen as a working manuscript rather than a finished product. For this reason, in *The Book of Five Makings*, Gurney's suggested additions to poems are included by showing a slash before and after the alternative word. This approach has been followed below, with the alternative words in italics.

Thornton and Walter explained that these additions showed that Gurney, 'valued truth and accuracy of the observation above metrical regularity' (in other words, that his additions often disrupted the flow of the poem!)

It is also worth adding that the *Unfamiliar Camp* mentioned is probably not Uley Bury (Uley is not a *small camp*). Despite these provisos, the poem is included here since it gives a feel for Gurney's curiosity about archaeological remains, merged always with his deep sense of the Cotswold landscape.

## The Unfamiliar Camp

Some day (I know) they will dig up the ramparts perhaps
To find money hidden or broken swords or spear tips –
And renew an old honour of tales, which now /
  (there's a glow) /
Is but of comradeship with the stars and/ *unseen*/ dew
Of dawn, the eternal watching to the Welsh mountains
  and great tops.
But to me it will be / *surely*/ but the small camp left aside,
For the toil of climbing, jumping of the brambles, and
  / *so*/ slow
Change of the love's colour there from May to May's
  return slow …
(Wonderful colour staying long in drenched miraculous
  glow.)
                (BP)

Apart from its northern corner, the Bury is surrounded by steep natural slopes. The hillfort was created by terracing a double line of ramparts – more than a mile in length overall – into the hillsides. Excavations carried out on the north-eastern rampart during the 1970s (echoing

*Uley Bury, a sketch by Edward Burrow, 1924*

Gurney's prediction that *some day they will dig up the ramparts*) found evidence of how the ramparts were constructed. Finds during this excavation included a crouched burial, iron currency bars, quern stones, a brooch and large amounts of pottery. Finds made at other times included a gold coin of the *Dobunni* (one of the Iron Age tribes living in southern England prior to the Roman invasion) and a silver Roman coin. Aerial photography has revealed extensive crop marks suggesting that there were once numerous circular dwellings in the interior of the hillfort; however, these have not yet been excavated.

⑦ If you walk along the western edge of the Bury, you can enjoy fine views across to Cam Long Down. Bear right downhill by the information board and find a gate and path back to the layby parking area at which you started.

*The view from Uley Bury, showing Downham Hill*

# Coaley Peak and Frocester Hill

**Cotswold Slopes** (*extract*)
Wonderful falls makes Cotswold edge, it drops
From the roadway, or quarry or young beech copse
It gestures, and is below in a white flash
Of lucky places.

(RW)

This walk is an extension to the Uley walk, taking you northward along the Cotswold Way as far as Frocester Hill and Coaley Peak, high on the Cotswold Edge to the south of Stroud. Gurney was inspired by the far-flung views, the hidden hollows below the scarp edge and, particularly in summer, the green and radiant countryside. Although he knew this area before the war, most of his writing about it refers to the post-war period.

*Rewards of Wonder* draws together many poems (such as **Cotswold Slopes**) that were written by Gurney when his mental state was deteriorating, just before he entered the asylum. These were edited and refined in Dartford and collected by Marion Scott and Ralph Vaughan Williams (although not published as a full collection until long after Gurney's death). George Walter, editor of *Rewards of Wonder* (2000), suggests that Gurney's illness (now believed to be a bipolar condition) allowed him to retain control of certain cognitive functions, including those linked with his creativity and the inspiration gained from his surroundings. Gurney clearly had this Uley-Coaley-Frocester Hill area in mind when he wrote **Cotswold Slopes** which presents a journey from the scarp edge onto the high plateau regions. Gurney uses the first four lines (see above) to paint a picture of the steep edge in all its guises, whether road or white track, quarry or grassland with beech copses – all of which can be seen on this walk.

This is an energetic walk of 3.8 miles with numerous steep climbs, starting from the Cotswold Way near Uley Bury and running along the scarp edge through beautiful beechwoods, out onto the high hilltops of Frocester Hill and Coaley Peak with their panoramic views, and passing the two Neolithic Long Barrows of Uley and Nympsfield. The return journey takes in scarp-edge fields and the Frocester Hill Nature Reserve before climbing back up the steep slope to Uley Bury.

*'a white flash of lucky places' – the edge falling from the
Stroud–Dursley Road*

**Route Details**

DISTANCE/ TIME:
6.2kms (3.8 miles)/ 2.5–3 hours.

MAPS:
*OS Explorer 167, 1:25 000, Thornbury, Dursley & Yate*
*OS Landranger 162, 1:50 000, Gloucester & Forest of Dean*

START AND PARKING:
The walk starts in the layby next to the Cotswold Way near
Uley Bury (SO 787994; GL11 5AN) to the west of Stroud
– the same starting point as Walk 8. An alternative parking
place is Nympsfield Long Barrow (SO 794014; GL11 5AU)
on the B4066 to the north.

TRACKS AND PATHS:
Well-used paths and grassy tracks. Some are very steep and
maybe muddy when wet. This is a challenging walk, with
about 230m of height gain. One stile (Point 6) but next to a
gate which usually opens.

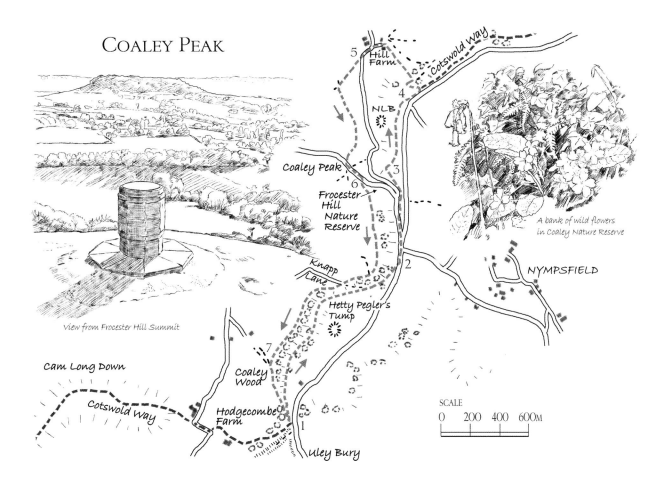

# COALEY PEAK

Hill Farm

Cotswold Way

5

4

NLB

Coaley Peak

3

6

Frocester Hill Nature Reserve

A bank of wild flowers in Coaley Nature Reserve

NYMPSFIELD

2

Knapp Lane

Hetty Pegler's Tump

View from Frocester Hill Summit

Cam Long Down

Cotswold Way

Coaley Wood

7

Hodgecombe Farm

1

Uley Bury

SCALE

0   200   400   600M

## The Walk

① From the layby (SO 787994), walk down to the seat and viewpoint on the Cotswold Way, then follow this northward (right) through beech woods, pale green and bluebell-strewn in spring, and brown and orange with falling leaves in autumn. You are in the 22-hectare Coaley Wood, an ancient, semi-natural beech woodland managed by the Woodland Trust. The path contours along the wooded slope with the ground plunging dramatically down to your left and climbing steeply uphill to the right. After a few minutes, you will see limestone cliffs on the uphill side with Hart's Tongue fern at their base.

> Note that **Uley Long Barrow**, otherwise known as Hetty Pegler's Tump, lies up behind the woodland to your right, but cannot easily be reached this way. It is better accessed from the B4066 where there is a small layby and footpath. Uley Long Barrow is a partially reconstructed Neolithic chambered mound, 37m long and standing high above the Severn Valley. It is known locally as Hetty Pegler's Tump, after Hester Pegler who owned the land in the seventeenth century. The barrow as seen today is largely the result of the excavation and reconstruction undertaken by Dr John Thurnham in 1854 and subsequent repairs in 1871, 1891 and 1906.

*Looking back along the pathway through Coaley Wood*

• The path in the woods is undulating at first then drops to a gate and path junction. Follow Cotswold Way signs up to the right and climb steeply to the road. Be careful, as you will emerge at the busy road junction of the B4066 with the Frocester and Nympsfield roads, *where the roadways clash* (1.5km from start).

② From the road junction, follow the Cotswold Way signs onto the grass verge between the roads and eventually along a narrow path and down steps to avoid walking on the busy Frocester Road. Find a good place to stop and read **Cotswold Slopes** (see overleaf). This is not an easy poem and explanatory notes accompany the poem.

• After the steps, join a stony limestone path. Go through a gate and pass limestone cliffs off to the right The path rises as you climb up to Frocester Hill summit and viewing point, owned by the National Trust.

③ From Frocester Hill there are magnificent views across the Severn Vale and Forest of Dean with the village of Coaley lying beneath you. There is a topograph to help you identify landmarks, including looking back to Cam Long Down (Walk 8) with its distinctive band of woodland

emphasising its shape; and, behind it the sinuous curves of the River Severn gleaming in the Vale, possibly with clouds like banners streaming. In France, Gurney longed to return to such experiences.

*The view from Frocester Hill with Cam Long Down ahead*

**Cotswold Slopes** (*extract*)

Wonderful falls makes Cotswold edge, it drops
From the roadway, or quarry or young beech copse
It gestures, and is below in a white flash
Of lucky places. But where the roadways clash
By Frocester Hill, flatness is flatness' self,
With thorn bushes and rabbits in haunt of elf
And kind hobgoblin continual corners:
Where rest calls out to beggars and seldom sorners;
Working or walking their way through the June's palaces
To red-brick dosshouses or the cheaper workhouses.
While here all wonder with clean sheets spreads a pallet
Tiredness to soak content, no ill to befall it;
Swept over all night by soft wrapping dim airs …
Till dawn takes one onward a mile, and the day-lit
Cotswold shows all that county, with towns and inns:
Tunes and tales in the quick mind eager desire begins;
Who walked here, and debated his sword, or who
   walked poor student to Oxford,
Who debated a country's fate and kept death in heart
   unfeared

What squire watched his loved land and cared for his
   hid ways and cairn stand?
The beech copses are they not better than thorn,
   confess!
And the flat thousand feet up plain, whose barns
Front light like Thebes' self or strength of Timgad
Runs on to waterless, treeless gray [sic] spaces,
And to acre ploughlands square with gray [sic] walls –
   Cotswold walls –
And light mists on commons and fallow sad places
With some change seen in the grass colours and farm
   faces.

(RW)

As explained, the inspiration for **Cotswold Slopes** came directly from this Uley-Coaley-Frocester Hill area. After setting the scene with its *Wonderful falls* of *Cotswold edge*, Gurney describes *where the roadways clash / By Frocester Hill*. This is the road junction of the B4066 with the Frocester/ Coaley roads and the minor road from Nympsfield (Walk, Point 2).

George Walter suggests that one characteristic of Gurney's mental illness is that he often became obsessed with one topic or word – in this case, the fate of returning soldiers. 'Sorners' may be a derivation of 'sojourners', so *seldom sorners* means those who don't stay long and is a reference to former soldiers still unemployed and homeless, wandering the roads as beggars. Gurney contrasts the *palaces* of the June countryside and the *clean sheets* of Cotswold grassland with the *dosshouses* and *workhouses* of the towns.

This is a strange, rambling poem, perhaps a reflection of the mental distress Gurney was suffering in the asylum and from his banishment from Gloucestershire. In the section beginning *Who walked here*, Gurney may be referring to his reading in the asylum. We know that Marion Scott brought him books and that he read avidly. Perhaps he references

Shakespeare's King Lear (*debated his sword*?) or Thomas Hardy's Jude (*who walked poor student to Oxford*?).

Later in the poem, he introduces us to the high but flatter Cotswold plateau, as experienced around Nympsfield. By alluding to Thebes, an ancient Egyptian city of about 3500BC located on the Nile, and to Timgad, a Roman colonial town of AD 100 sited in modern-day Algeria at about 1,000m above sea-level, Gurney is making the link between these remnants of antiquity and the fine Cotswold stone barns on the high plateau. The allusion creates a glow of grandeur and mystery. Remember that when Gurney walked here, the high plateau areas may have seemed even more remote and wild than they do today.

This poem represents the strange mixture of landscape memories, reading and wartime experiences that so often colour Gurney's asylum poetry.

**Time and the Soldier**

How slow you move, old Time;
Walk a bit faster!
Old Fool, I'm not your slave …
Beauty's my master!

You hold me for a space …
What are you, Time?
A ghost, a thing of thought,
An easy rhyme.

Some day I shall again,
For all your scheming,
See Severn-valley clouds
Like banners streaming.

And walk in Cranham lanes,
By Maisemore go …
But Fool, decrepit Fool,
You are SO SLOW!!

(K2004)

• Leaving the summit, walk back to the main path and through the gate into the Coaley Peak area, which offers 4.9 hectares (12 acres) of wild flower meadow. The land was farmed for arable crops before Gloucestershire County Council turned it into a wild grassland area and picnic site, maintained by sheep grazing. Coaley Peak was adopted as a nature reserve by Gloucester Wildlife Trust in 2016. Below the nature reserve is a National Trust-owned area of unimproved limestone grassland.

• Walk across the short grass, enjoying the open landscape and views. The path curves around the hill edge passing the parking area to your right. For many years this was a seasonal home to a community of New Age travellers, who were evicted in around 2002. Walk past the car park, to find the Nympsfield Long Barrow (see opposite).

• Leaving the Barrow, carry on along the Cotswold Way, following signs on wooden posts across the grassland, to reach a wooden gate.

**Nympsfield Long Barrow** (given the acronym 'NLB' on the OS map) lies at the edge of woods and is one of the earliest examples of a barrow with several separate chambers. It was constructed around 2800BC and is in the guardianship of English Heritage. The barrow is almost oval in plan, measuring 30m (98ft) from east to west, 25m (82 ft) from north to south at the western end. The roof was removed at some point, so the chambers remain uncovered today allowing the layout to be seen clearly. At the eastern end is a forecourt flanked by two arms of the mound. This leads into an east-facing entrance defined by two standing stones. Beyond the entrance is a stone gallery that leads into a pair of side chambers and an end chamber, all constructed of the local oolitic limestone, probably quarried nearby. (For more information visit the English Heritage website: www.english-heritage.org.uk/visit/places/nympsfield-long-barrow/history/).

When researching this walk, the author spoke to a local man who claimed that one of the two standing stones near the Barrow entrance is known as the 'Wizard Stone'. If you stand with your back to the Barrow entrance and look

outward (eastward), the left-hand standing stone has a distinctive 'face'. The 'Wizard' protects the Barrow. I think Gurney would have enjoyed this story.

*The Wizard Stone, Nympsfield Long Barrow*

④ Go through a gate with a noticeboard explaining that you are leaving Coaley Peak Nature Reserve and entering Stanley Wood (managed by the Woodland Trust). Follow the Cotswold Way round to the left and down some steps to reach a path junction. The Cotswold Way goes up to the right to a gate, but take the path down to the left and round a horseshoe bend, along a wide, wooded track with mature beeches and leaf litter. Continue down round another bend.

*Taking the wide, wooded track in Stanley Wood*

Gurney found inspiration in the ever-changing sights and sounds of the trees on the Cotswold Edge. An essay he wrote in 1921 ('Springs of Music') referred to the music he discovered in the Cotswold trees.

> Autumn is strongest in memory of all the seasons. To think of autumn is to be smitten through most powerfully with an F sharp minor chord that stops the breath, wrings the heart with unmeasurable power. On Brahms it is so strong, this royal season; has given him so much, worthily and truly translated. What! Do you not know the Clarinet Quintet, the Handel variations, The C minor symphony? And do you not smell Autumn air keen in the nostrils, touch and wonder at leaves fallen or about to fall? Have you not hastened to the woods of the F minor Quintet?

If you are walking this route in autumn, consider your own response to the sights and sounds of Stanley Wood. Autumn storms were dramatic events for Gurney. He relished walking in the wind and participating in the drama of flying leaves and windswept branches, finding it a relief from depression or anxiety – *The sick mind grows whole*, as the poem **October** reveals.

October (*extract*)
The sick mind grows whole in October gales
And memory comes
With tides of wind and music whenever fails
The body, despises mean men and spirits safe in
   homes –
Leaves flung riotously and for once carelessly
Send the arm out to touch them lovingly, waveringly:
The blood warms at them – so England's autumn
   comes;

And the [he] loves to watch the tossing passion-
   wind-beaten glooms,
A man's life blessing the tree's life high
A man's music coming out of the war of wind, earth
   and sky
On Roman and all powerful rampart outflung –
Fitting the praise of great triumphing night strengths sung
Of Autumn's boyish mood

(RW)

This is another difficult poem. Gurney throws out images almost before the words are formed. If it is read for the atmosphere rather than the strict meaning, it provides a moving image of Gurney who *loves to watch the tossing passion-wind-beaten glooms*, walking in dark woods with music and poetry *coming out the war of wind, earth and sky*. For me, there are echoes of Housman's **On Wenlock Edge** (*the wood's in trouble*).

• Eventually, leave the woods onto a grassy track with steep-quarried slopes up to the left and reach Hill Cottage.

• Keep right of Hill Cottage, through two gates and out onto a tarmac lane. Walk along this to reach the busy Frocester road and turn up to the left. Your aim is to reach a footpath off to the left, about 100m uphill. Look out for traffic.

⑤ Take the footpath into a field (the pedestrian gateway is to the right of the main five-bar gate).

• Contour round to the left on a faint, grassy track and gradually drop down to a gate. Don't go through it but turn left to follow a natural valley up the slope to another gate in the fence on the right. Go through this and past several houses, before reaching a small lane. Don't take the obvious bridle path opposite but walk on up the lane past two or three houses. On the left you may notice a footpath sign for NT Coaley Peak. Ignore this (unless you want a stiff scramble back up to the edge at Coaley Peak). Find a gateway on the right with a stile leading into Frocester Hill Nature reserve.

⑥ Enter the Reserve, go through another gate and follow the enchanting-looking path through low-growing shrubs, bramble and bracken. This footpath runs parallel but just below the Cotswold Way woodland path you were following on the outward journey. The natural limestone rock and soils provide a rich base for a variety of lime-loving plants clustering on the lower slopes of the edge.

• Soon (after 0.5km) the path enters woodland, and shortly Knapp Lane joins from the right, with cars parked on the lane side. Walk past the end of the lane, ignoring footpaths uphill to the left. Keep straight ahead on the lowest of the woodland tracks. You should follow this for 1km all along the bottom edge of the woods. On a clear day, there are fine views out from the woods onto sloping fields with Cam Long Down in the distance (see the photograph of *Sheer Falls of Green Slope* on p. 100).

⑦ Eventually you reach a bigger track at a T-junction. Turn left and follow this steeply uphill to regain the seat and Uley layby, where the walk began.

# WALK 10

# Brimscombe and Bisley

**Brimscombe** (*extract*)

One lucky hour in middle of my tiredness
I came under the pines of the sheer steep
And saw the stars like steady candles gleam
Above and through them; Brimscombe wrapped (past
life) in sleep:

(K2004)

This walk begins at Brimscombe, a small, former industrial village in the Frome valley south-east of Stroud. We know from Gurney's letters that he sometimes attended musical and literary events in Stroud and that in the post-war period he frequently walked on the hills above Stroud – for example Cam Long Down and Coaley Peak (Walks 8 and 9) and near Bisley and Painswick (Walk 11), often hoping to forget the depression he was feeling. One of the stained-glass window panels, produced by Tom Denny in Gloucester Cathedral, remembers Gurney's night-time walk above Brimscombe when, as the explanatory notes state, 'the pure clemency of the moment enabled him to forget the blackness and pain of France' (see p. 20).

The so-called 'Golden Valley' of the Frome is the largest of the five valleys that converge on Stroud, and formed the centre of the textile industry from the seventeenth to the nineteenth centuries. At the height of production, the numerous mills on the floor of the narrow valley were served by the railway and the canals, and Brimscombe Port was the hub of the canal system. Cargo was transferred from Severn trows (a type of masted cargo boat used on the Severn) at Framilode and travelled via the Stroudwater Navigation to Thames barges which carried the goods eastwards, using the Thames and Severn Canal, towards London. For Gurney, Brimscombe was at the junction of his different Gloucestershire landscapes. To the west was Stroud, his beloved Severn Valley and the village of Framilode (Walk 7), where he kept the sailing boat for his expeditions with Harvey. The Thames and Severn Canal and the various streams flowing in from the northern slopes of the Frome valley all pointed eastwards towards his walking routes on the high Cotswolds.

This walk climbs through beautiful beech woodland up one of these steep-sided valleys (the Toadsmoor Valley) to reach the small village of Bisley where, as Gurney wrote in a letter to John Haines, 'Roger Bacon might be born, and my mother was' (February 1921). It then returns down the valley by a different route, including a stop on the hill shoulder by the pines, to view Brimscombe from above, as Gurney did on his night walk. It is a long walk with several stiles and some muddy paths.

*The village of Bisley*

## Route Details

DISTANCE/ TIME:

12.7km (7.9 miles)/ 4.5 hours. This could be done as two separate walks – one up the valley and one down.

MAPS:

*OS Explorer 168, 1:25 000, Stroud, Tetbury & Malmesbury and 179, Gloucester, Cheltenham & Stroud*
*OS Landranger 162, 1:50 000, Gloucester & Forest of Dean and 163 Cheltenham & Cirencester*

START AND PARKING:

Park and start from a large layby in Brimscombe on the A419 Stroud to Cirencester road, after passing the left turn for Bisley and Chalford Hill (SO 877022; GL5 2TL approximate postcode). The walk starts on a small footpath signposted up some steps next to a house called St Kilda.

TRACKS AND PATHS:

Well-used woodland paths and grassy tracks. It can be muddy and steep. Eight stiles but sometimes gates are open alongside.

# BRIMSCOMBE AND BISLEY

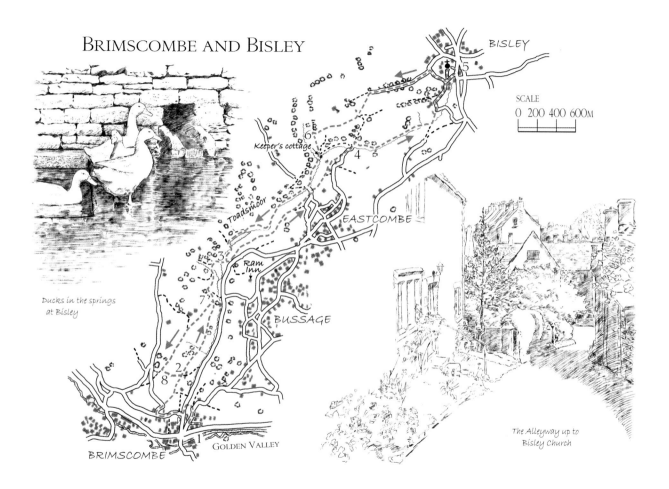

BISLEY

5

SCALE

0 200 400 600M

6

*Keeper's cottage*

4

*Toadsmoor*

EASTCOMBE

3

Ram
Inn

BUSSAGE

*Ducks in the springs
at Bisley*

7

2

8

1

BRIMSCOMBE    GOLDEN VALLEY

*The Alleyway up to
Bisley Church*

## The Walk

① Walk along the layby in the Chalford direction to find the steps next to a house called St Kilda (if you reach The Pavilion Indian Restaurant you have gone too far!) Climb up the steps, turn left into a lane and after about 200m turn right at a T-junction. Walk uphill for a few minutes until you reach steps down to the left. Follow these to a road, cross the road and turn downhill for 100m to find Bourne Lane. Now walk uphill following the road round a left-hand bend and past a post-box. Eventually you reach Quarhouse Lane on the right. Walk up it until the road veers left, at which point you go straight ahead on the higher track passing by Thumper's Cottage on the corner and Highcroft and Loft House before reaching two stone gateposts and a gravel track. Near the end of the track is a gate and a stile and footpath sign to the left, reading 'Toadsmoor Woods/ Bussage'.

② Now the walk takes you into the pleasant Cotswold beechwoods of Lawrenceland, a beautiful experience in spring with pale green beech leaves and bluebells, and in autumn when the brown and red hues are dominant. The path is soft and leaf-strewn, sometimes muddy in wet weather but one is always aware of the steep wooded slopes to the left and the gleam of the brighter valley bottom below to the right. At one point the path descends slightly to cross a stream then rises again.

• Gurney found that walking in natural landscapes brought him both physical exercise and mental stimulation. The subsequent act of writing provided a distraction in madness. A poem of 1922 expresses these possibilities; but, as always with Gurney, gives us a hint of his underlying fragility.

*Lawrenceland woods in the Toadsmoor Valley*

**Old Times**

Out in the morning
For a speed of thought I went,
And a clear thought of scorning
For home-keeping; while downward bent
Grass blades with dewdrops
Heavy on those delicate
Sword shapes, wonder thereat
Brightening my first hopes.

A four hours' tramping
With brisk blood flowing
And life worth knowing
For all that something
Which let happiness then –
Sometimes not always,
Breath-on-mirror of days –
And all now gone, since when?               (K2004)

• At a fork in the path, go right and downhill and find a stile by a metal gate. Here, go left up the hill and at another junction keep right, so staying on the lower edge of the woods. Soon the path comes out by a grey garage beside Dove Cottage. (Your return path joins here.)

③ From here, cross to the other side of the valley, walking up the lane to a T-junction. Look straight across it to find a small rough path leading to another lane. Before you reach the lane, turn left to join a track that now contours along the valley side (the opposite side from where you were before), passing fields that may contain horses, sheep and cattle. The track is rising steadily so that you are now high above the valley floor to the left. Pass Bismore Farm and continue until you reach a small lane by a cottage. Cross the lane and carry on up the path into woods and gaining height. At some houses where there is a track running left, don't take it but go straight on, eventually coming out onto a road. Follow this road and cross the stream at the bottom near Hawkesley House.

④ Keep walking up a concrete track and find the first footpath sign on your right (not the one on your left). This is a rough path with tree roots and mud but it soon takes you through a gate into a meadow beside the stream. There are various paths here but keep to the left of the stream and uphill, and eventually onto a muddy track. Follow this up to come out at the lower edge of Bisley. The lane leads upwards past Hartwell House and veers right to find the Bisley Village springs, a mossy stone monument providing seven spring sources and a stone trough – a prime example of one of

Gurney's *strangest things in walks*. From the spring go straight on up into the High Street to reach a conveniently-placed seat with some stone steps that lead up to All Saints Church. Here is a good place to pause and rest – the village shop and Post Office (up the street on the right-hand side) sells hot drinks and snacks.

*'the strangest things' – Bisley spring in 2021 during the drought*

**Cotswold Ways**

One comes across the strangest things in walks:
Fragments of Abbey tithe-barns fixed in modern
And Dutch-sort houses where the water baulks
Weired up, and brick kilns broken among fern,
Old troughs, great stone cisterns bishops might have
   blessed
Ceremonially, and worthy mounting-stones;
Black timber in red brick, queerly placed
Where Hill stone was looked for – and a manor's bones
Spied in the frame of some wisteria'd house
And mill-falls and sedge pools and Saxon faces;
Stream-sources happened upon in unlikely places,
And Roman-looking hills of small degree
And the surprise of dignity of poplars
At a road end, or the white Cotswold scars
Or sheets spread white against the hazel tree.
Strange the large difference of Up-Cotswold ways;
Birdlip climbs bold and treeless to a bend,
Portway to dim wood-lengths without end,
And Crickley goes to cliffs are the crown of days.

(K2004)

Bisley is a small village at the head of the Toadsmoor Valley. The epithet 'charming' is often used to describe this village, because of the numerous historic buildings of Cotswold stone, the network of tiny lanes ascending and descending Bisley's hilly site, the imposing church and the sense of it being a miniature town rather than a village. In fact, before the wool trade developed, Bisley was a more important centre even than Stroud and was visited by Henry VIII who stayed in Over Court in 1542. There is a persistent local legend that the baby Princess Elizabeth took ill and died at that time, and was replaced by a baby boy – the 'Bisley boy'. It is worth walking around the village, particularly on a sunny day when the grey stone takes on a lighter hue and the views out to the surrounding countryside are clear. This walk takes you through the churchyard of All Saints Church which may originally have been an Anglo-Saxon minster but was largely rebuilt in the 1860s. Other points of historic interest are the Bear Inn (dating back to the sixteenth century), the village lock-up – a structure which replaced the original prison that was in the churchyard – and a Saxon wayside cross located on the wide verge of Bisley Road, south-west of Stancombe Toll House.

The Bisley Springs with its seven spouts was already noted.

For Gurney, Bisley was significant as the childhood home of his mother, Florence. Some jottings on a piece of paper in the archives show Gurney considering the origins of his mother's maiden name, Lugg. 'Huguenot I suppose' he has written, 'Flemish weaver – cloth in Stroud valley. So, with Maisemore, Upleadon, Ashleworth – Bisley I am proud'. Research by Phil Richardson (*The Ivor Gurney Society Newsletter*, 2023) suggests that William and Mary-Ann Lugg (Gurney's great grandparents) were both born in Bisley and that they had five children, of whom Florence was one. According to the records, two of the sisters, Mary (1857) and Florence (1860) were born in Stroud, although it is not clear if the family were living there then or still in Bisley. Gurney clearly thought his mother was born in Bisley. Certainly, by 1871 the Lugg family (parents and five children) were living in Yew Villa, Bisley. The question of how Florence Gurney met David Gurney (Ivor's father) is answered by the fact that the Lugg family had moved to Gloucester by 1881 and were living at Vauxhall Road, Barton St Mary. Both Florence Lugg and David Gurney attended All Saints Church, Gloucester and sang in the choir there, so it was not surprising that they met and that their wedding took place at this church in January 1886. What is surprising, however, given that many of both Florence's and David's relatives lived in the Barton Street area, is that there was no one to act as godparents and Alfred Cheesman was asked to stand in this role. For Ivor Gurney, the choice of Cheesman as his godparent was a huge advantage. (Note the strange coincidence that All Saints, Bisley has the same name as the Gloucester church in which Florence Lugg married David Gurney in 1886).

⑤ From the seat, go up the steps into the churchyard and, after viewing the church, walk in front of the church to the pathway next to the stone wall at the far end of the churchyard. Follow the steps down to the lane, and turn right. The lane bears left and joins Well Street. Eventually at a junction take the right-hand lane (Back Lane) and walk along with woodland on your left. Soon the entrance gates of eighteenth-century Jayne Court (formerly the site of the

medieval Nether Manor) appear on the right and, shortly after, turn left down a long avenue bordered with chestnut trees to reach one large tree and a footpath to the left through a gate with a cattle grid.

• Follow this pleasant path down a track lined with poplar trees, recalling Gurney's lines in **Cotswold Ways**: *the surprise and dignity of poplars at the road end*. Another poem, **The Poplar**, written in hospital in 1918, celebrates the glory of a single poplar tree. Where the track bears right, cross the

*the track lined with poplars*

grass to find a stile and footpath sign pointing across the fields. A grassy walk contouring across the high slopes allows you to enjoy the view of Cotswold woodland clothing the slopes below Bisley before you reach a stile at the field edge.

**The Poplar**
A tall slim poplar
That dances in
A hidden corner
Of the old garden,
What is it in you
Makes communion
With this wind of autumn
The clouds, the sun?

You must be lonely
Amidst round trees
With their matron-figures
And stubborn knees,
Casting hard glances
Of keen despite
On the lone girl that dances
Silvery white.

But you are dearer
To sky and earth
Than lime-trees, plane-trees
Of meaner birth.
Your sweet shy beauty
Dearer to us
Than tree-folk, worthy,
Censorious.

(K2004)

⑥ Once in the woodland, walk down to the main path and turn left, walking steeply downhill to the Keeper's Cottage. Now the path follows the Toadsmoor Valley again, through woodland and crossing a stream until (3–4km from Bisley) you walk alongside Toadsmoor Pool (overleaf), a mysterious and peaceful lake alive with water birds and plants.

• The path takes you briefly across to the other side of the valley and to the turning you took going out. But follow the road back across to the western side of the valley, revisiting Point 3 from your outward journey. Back in the woodland again, you eventually reach a path junction at the stile and metal gate. From here, walk slightly left uphill. Just below the brow of the hill, where your outgoing path came in, there is a right turn which will take you, in about 500m, to a field.

*Toadsmoor pool*

⑦ Take this right turn and follow the path uphill and out of the woods into fields. Walk through three or four fields (depending on temporary animal fences). Over to your left views of the settlement of Bussage are seen straggling across the Toadsmoor Valley sides. Just before you reach a gate in the last field of rough pasture, a view begins to open out over the brow of the hill ahead and to the left. You are reaching Quarhouse. Don't go through the gate but take the smaller path across the field to the left and you will arrive right on the brow of the hill.

⑧ At this point, there are pines in front of you and a long view down to Brimscombe. As Gurney discovered, this (or somewhere very similar) is where the lights of Brimscombe will be twinkling below you if you are coming down from the high Cotswold plateau near Bisley and walking at night.

**Brimscombe**
One lucky hour in middle of my tiredness
I came under the pines of the sheer steep
And saw the stars like steady candles gleam
Above and through them; Brimscombe wrapped
  (past life) in sleep:

Such body weariness and bad ugliness
Had gone before, such tiredness to come on me:
This perfect moment had such pure clemency
That it my memory has all coloured since,
Forgetting the blackness and pain so driven hence.
And the naked uplands from even bramble free,
That ringed-in hour of pines, stars and dark eminence.
Wonder of men had walked there, and old Romance.
(The thing we looked for in our fear of France).

(K2004)

*The view from Besbury in 1900 with the hillside where Gurney looked down on Bourne and Brimscombe (© The Francis Frith Collection)*

The theme of this poem is the despair and depression (*body weariness and bad ugliness*) that have preceded this night walk, and the relief of finding some peace on the dark hillside above Brimscombe. In its simplicity, this poem reminds us that in this immediate post-war period, Gurney could find solace but not a complete cure for his mental state. As mentioned, the artist Tom Denny chose this poem to illustrate in his stained-glass Gurney memorial window for Gloucester Cathedral – a striking image of deep blue.

The photo (previous page) shows an early twentieth-century view of Bourne Mill taken from the south side of the main valley (the mill is no longer there), and behind it the slopes of Quarhouse where Gurney must have stood to view the lights through the pine trees.

• Cross the stile and cross a field but just before the next stile and some houses, turn down to the left at another stile and through the woods. It is very steep for a while before you emerge into a field and walk diagonally left down the field to one more stile and join Point 2, near the beginning of the Toadsmoor Valley path you used on the way up. Make your way back through the houses and lanes to the layby at Point 1.

# Part Four: The High Hills

The High Hills explores the Cotswold Edge between Painswick and Crickley Hill, an area that Gurney discovered as a young boy walking or cycling by day and night from his home in Barton Street, Gloucester. He would leave his Barton Street home, following the Painswick Road (now the B4073) or the ancient Portway, and up the steep hill. Here he would have had his first encounters with scarp-edge views from Cooper's Hill or Painswick Beacon and the rich colours of Cranham beechwoods, contrasting pleasingly with the softer landscapes and colours of the Severn Vale. The poem **Dawn** (p. 146–7) recounts one such journey made by bicycle at night while all the Gurney household was sleeping.

Cooper's Hill and Crickley Hill took on huge significance while he was away in France and during the post-war period when he tried to live in a cottage under the steep slopes of Crickley Hill.

**The High Hills**
The high hills have a bitterness
Now they are not known
And memory is poor enough consolation
For the soul hopeless gone.
Up in the air there beech tangles wildly in the wind –
That I can imagine.
But the speed, the swiftness, walking into clarity,
Like last year's bryony are gone.

(K2004)

This is a short but intensely moving poem with its first two lines *The high hills have a bitterness / Now they are not known*. Written at a time of low mood sometime between 1920 and 1922, it is clearly both the cry of the blocked writer who cannot express his feelings, but also perhaps a premonition of the anguish of leaving the high hills, and so of losing the inspiration from his life and the possibility of *walking into clarity*.

Walk 11

# Great Painswick

**Dawn**

Great Painswick standing up in the dim light for ever fast
And Roman calling to me, and challenging …
Free ever of beeches, save where the dead leaves cling
Of winter, that Spring left and Summer ever

(GA)

In the 1918–22 period, Gurney frequently visited
Painswick Beacon and the fields and woodland paths
around this Cotswold village. 'I walked over Horsepools
today and Painswick, Cranham, Coopers with King Lear
and Chapman', he explained to Marion Scott in a letter
dated 19 April 1921. Gurney frequently walked to relieve
stress, often with a book in hand, sometimes reading
from it or declaiming verse to the countryside. In an
essay (Springs of Music, 1922), Gurney explains how such
early experiences formed his inspiration: 'The springs of
music are identical with those of the springs of all beauty
remembered by the heart'.

*Painswick Beacon – one of Gurney's 'high hills'*

This walk takes you from St Mary's Church in
Painswick across fields following the Cotswold Way to
Wash Brook Farm. It guides you uphill alongside Wash
Brook through fields and copses before climbing out of
the valley to find Holcombe Farm and Holcombe House
and, eventually, reaching the B4073 road along which

Gurney often cycled from Gloucester. The last two miles of the walk climb to the high point of Painswick Beacon with magnificent views across the Severn Vale, before descending steeply back to Painswick.

*Painswick seen from Edge, with the beechwoods of Sheepscombe behind*

## Route Details

DISTANCE/ TIME:
8.7km/ 5.4 miles, 3–3.5 hours

MAPS:
*OS Explorer 168, 1:25 000, Stroud, Tetbury & Malmesbury and 179, Gloucester, Cheltenham & Stroud*
*OS Landranger 162, 1:50 000, Gloucester & Forest of Dean and 163 Cheltenham & Cirencester*

START AND PARKING:
This walk begins in Painswick's main public car park in Stamages Lane (SO 865096; GL6 6UT). Painswick is a small town on the A46 7.2km (4.5 miles) north of Stroud. From the car park, walk through into churchyard and town centre.

TRACKS AND PATHS:
Mainly well-marked footpaths in meadows and woods, with occasional sections of country lane and some steep hills. Potentially muddy and wet sections (for example at Point 3). Five stiles.

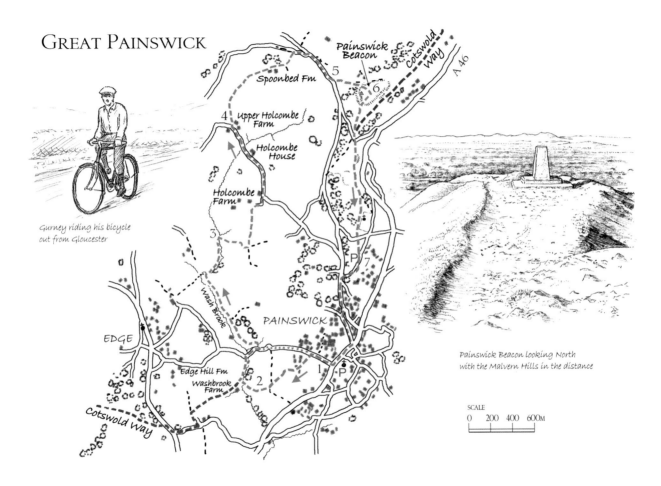

# GREAT PAINSWICK

Gurney riding his bicycle
out from Gloucester

Spoonbed Fm

Painswick
Beacon

Cotswold Way

A 46

5

6

4 Upper Holcombe
Farm

Holcombe
House

Holcombe
Farm

3

P 7

Wash Brook

PAINSWICK

EDGE

Edge Hill Fm

Washbrook
Farm

2

1

P

Cotswold Way

Painswick Beacon looking North
with the Malvern Hills in the distance

SCALE

0    200  400  600m

140

## THE WALK

① The walk starts at the south-west corner of the churchyard which contains a fine set of carved tombs. The lych gate has gone but the name 'Lych Gate Cottage' remains. St Mary's Church dominates the view, though partially hidden behind the famous 99 yew trees (legend states that the Devil will always destroy the 100th tree).

Painswick Church was owned by Llanthony Priory, Gloucester from the twelfth century to the Dissolution, but the original Norman structure was replaced in the fourteenth and fifteenth centuries, and the seventeenth-century spire had to be renovated in 1833 after being struck by lightning. This could account for the tone of **Unvisited Church** (RW) a poem written in the early 1920s and believed to refer to Painswick. It begins: *Disappointment comes to all men* and continues, *But now the thing is seen and the regret taken: / The hill known nobler than the guarding tower.* Gurney seemed to prefer Painswick Beacon!

### Queen of Cotswold

Painswick itself is situated on the gentle slopes above the Painswick Stream which flows south-westwards to join the Frome in Stroud. Walk around the town to admire its network of narrow streets and fine houses of the sixteenth–eighteenth centuries, built at a time when the Painswick woollen industry, founded on Cotswold sheep, was at its height. The Pevsner Architectural Guide (Verey and Brookes, 2000) suggests that the epithet of 'Queen of the Cotswolds' is well-deserved by Painswick, and devotes 18 pages to its architectural and historic features. Gurney's poem with the same title (overleaf) gives a less glowing picture of the town in the early twentieth century.

**Queen of Cotswold** (*extract*)

Only at certain times the tourists go there,
And the town lives feebly on unemployment pay,
Housed in the old gettings of wool ware,
Wearing such vesture of our Elizabethan day –
And looking for the good times to recover
Some fortune worthy of such nobleness' array.
Splendours gone hollow,
With despair to follow
Heavy on hope not blind to a past of great kind.
Heavy on hearts that loved churches set apart –
  Beloved
By many a squire and squire's son who had his way
Of tending land, or serving so loved an England –
  moved
Whether by Northleach, Daylesford or by
  Massachusetts, Virginia to a word.

They took their faith in hand and received just pay.
Names on old, honoured tombstones naming known
  cities.
Families serving the good soil, taming the clay,
These went out – taught by stone
And the Cotswold good done –
Made New States fortunate, Cotswold sad in her fate.

                      (RW)

**Queen of Cotswold** is in the *Rewards of Wonder* collection prepared by Gurney in Dartford asylum. George Walter, who edited the 2000 publication of this collection, assumes that it refers to Chipping Camden but I would suggest it is more likely to be Painswick. The description reveals how small towns dependent on the wool trade had suffered severe decline with the opening of New World trade.

• Leaving the churchyard by the lych gate, cross the main A46 and take the Cotswold Way following the Edge road. Soon a view opens out over the stone wall to the left, with fields in the foreground and the edges of the Cotswold escarpment in the distance. Opposite a gravel driveway find the Cotswold Way sign and a gate to the left. Follow this through the meadow, over a stile and along a narrow path confined by hedges into an open field. Walk down to another stile and, having crossed it, look downhill towards the Wash Brook valley.

• Walk down the slope, veering to the right and following the edge of the shrubby woodland which borders the brook, to find a gate, a path and a bridge to take you to Washbrook Farm.

② The oldest wing of Washbrook Farm was a seventeenth-century mill using the local water power (it is now Grade-II Listed). The whole three-storey property has now been renovated as a private dwelling. Turn right on reaching the roadway and follow the track above the Brook for about 0.5km to reach a lane.

• Cross to the other side and find some wooden steps into rough pasture. The path leads uphill then turns left onto a small path overhung with trees. Follow it alongside the valley.

*'Coppices that hear awhile and then lie as still' – walking the Washbrook valley*

**Walking Song**

The miles go sliding by
Under my steady feet,
That mark a leisurely
And still unbroken beat,
Through coppices that hear
Awhile, then lie as still
As though no traveller
Ever had climbed their hill.

My comrades are the small
Or dumb or singing birds,
Squirrels, field-things all
And placid drowsing herds.
Companions that I must
Greet for a while, then leave
Scattering the forward dust
From dawn to late of eve.

(K2004)

• Gurney's **Walking Song** sums up the sense of peace and tranquillity that he found moving through such landscapes. Given a bright spring day, with birdsong and the sound of sheep, the walker can still find such peace here; although possibly nowadays broken by the noise of the A46.

• Do not go left at a path junction, but keep straight ahead into an old orchard. After leaving the orchard by a gate, cross four pasture fields where sheep may be grazing and, in the autumn, there is often a wonderful crop of field mushrooms. At the end of the fourth field, an old wooden summerhouse appears on the left, and a house in the distance. The footpath takes you round to the right, down to a wooden bridge over Wash Brook. Cross the wooden bridge and follow the path, first through some woodland then round to the left and uphill. After crossing two more fields, enter a copse and find a small bridge down to your right.

③ Cross this bridge and walk uphill. The path from Wash Brook runs in a deep groove cut in the hill slope. In the summer the path is dry, but in autumn and winter, when the water table is high, it may be partially occupied by running water joining the Brook.

• At the top of the slope, ignore a footpath to the right but take the next one left, leading across a grassy meadow to reach the Holcombe Farm buildings. This is typical Cotswold Edge countryside – sloping pasturelands with grazing animals, hedgerows and coppices, and the occasional farm settled into the hillside. The footpath signs take you around Holcombe

Stables to the lane passing Holcombe Farmhouse itself. Go straight on along the lane, which soon leads you downhill past Holcombe House on the right.

**Holcombe House** was built for a wealthy clothier from Painswick in the late 1600s but was later enlarged and remodelled in the early 1900s by Detmar Blow in the Arts and Crafts manner. Writing in *Country Life* (December 21, 1940), Christopher Hussey described the house as 'one of these gems of masonry tucked away among the steep pastures that grew the wool which paid for the building of them all'. There is a painting of Holcombe House in Gloucester Museum, done by Charles Gere in 1930.

Many of the Cotswold farm buildings we have passed have become desirable residences for commuters of Gloucester, Cheltenham and Stroud, or hideaways for celebrities and businesspeople. Even in Gurney's day, it was no longer just farm workers who lived in the villages and outlying cottages. There were experiments in communal living – as at Whiteway

near Gurney's mother's village of Bisley – and there were increasing numbers of artists, designers and writers who were taking themselves off to rural hideaways, including William Morris at Kelmscott, and Ernest Gimson and Sidney Barnsley at Sapperton.

*Holcombe House – 'one of those gems of masonry'*

• Make your way up the lane towards Upper Holcombe farm, another fine building which is Grade-II Listed and dates mainly from the late seventeenth or early eighteenth centuries.

④ At Upper Holcombe Farm, veer right away from the lane and take the footpath over a stile out of the farmyard. Follow this uphill, noticing Painswick Beacon appearing up to the right, adorned with a long curve of woodland. At the edge of the field, cross a stile and go up the farm track beyond it through some newly-planted woodland alongside fields.

• Eventually, the track veers left but an information board signposts two smaller paths into the woods. The public footpath is the red route (right) but the landowner is encouraging walkers to take the left-hand path (green) avoiding the Spoonbed buildings. Whichever route is taken, reach a path junction to the north of Spoonbed and here go straight ahead (not right on the marked footpath) to join a small lane (and joining the Wysis Way). Turn right and follow a path along by the wall to join the B4073 road from Gloucester. Cross the busy road carefully, find the footpath set back from the road, and follow it to the grassland below Painswick Beacon.

⑤ On reaching a safe place near the Beacon information board, stop to consider 'Great Painswick' rising above you, alongside the road up which Gurney frequently cycled or walked from his home in Gloucester.

In Dartford asylum, Gurney's mind increasingly roamed back over his childhood, analysing, as he saw it, the roots of his well-being and creativity in the Cotswolds and Severn Valley landscapes.

A poem written in the Dartford asylum in 1925 provides a tantalising glimpse of the young Gurney stealthily leaving his home at night and cycling up the Painswick Road from Gloucester to find Painswick Beacon.

**Dawn** (*extract*)
It is I have stirred restlessly in my bed,
At midnight, and dressed softly not to awaken
Others, and gone out to see Pegasus overhead
And tiny stars by no wind stirred or shaken.
With my bicycle taken

Carefully over rough stones not to make a sound
Nor waken my still sister, girl in her deep
Sleep, with hope of high beeches and Cranham
 instead
Of her dreams. (I did not dare at a girl's sleep)
Not resting, riding; mounting, walking till I had
 passed
Great Painswick standing up in the dim light for
 ever fast
And Roman calling to me, and challenging …
Free ever of beeches, save where the dead
 leaves cling
Of winter, that Spring left and Summer ever.
(That camp dipping nobly centrewards like a cup)
To pass that, and swift as running horse be driven
By quarry and sleeping house, and quiet
 townend –
Eastward, eastward, northward till I found my
 friend.

The cross-roads of Cranham, and Cooper's and
 Prinknash (said Prinnadge)
To find my Roman nobleness, and to find music
At last, my dear thought flowing in my mind quick.
Looking up at the bright stars, beech twiggen, and to
 have knowledges
Of all the ages of life not told in pages.
My friends, the sentinels, and the corporal my
 courtesy.
To find at last on Coopers Heath a peace
Which enrapt me all in a cloak, my honourers
The dead Romans …

(GA)

Gurney often walked or cycled at night. This time, he seems to be looking for the beech woods of the Edge and takes the Painswick road out of Gloucester. The road climbs steeply within a couple of miles – hence the alternation of *mounting* and *walking* – before he passes Painswick Beacon on his left (Great Painswick), rising steeply from the road with many little paths climbing the rough slopes. Gurney was keenly aware of the Roman associations all around him (*Roman calling*); Roman Gloucester itself, farmhouses, villas (like Upton St Leonards and Witcombe) and roads.

The summit of Painswick Beacon, then as now, was a grassy hilltop (*free ever of beeches*) and the site of an Iron Age fort was surrounded by ditch and rampart – Gurney refers to *that camp dipping nobly centrewards like a cup*. Soon he cycles downhill into Painswick *swift as a running horse*, and *by quarry (Beacon quarry alongside the road). His route passes the quiet townend* before he turns north-east along the main road (now the A46) between Cheltenham and Stroud.

Gurney's 'friend' is the road junction at Cranham Corner, where roads turn off for Cranham, High Brotheridge and Coopers Hill. This junction at the top of the ancient Portway gave him access to all the Cotswold Edge in this area – north-east to Cooper's Hill, Birdlip and Crickley; eastwards to Cranham, Syde (called *Side* here) and Sheepscombe; south-west to Painswick, Edge, Slad and also his mother's family village of Bisley.

He is inspired by the surroundings, finding music and his thoughts *flowing in my mind quick*. He may have cycled down the main road to Coopers Hill Lane (past Prinknash Park, *said Prinnadge*) and reached the grassy commons of Cooper's Heath that way. But I like to think he cycled along the Birdlip road to Buckholt and took the adventurous route on an old Roman track through the dark beechwoods, to emerge on the Coopers Hill summit and watch the lights of sleeping Gloucester until the dawn came up in the east.

Gurney does not tell us about his return journey, but the quickest way was down Coopers Hill Lane and through Upton St Leonards to join the Portway, and so back to the sleeping household before it awoke.

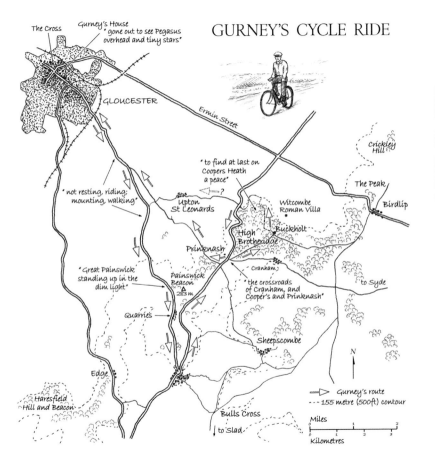

# GURNEY'S CYCLE RIDE

The Cross

Gurney's House
"gone out to see Pegasus overhead and tiny stars"

GLOUCESTER

Ermin Street

Crickley Hill

"to find at last on Coopers Heath a peace"

The Peak

Birdlip

"not resting, riding; mounting, walking"

Upton St Leonards

?

Witcombe Roman Villa

Buckholt

High Brotheridge

Prinknash

to Syde

"Great Painswick standing up in the dim light"

Painswick Beacon
△ 283 m

Cranham

"the crossroads of Cranham, and Cooper's and Prinknash"

Quarries

Sheepscombe

N

Edge

Haresfield Hill and Beacon

Bulls Cross

→ Gurney's route
--- 155 metre (500ft) contour

to Slad

Miles
0    1    2
Kilometres
0    1    2    3

*Looking back from the Beacon to the road
up from Gloucester*

⑤ (continued). From the information board there are many scrambling routes up the grassy slopes, but also two more prominent tracks to the left. Take the right-hand of these two (the Wysis Way) for a few metres, but almost immediately it rises to the right and contours round the hill to reach the summit of Painswick Beacon. As you climb, pause to look around as a wide-ranging view unfolds to the south-west, revealing Haresfield Beacon, Standish Woods, the lower Severn, May Hill and Robinswood Hill.

⑥ Arriving on the summit of the Beacon at 283m, an even more spectacular view appears. Given a clear sunny day you can see Gloucester and its cathedral below you, the outliers of Robinswood Hill and Chosen Hill, the small hills west of the Severn and, away in the distance, the rampart of the Malvern Hills, Bredon Hill, and the faint line of the northern Cotswold Edge.

**Heights**

I'll take my love on Painswick Beacon
And show her all the earth so fair,
May Hill, Maisemore, Malverns, Bredon,
Lying so tranquil-hearted there.

And still we'll lie with great clouds sailing
Like tall proud ships high over the crest.
Till beauty hurts my heart, I'll wonder …
Then hide my face on her soft breast.

(CPW)

• Painswick Beacon was and still is a favourite beauty spot and, in this poem, Gurney imagines bringing his love here. Given the date of 1917, he is probably referring to Annie Drummond, the VAD nurse who cared for him at Edinburgh War Hospital and with whom he fell in love, when he returned from Belgium having been gassed at St Julien in September 1917. The relationship didn't last, but in November 1917 Gurney was undoubtedly hoping it would – and that, as he says in this poem, he could share with her his love for Gloucestershire.

• Walking back down the narrow ridge from the summit, the ditch and rampart structures of this large, former Iron Age hillfort are clearly visible. Dating from the first century BC, the Kimsbury Fort site is about 2.8 hectares (6.9 acres) enclosed by a triple set of ramparts on the east, south and west sides but only a single line on the north side. The main entrance was on the south-east corner.

• The Beacon landscape has been damaged by quarrying on all sides, especially at Catbrain Quarry which we will pass shortly. Many of the substantial buildings of Stroud, Painswick, Gloucester (including Llanthony Priory) and Cheltenham were built from the fine oolitic stone.

• Cross the lane that provides access to the Beacon. The rolling limestone slopes and short grass provide the ideal conditions for golf (Painswick Golf Club opened in 1891), so proceed with caution. Follow the Cotswold Way signs which, disappointingly, redirect walkers around the rather gloomy eastern edge of Catbrain Quarry rather than following the splendid ridge (which Gurney would undoubtedly have taken!) more naturally southwards to Painswick.

• After Catbrain Quarry, the Cotswold Way runs through some shrubby woodland, onto the lower slopes above the Golf Club, then into the wooded walkers' car park.

⑦ From here, walk down to join the B4073, then via Gloucester Street and Bisley Street into the heart of Painswick. Bisley Street was the former main street carrying trade from Gloucester through the old marketplace off Friday Street and out via Greenhouse Lane to Bisley (Walk 10).

• Return to the churchyard and car park.

*St Mary's Church, Painswick*

# High on Cooper's

**That Centre of Old** (*extract*)
At a strafe end grateful for silence and body's grace
(Whole body – and after hell's hammering and
   clamouring).
Then memory purified made rewarding shapes
Of all that spirit runs towards in escapes,
And Cooper's Hill showed plain almost as experience.
Soft winter mornings of kind innocence, high June's
Girl's air of untouched purity, and on Cooper's Hill
Or autumn Cranham with its boom of colour …
Not anyway does ever Cotswold's fail – Her dear blue
   long dark slope fail –
Of the imagining promise in full exile.

(K2004)

Cooper's Hill is a distinctive grassy promontory high on the Cotswold Edge above Gloucester. The hill wears a thick mantle of beech woodland that hides an impressive Iron Age hillfort. Gurney loved climbing Cooper's grassy summit, wandering through the wild flowers and sweet-scented beech woods in *high June* or revelling in the soft quietness of winter snow.

The long extract from **That Centre of Old** clarifies that this poem refers to a battlefield experience. Essentially it is a war poem, but one in which the frightened young soldier *after a strafe end* still alive (*grateful for … body's grace*) turns to Cooper's Hill *plain almost as experience* and to *autumn Cranham with its boom of colour* to save him from the terror and noise of war. It is as if the Cotswold Hills have become the ideal places of memory, the touchstones of hidden happiness (or at least of an identity), that he could cling to whenever a sight or sound sparked off his imagination. It was something he could rely on – *not anyway does ever Cotswold fail.*

After the war, he often visited the hill, easily reached by the old Portway from his home in Barton Street, Gloucester. The ancient beech woodlands running towards Cranham were a particular source of creative energy. *Autumn would clang a gong of colour between*

*Cranham and the Birdlip curve* he explained in **The Bronze Sounding**. The mixed images of glowing colour and mellow sound summon up precisely the sight and sense impressions of Cooper's and Cranham woods.

This walk starts at the village pub (the Black Horse) on the edge of Cranham Common and presents a cross-section of the diverse landscapes of the Cotswold Edge. Crossing Painswick Stream, it climbs up into the ancient beechwoods of Buckholt and Witcombe Wood, then skirts the edge of High Brotheridge Iron Age Camp, hidden beneath the trees. After passing the remains of Witcombe Roman Villa, it reaches the hamlet of Cooper's Hill and climbs to the open grassy summit of the famous cheese-rolling slope. The return route takes you across the ditches and banks of High Brotheridge, traversing the edge of the disused Cooper's Hill quarry before dropping down the wooded slopes of Buckholt Woods back to Cranham.

*High on Cooper's in 'June's scented silence'*

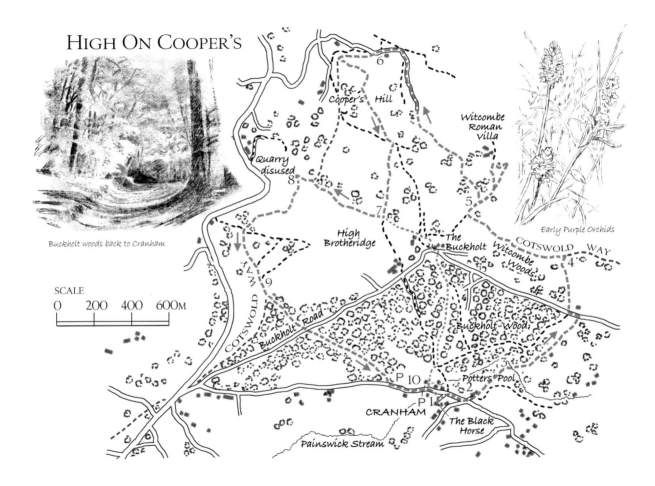

# HIGH ON COOPER'S

*Buckholt woods back to Cranham*

*Early Purple Orchids*

Cooper's Hill

6

Witcombe
Roman
Villa

Quarry
disused

8

7

5

COTSWOLD WAY

The
Buckholt

Witcombe
Woods

4

High
Brotheridge

COTSWOLD
WAY

9

Buckholt Wood

Buckholt Road

3

P 10

Potter's Pool

2

P 1

CRANHAM

The Black
Horse

SCALE

0   200   400   600M

Painswick Stream

## Route Details

DISTANCE/ TIME:

7.5km (4.6 miles)/ 3–3.5 hours. This is a challenging walk with several steep climbs.

MAPS:

OS Explorer 179, 1:25 000 Gloucester, Cheltenham & Stroud
OS Landranger 163, 1:50 000 Cheltenham & Cirencester
OS Landranger 162, 1:50 000 Gloucester & Forest of Dean

START AND PARKING:

Start at the Black Horse Inn (SO 896130; GL4 8HP) in Cranham. Park in the pub car park up to the right, if visiting for refreshment. There is alternative parking beside the B-road at the west edge of Cranham (Point 10), or on Cooper's Hill (Point 6 – two or three cars only).

TRACKS AND PATHS:

Mainly woodland paths, grassy common and country lane. Steep hills and mud in wet periods (e.g. the 'shortcut' pathway back into Cranham village from Point 7). No stiles.

## THE WALK

① Looking down at the village from the Black Horse Inn, notice how the settlement seems to be enclosed by beechwoods. For Gurney, these encapsulated the beauty and stability of the Cotswold countryside, evoked in many poems: *autumn Cranham with its boom of colour* (**That Centre of Old**); *And Cranham, Cranham trees, And blaze of autumn hues* (**The Fire Kindled**, *S&S/ WE*).

• Walk straight along the road outside the pub (not downhill). At the junction with the main street, turn right and walk up to find a grassy track on the left between two houses, before you reach the road junction. A small diversion (50m) down this track takes you to the spring at Potter's Pool, which is the source of Painswick Stream and one of the main reasons for Cranham's site, on the spring line where the oolitic limestone meets the lias sands and clay. Return to the road and notice the old Village Pound ahead of you, before turning left along a bridleway.

② Looking up to the right, you will see typical Cotswold common land with rough grass, wild flowers such as cowslips and various orchids in profusion in the spring and summer,

*The Potters' Pool, Cranham*

blackberries and wild raspberries in the autumn, and sightings of the Chalk Hill Blue butterfly. The Common was purchased by the villagers in 2008 and is now owned by the Cranham Common Trust and managed by Cranham Common Management Committee. The common is maintained by continuous grazing by cattle and sheep. Carry on down the path into the woods to the wooden bridge over the stream.

③ In a clearing by the stream, there is a fine mature beech tree which has provided swinging and climbing facilities for generations of Cranham children. A notice board explains that Buckholt and Rough Park Woods are part of the Cotswold Commons and Beechwoods National Nature Reserve.

• Follow the steep, stony track uphill. This is Monk's Ditch, an ancient track that runs from the village up to the Birdlip road and seems sunken into the hillside. After heavy rain, it may be full of rivulets which scour the limestone, but after the entrance to Monk's Ditch House, it has a tarmac surface. At the top of the track, veer left around a parking area to reach the Birdlip–Cranham road. Cross this to find a signposted track and walk downhill past a large new house on the right (a ruin in the woods when I walked here in the 1960s). Once through the gateway you are in Witcombe Wood, part of the Witcombe Estate, owned for generations by the Hicks-Beach family. Take either path downhill to join the Cotswold Way.

④ Follow the Cotswold Way to the left along the bottom of the woods to Cooper's Hill. To the right, you should see glimpses of pastures and the reservoir in Witcombe embayment below you. In the summer, this can be a delightful experience, peeping out from the rich, shady woodland into the brightly-lit meadows with the blue gleam of the reservoir. Gurney's poem **Possessions** regrets the wartime demand for timber that led to many of the Witcombe trees being felled, particularly on the steep slopes to the east.

### Possessions

France has Victory, England yet firm shall stay,
But what shall please the wind now the trees are away
War took on Witcombe steep?
It breathes there and wonders at old roarings
October time at all lights; and the new clearings
For memory are like to weep.
War need not cut down trees, three hundred miles
   over Seas
Children of those the Romans saw – lovely trunk and
   great sail trees!
Not on Cranham, not on Cooper's of camps;
Friend to the great October stars – and the July sky
   lamps.

(RW)

• The track can be muddy and rutted in the winter months. In spring, the delicate colour of the new beech leaves gives a pale lemon glow to the woodland – *Lemon-green the morning drips / Wet sunlight on the powder of my eye* as another Cotswold poet, Laurie Lee, described these Cotswold woodlands (**April Rise**). Later in May and June,

*Wild garlic in Witcombe Wood*

whole areas are awash with the blue haze of bluebells and the wild garlic flourishes, providing the strong smell for which these woods are famous. In my childhood, we knew them as 'the onion woods'. In spring and summer, the path is full of woodland flowers, such as wood anemone, wild geranium and celandine, and in the autumn it is rich with shades of red and brown leaves; or, as Gurney described it, *Autumn, dear to walkers with your streaks and carpets / Of bright colours* (**Autumn**). Even in winter, the delicate tracery of beech twigs and branches presents a stark splendour, often lit by low sunlight.

⑤ After descending into a valley occupied by a stream (known to Cooper's Hill children as the 'onion stream'), reach a path junction. Take the right-hand fork down to a field gate leading into a sheltered embayment and the site of the Witcombe Roman Villa, well-known to Gurney who was fascinated by the signs of Roman life. Since his day, the site has been excavated to reveal a luxurious Roman villa at the heart of a large country estate. For now, enter the site and walk around to enjoy the deep calm of this valley, with its sunny aspect and protective woodlands.

**Above the Villa** (*extract*)
The wind of autumn has touched there, the beech
  leaves have changed.
All the willowherb of all the world falling steep to the
  Villa
Where once the Romans ranged, is a wonder of light
  chanced
Upon … O friend are you not drunken with the sea of
  far lost mystic colour?

And I with the Roman unknowing in me then,
  watched the fall
Of the high hill to pasture, and wondered if master
I might ever be of the thoughts in me did fire and thrill
To have black on paper, golden in fame my dear
  dreams and flooding faster.

(GA)

Gurney's poem refers to an autumn visit to one of the villas he knew – it may have been Witcombe or Dryhill (Walk 13), but the description seems to fit Witcombe. He mentions the frustrations of trying to capture the *fire and thrill* of his emotions and of paying due respect to the *glory of the hidden and noble sword [that] was Rome's.*

**Great Witcombe Roman Villa**, built in AD 250, was one of the largest and most luxurious Roman houses in Britain, and was part of a cluster of very wealthy villas in the Cotswolds area. It was discovered in 1818 by farm workers, and explored by the antiquarian, Samuel Lysons. The Hicks-Beach family agreed to public ownership in 1919 and further excavations took place in 1938 and 1960–73.

A rich family lived here, together with their slaves and freedmen, for around 200 years, until the end of the Roman period in Britain. The original plan of the main villa was a symmetrical U-shape, carefully terraced into the hillside. The west wing consisted almost entirely of two bathhouses. The east wing comprised kitchens and storerooms. A rectangular dining room projected from the north side of the central range, with a covered walkway and view down the hillside. Both wings had an upper floor where the family lived. Amongst the excavation finds were the shrine of, perhaps, a water spirit, and an exceptional mosaic depicting many sea creatures.

*Great Witcombe Roman Villa*

The villa can be viewed, including the mosaic, through the main entrance from the Birdlip road (SO 902158) with a car park and footpath to the site. (More information from English Heritage: www.english-heritage.org.uk/visit/places/great-witcombe-roman-villa/history/).

• Return to the woods and rejoin the main track. Follow the undulating path, passing an isolated cottage (Woodcot) before leaving the woods and reaching the lane. Walk into the main village, noting the view of Brockworth and the Vale of Gloucester, dominated now by the post-1945 factories and houses that have marched across the vale. When Gurney roamed here, Coopers Hill seemed remote from the settlements below.

⑥ At the village notice board (SO 893148) turn up past a small car park and follow the Cotswold Way along the bottom of the Cheese Roll. On the May Bank Holiday, large Double Gloucester Cheeses are rolled down the steep slope to be chased by local people. Marvel at the steepness of the slope and the courage (or madness!) of those who throw themselves down it, for the sake of glory and a 7lb cheese!

• Go through a gate and climb steeply through the woods to the side of the Cheese Roll, bearing left where the Cotswold Way goes straight on. Eventually emerge onto Cooper's Hill summit by the flagpole where the cheeses are launched. The teenaged Gurney stood here and watched how *Gloucester slept below with her strange patterns of light* during his night-time cycle ride described in the poem, **Dawn** (see Walk 11). This

is one of the best views in Gloucestershire, taking in the Vale of Gloucester, the city itself with the cathedral glimpsed if the light is right, the Malvern Hills to the north-east, the outlier of Churchdown Hill, and the Cotswold Edge to the north.

• Leaving the flagpole, ignore the path leading half-right into the woods. Go straight ahead into the remains of Cooper's Hill Common, which was much more extensive when Gurney walked here (he refers to it as *Cooper's Heath* in his poem, **Dawn**). Cross several bank and ditch structures – you are now traversing one of the inner earthworks of the High Brotheridge Iron Age Camp (or *Oppidum*) which once occupied the whole of the high promontory of Cooper's Hill and Buckholt. Historic England research records refer to this feature and to the debates about its extent and origins (www.heritagegateway.org.uk). Gurney often mentioned High Brotheridge.

• Alongside the path, you may find many limestone-loving wild flowers, including the early purple orchid, 'hen and chickens', scabious and wild strawberries. When I was a child, we called this area 'the wilderness' and Gurney's poem with this title evokes these memories well:

**Wilderness** (*extract*)

The wildest place for brambles, the sweetest for
  strawberries
With the great edge of Wales, and ridgy Malverns, ...
O Common of thousand flowers, and the great love of
  June,
Which gave all things to the Hill – and later all
  blackberries.

(GA)

• Leaving the common, you are back in the ancient beeches of High Brotheridge woodland, with dead leaves beneath your feet. The path is indistinct, but once in the woods, veer slightly left and then pick up a green and white ground marker next to a muddy patch. Go straight ahead in a southerly direction but when the green and white marked path turns right, don't follow, but keep straight ahead through another muddy patch and then gradually uphill towards a dilapidated wall on the left. Eventually, the path runs alongside the wall. At one point, you cross a High Brotheridge earthwork topped by crumbling stone. In May you will be rewarded by a sea of bluebells and in autumn by a boom of colour.

*The 'wilderness' on Cooper's summit, with
views to the vale through the trees*

⑦ After about 1km, meet a path junction and the field edge of High Brotheridge Farm, and turn right for the main walk or turn left for a shortcut back to Cranham.

**Shortcut**

A left turn takes you to Buckholt where, until recently, there was a house of the same name (the name meaning 'deer wood'). According to the archaeologist, Gordon Harding (1978), here was once an impressive 'guarded entrance' to High Brotheridge Iron Age Camp. The gate mounds sat astride an ancient paved trackway (probably Roman) proceeding eventually to Birdlip, Cranham and Painswick, and predating the Ermine Way from Gloucester to Cirencester. Recent redevelopment of the Buckholt House site has destroyed the gateway mounds. Cross the road at Buckholt and walk a few metres to the left to find a footpath sign directing you down into the woods on the other side of the road. Take care walking down as the path can be rough, stony and muddy, particularly in the winter. You come out by the Cranham Scout Hut and the village street. Walk back up to the Black Horse.

• If you are doing the full walk, turn right and follow the field edge path in the other direction first through a grassy area and then a steep downhill section in woodland on a rough path with tree roots. On meeting the Cotswold Way near piles of old logs, follow it to the left across the head of a field.

⑧ Go through a gateway and follow the Cotswold Way, now bumpy and rutted. A wire fence appears to the right and the disused and inaccessible Cooper's Hill quarry lies behind it in the brambles and woodland, with the main A46 road beyond (you may hear the traffic). Pause in the woodland and read Gurney's poem referring to the quarry as one source of the stone for the abbey (Gloucester Cathedral).

### The Abbey

If I could know the quarry where these stones grew
A thousand years ago: I would turn east now
And climb Portway with my blood fretted all grew*
With the frightened beeches with that strange wind-
   kindled rough row.

And there, grown over with blackberry and perhaps
   stray ferns
Willowherb, tansy, horehound, other wonders (here to
   come)
I should find a wide pit fit for a masque** (if the turns
Of such should ever come again) with tree screens and
   robing room.

(RW)

* *grew*: gruesome i.e. frightening ** *masque*: Elizabethan short play

Another poem called **Twyver Begins** (GA) refers to the tiny stream that rises on these quarried slopes and, according to Gurney, bore down to Gloucester the raft of stones to build the abbey.

• Continue along the Cotswold Way, still following the edge of High Brotheridge Farm fields. About 0.5km beyond the quarry, there is a stiff climb and the highest point of High Brotheridge camp (282m) is in the middle of the fields you are walking around. After the climb, the path gradually runs downhill until you leave the Cotswold Way at a distinct left turn.

⑨ Follow this path, still in woodland, and cross the Birdlip/Cranham Corner road at a layby and information board. Follow any of the paths heading downhill back to Cranham village.

One of Gurney's best-known poems draws on his memories and images of these woodlands to compare with the horror and desolation of the war-devastated landscapes he found in France. He seemed personally wounded by the scenes he saw – 'You cannot think how ghastly these battlefields look under a grey sky. Torn trees are the most terrible things I have ever seen. Absolute blight and curse is on the face of everything.' (Letter to Marion Scott, 10 March 1917). In **Trees**, he tries to recall, instead, the fine beechwoods on the Cotswold Edge at Cooper's Hill and Cranham.

**Trees**
The dead land oppressed me;
I turned my thoughts away,
And went where hill and meadow
Are shadowless and gay.

Where Coopers stands by Cranham,
Where the hill-gashes white
Show golden in the sunshine,
Our sunshine, God's delight.

Beauty my feet stayed at last
Where green was most cool,
Trees worthy of all worship
I worshipped … then, O fool,

Let my thoughts slide unwitting
To other, dreadful trees, …
And found me standing, staring
Sick of heart – at these!

(S&S/ WE)

Gurney wrote this poem when stationed at St Quentin on the Somme, and sent it to Marion Scott 12 days after his letter describing the trees. Paul Nash, the artist, who was serving further up the Western Front at Ypres, was similarly moved at about the same time, and wrote a letter to his wife on 7 March 1917. He described 'a wood passed through on our way up, a place with an evil name, pitted and pocked with shells, the trees torn to shreds, often reeking with poison gas – a most desolate ruinous place…'. It was this experience that inspired him to make the drawing (at a place known as Inverness Copse) that would form the basis of his celebrated painting, 'We Are Making A New World'. Both Gurney and Nash were shocked by the devastating impacts of mechanised warfare – not only on the people caught up in the horror, but also on the natural environment.

*'Trees worthy of all worship' – Cranham Woods in early autumn*

⑩ Eventually you come out at one of the suggested parking places on the edge of Cranham village. If you parked here, finish your walk now, or walk back through the village to the Black Horse.

# On the Roman Hill: Crickley

**Crickley Hill** (*extract*)
The orchis, trefoil, harebells nod all day,
High above Gloucester and the Severn Plain.
Few come there, where the curlew ever and again
Cries faintly, and no traveller makes stay,
Since steep the road is,
And the villages
Hidden by hedges wonderful in May.

(K2004)

This walk is focused on Crickley Hill, Gurney's high playground and place of retreat, where he often walked on his own at day and night, particularly post-war. It is one of the places featuring most frequently in his poems, often named directly (as in *Crickley Cliffs*, *Crickley Morning*) but also spoken of as *the Roman Hill*, where Gurney sensed the ghost of Roman soldiers and farmers.

The poem, **Crickley Hill**, written in 1918 when Gurney was recovering in the Lord Derby's War Hospital, Warrington, recalls the way in which his relationship with Crickley was suddenly revealed to him when *At Buire-au-Bois a soldier wandering / The lanes at evening talked with me.*

**Crickley Hill** (*extract, 4th and 5th verses*)
When on a sudden, 'Crickley' he said. How I started
At that old darling name of home! and turned
Fell into a torrent of words warm-hearted
Till clear above the stars of summer burned
In velvety smooth skies.
We shared memories
And the old raptures from each other learned.

O sudden steep! O hill towering above!
Chasm from the road falling suddenly away!
Sure no two men talked of you with more love
Than we that tender-coloured ending of day.
(O tears! Keen pride in you!)
Feeling the soft dew,
Walking in thought another Roman way.

(K2004)

In 1920, Gurney briefly tried to make Crickley his home but the attempt at such simple happiness failed. Crickley Hill came, instead, to represent a major transition in his life – from a scholar at the Royal College of Music to a farm labourer; from the solitary creator to the lonely writer; and from someone showing signs of instability to someone with mental problems severe enough to warrant being committed to an asylum.

The walk is a short one, but what it lacks in length it makes up for in the diversity of scenery and the richness of Gurney allusions. The route begins amidst the remains of an important Iron Age settlement, standing high above the vale and looking down on the Roman Ermin Street. It descends the 'nose' of Crickley, passing a cottage that I believe was the one Gurney lived in briefly, crosses the fields under the steep slopes of the Edge and pauses at Dryhill Farm where Gurney worked as a farm labourer. Climbing back up the scarp slope via the ancient drover's road, the Greenway, the walk follows the Cotswold Way along the high edge, passing through the magnificent, mature beechwoods, now being protected in Crickley Hill Country Park.

## Route Details

DISTANCE/ TIME:
5km (3 miles)/ 2–2.5 hours

MAPS:
*OS Explorer 179, 1:25 000, Gloucester, Cheltenham & Stroud*
*OS Landranger 163, 1:50 000, Cheltenham & Cirencester*
Gloucestershire Wildlife Trust has produced a useful map and leaflet (www.gloucestershirewildlifetrust.co.uk/explore-crickley-hill)

START AND PARKING:
Start at the information centre at Crickley Hill Country Park (SO 929163; GL4 8JY). There is ample parking in the upper and lower car parks. (Please note that in 2023, a major new A417 road junction was under construction. This will result in the clearance of the Air Balloon pub, the repurposing of the old A417 as a pedestrian and cycling trail, and the rearrangement of access roads. Check how to approach Crickley Country Park when you do this walk).

TRACKS AND PATHS:

Grassland and woodland paths. No stiles. However, there are steep, stony and sometimes muddy slopes down to Cold Slad (Points 3–4). To avoid the steepest slopes, walk from the lower car park along a track directly down to Point 4 (see map).

*Crickley Hill – 'High above Gloucester and the Severn plain'*

## THE WALK

① From the Information Centre, walk down the road a short way to join a marked walk off to the left, leading to a viewing platform describing the amazing 180-degree panorama of the vale and distant hills. The eye travels from Cooper's Hill on the far left to Bredon Hill on the far right, taking in the Forest of Dean, the Welsh hills of Sugar Loaf and Blorenge, the 'outliers' of Robinswood Hill and Chosen Hill in the Severn Vale, Cleeve Hill, and the striking silhouette of the Malverns. You may also catch a glimpse of Gloucester Cathedral.

• The distinctiveness of this scarp edge owes much to its geology. Crickley Hill marks a geological transition and so also a landscape transition, west to east, from the Liassic clays of the Vale of Gloucester to the oolitic limestones of the Cotswold Hills (see Introduction). Rising to 267m, Crickley Hill is not the highest point on this edge (Cleeve Hill is, see Walk 15) but it is a significant point. Gurney, viewing the scarp edge from below, claimed that *the Cotswolds stand out eastward as if never / a curve of them the hand of time might change / Beauty sleeps most confidently for ever* (**Above Ashleworth**). Despite Gurney's hopes, the hand of time has already changed the landscape here as the main A417 road,

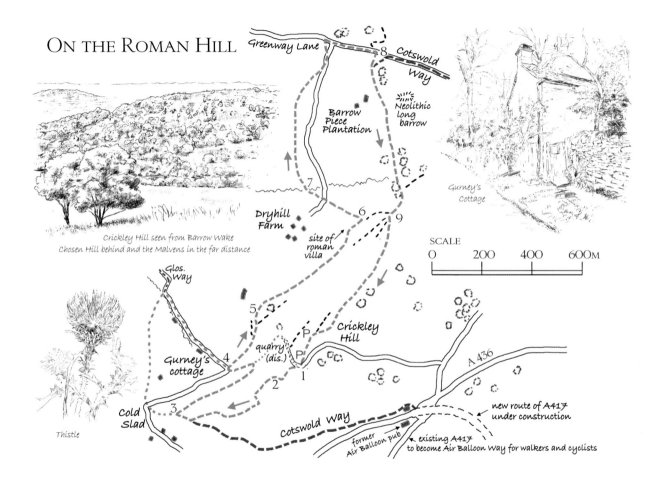

# ON THE ROMAN HILL

Greenway Lane

8 Cotswold Way

Barrow Piece Plantation

Neolithic long barrow

Gurney's Cottage

7

Dryhill Farm

6

9

site of roman villa

Crickley Hill seen from Barrow Wake
Chosen Hill behind and the Malvens in the far distance

Glos. Way

SCALE

0    200    400    600M

5

Gurney's cottage

4

quarry (dis.)

P

P

Crickley Hill

A 436

2

1

Cold Slad

3

Cotswold Way

new route of A417 under construction

former Air Balloon pub

existing A417 to become Air Balloon Way for walkers and cyclists

Thistle

seen below you, uses a geological weakness (a fault-line) to drive through the Edge on its way to Oxford

• Carry on along the path.

② Pause at the information board describing the remains of the Iron Age fort and town. The Cotswold Edge was attractive to earlier settlers, partly for defensive reasons and partly because the lighter and thinner soils of the top were generally easier to till than the thick clays of the vale.

### Crickley Hill – Early Settlement

In Gurney's day it was clear that the mounds, ditches and banks were evidence of earlier peoples, but there was disagreement as to whether this was a burial site or a fort. Archaeological excavations during 1969–93 show two main areas of settlement. At the narrow end of the promontory, there are signs of settlers living in a Neolithic causewayed camp dating from about 4000BC, with two phases of occupation being apparent. The 'evidence from the second

main enclosure suggests that by 3500BC Crickley Hill was nothing less than a small, fortified village' (Darvill, 1987) with strong defences on the eastern side and rows of burial mounds. This settlement was destroyed and burned during the so-called Battle of Crickley Hill sometime between 3495–3415BC. The main Iron Age hillfort was constructed further east in the seventh century BC (Dixon, 1979). There was a fortified Iron Age town with an imposing double gateway and a main street lined with long houses. The walls were made of limestone rubble and timber. Later, roundhouses were also built here, probably by a different group. Eventually, sometime in the third century BC, the site was abandoned and not subsequently reoccupied on a large scale again.

After AD 43 the Romans gradually spread out from south-east England and by the start of the second century AD, the Celtic *Dobunni* kingdom had been taken over by the Romans. There are signs of Roman activity at the site – possibly a village behind the Iron Age ramparts and a second settlement in the west of the site where there was a guard house and living areas. Gurney seems convinced that Roman soldiers were stationed here, frequently mentioning their presence on the cold Crickley hill-top. He also knew of the Roman villas at Witcombe and Dryhill, lying either side of Ermin Street, as it makes a bend to climb up Birdlip Hill. *The bare line of the hill / Shows Roman and / A sense of Rome hangs still over the land*, as he described it in **The Bare Line of the Hill** (K).

• On the hill summit, there are concrete markings where the postholes of the Iron Age buildings were found.

• Afterwards, veer to the right down an open grassy slope. This is classic limestone common land, with its assemblage of rough grass, wild flowers (such as harebell, cowslip and scabious) and occasional hawthorn and elder bushes. It owes its characteristics to the underlying rock and continual grazing by sheep and cattle, nowadays maintained by the Gloucestershire Wildlife Trust. The poem **Quietitude**

(Gurney's spelling), reveals what a special relationship Gurney had with Crickley Hill, referring to the limestone landscape, the trees and flowers, his joy at roaming with a notebook, and the fascination of past histories.

**Quietitude** [Quietude]
Up there on the Roman Hill all was quiet.
Only harebells nodded,
And the pieces of limestone scattered in the spaces white,
Wondered not what I did.

It was early Spring, below hedges breaking in green
The coppice clothing with light,
Where soon the children should gather yellow marigolds in,
And the willow sprouts show bright.

In my pocket my sketch book to write of all
Beauty that I could –
But after the long climbing – the place majestical
Made lazy my mood.

So trying to guess what village I had never yet known
Lay under a mile forward …
I mused, hoping at night to work well from the longing
Now, keeping no vow or word.

And thought of all the mailed sentries that had kept
In past times watch here – now …
When only through their vigilance danger slept,
Or went uncaring the plough.

(GA)

*Looking to Barrow Wake from Crickley Hill*

• Head straight down the 'nose' of Crickley, signposted as the Gloucestershire Way. Just before the path steepens, there is a stone wall on the left and on a clear day you can look across at Witcombe embayment (on the geological fault-line), Witcombe Wood, Cooper's Hill and, away to the left, Barrow Wake viewpoint near Birdlip. The next section of the walk is steep and potentially muddy. Descend the slope to reach a turning to the right with some steps (badly worn when I visited in 2022 so take care).

③ Go down the steps and follow the path to contour along the hillside above Cold Slad Lane.

NB the Gloucestershire Way – marked in a pecked line on the map – could provide an alternative route for those who want to retrace Gurney's steps as he walked up from Shurdington. It runs straight on down the hill (very steeply, so be careful!) and can be followed across the fields before turning back up an overgrown track, eventually leading up to the cottage I believe that Gurney lived in during 1920–21. Rejoin the main route at Point 4.

Gurney's poem noted the effects of a change in wind direction on the Crickley edge where *naked landslips* and quarrying have produced the characteristic uneven ground. The normal wind direction is south-west, when the slope would be sheltered.

**East Wind**
Cool air moves there up on Cotswold edge,
By Crickley's bastion or the Shurdington wedge,
Gray [sic] grass rustles, the harebells dance and the East
Wind has no good influences on the cattle at feast.

Naked landslides show, away downhill mist-shades cover
The land where South-West once moved high like a
  lover,
With colour and boy's glory and breath of renewal:
That also, that valley, for this dry air is a fuel.

But the great steeps keep one in right hoping still,
Mighty the upstanding curving of the golden-crowned
  hill
Crickley, where scabious and serious thistle nods,
And there is good hiding place for the old gods.

(K2004)

*The rough scarp slopes below Crickley Hill*

• As you walk along the narrow path, notice the signs of early industrial activity. Limestone was quarried here in the nineteenth and early twentieth centuries, and lime burning carried out, originally in two stone kilns which still survive under the vegetation. Later they were replaced by two tall iron kilns. The black gritty material under your feet is the remains of coke 'breeze' used in the kilns. Lime burning came to an end in the 1940s.

• The path eventually does a sharp turn to the left to reach a gate and a junction of paths with Cold Slad Lane.

④ At this junction turn down the track straight ahead. Cold Slad is where Gurney found *an old Cotswold stone house, under the shadow of the great rise of Crickley*, and experimented with living here on his own in 1920. I believe that I have discovered the actual cottage. The cottage is about 200m down the track on the left, hiding amidst shrubs and a small overgrown garden; it is now in poor repair but still in use (2021). The cottage has a gateway onto the track and from here a path once led across the fields direct to Dryhill Farm where Gurney worked as a farm labourer. Gurney found peace here, under the shadow of his favourite hill. We know that he wrote some poetry and that he worked on his *Gloucestershire Rhapsody*, an orchestral piece finished in 1921. From Gurney's letters and poetry, we learn that he wanted to write music rooted in this landscape: *All love from all memory called out*, as he described it in his poem **A Bit from my Gloucestershire Rhapsody** (BP). Once you are aware of Gurney as a musician you can hear the music in many of his poems.

**Crickley Cliffs** (*extract*)
Crickley cliffs blared a trumpet ever, ever golden,
A flourish of trumpets against the late afternoon light.
Rome spoke out intangibly yet matchlessly,
And defied land and high air with boy soldiers' might.
Such huge tramplings of brass sound about
Cliffs of white stone …

(GA)

### Gurney's Cottage, 1920–21

In April 1919, Gurney had found work at Dryhill Farm, and his letters to Marion Scott are full of enthusiasm. 'My wages (in money) are to be 5/- a week and keep; but O what a full competence and more of beauty! Aren't I lucky?' (22 April 1919). 'The loveliest place almost that ever was, the widest sweep of beauty before one' (late April 1919). He was convinced he had found a way of life in which the physical exercise of farm labour would keep his depression in check, whilst the landscape, with its beauty and ghostly Roman presence, would inspire his writing and composing.

He threw himself with vigour into this enterprise: 'Tomorrow to follow the plough, do an hour's Fugue perhaps and hammer out the Sonata on the rickety old piano here.' (22 April 1919). At that time Gurney was living at Dryhill Farm but his attention was drawn to a small cottage at Cold Slad, standing empty in 1919/20.

In Spring 1920 Gurney was briefly staying in High Wycombe, playing the organ at Christ Church. 'Well, in one of my fits of not being able to stand it any longer, I wrote a letter to the chief churchwarden at Wycombe, arranged for the service to be taken, and came here – to find out what might be found out. An old Cotswold stone house with one pretty good upper room, but draughty. There are holes in the floor – to be dodged. There are two square places in the roof which will need stopping. The garden was long ago a ruin, the stream dried up, and weeds grew in it; no one came save the curious; and now under the shadow of the great rise of Crickley – here am I. I am a bit afraid but hope to earn a little somehow to carry on.' (13 May 1920).

The cottage in Cold Slad lane meets his description, and the track and cottage are marked on the 1896 and

*Gurney's cottage at Cold Slad*

1919 OS maps. The main part of the building is Cotswold stone, possibly eighteenth-century, though there is a newer (possibly early twentieth-century) extension and the roof has been renewed at least once. There are windows looking up to the hill (though blinded now by overgrown vegetation), and a small garden crossed by an intermittent stream. Most importantly, the location is perfect, on the ancient trackway between Crickley and Little Shurdington, directly under the nose of Crickley and within a few minutes' walk of Dryhill Farm.

Gurney was living in the cottage from May 1920. There are no letters covering May–October 1920 but we do have Gurney's poetry. **Midnight** sees him rapt in writing, enjoying the sense and sounds of his own creative hideaway, though perhaps already beginning his downward spiral into mental 'pain'.

### Midnight

There is no sound within the cottage now,
But my pen and the sound of long rain
Heavy and musical, I must think again
To find so sweet a noise, and cannot anyhow.

The soothingness and deep-toned tinkle, soft
Happenings of night, in pain there's nothing better,

Save tobacco or long most looked for letter …
The different roof sounds. House, shed, loft and scullery.

(80P)

Did he intend to live here permanently? Was it an answer to Gurney's problems or an impossible dream, given his fragile mental condition and difficulty in holding down even the farm job on a permanent basis? What we do know is that in October 1920, he was back in London, and in Spring 1921 he was living with his aunt at Longford. The only further mention of the cottage that I can find (apart from in the poetry) is in a letter to Marion Scott of 9 September 1921:

No, I am not yet well; in spite of a journey to Crickley yesterday, where I found Cold Slad occupied, renewing, with two new, welcome windows looking up on the Hill. Mr Masefield was running Iphigenia in Tauris [a drama by Euripides] at Stroud yesterday and wrote to ask me over; but not being well and having a chance of Crickley, decided me not to go.

The dream was over.

• After visiting the cottage, return to the top of the track and turn left on the lane. After about 100m, the lane bends left but go ahead through a gateway onto the path under the scarp edge.

⑤ Just before the next gateway, turn left through a small gate onto a bridleway. As you climb up away from the gate and round to the right, look back to see Gurney's cottage amid trees. The footpath from the cottage ran across these fields.

• For the next 0.5km of the bridleway, you are on fields that belonged to Dryhill Farm, contouring above the farm and following a very ancient hedge boundary that marked the division between the open common land hill grazing and the enclosed fields. Notice the pollarded ash trees, formerly providing firewood and fencing stakes. Gurney helped with such tasks. In the poem **Above Dryhill** he compares the hedge-laying with composing music – *And there the high wild hedges I saw tamed / And cunning woven when the green buds flamed / With deft interweaving like a player's showing / Of Bach's fourstranded thought* (80P).

• From the field edge you can see the rooftops and outbuildings of Dryhill Farm, now a private house. These are the fields on which Gurney would have raked hay, gathered root crops or herded livestock, and wondered about the Romans whose villa was located just on the uphill side of the farmhouse and whose pottery and coins he occasionally found.

## Up There

On Cotswold edge there is a field and that
Grows thick with corn and speedwell and the mat
Of thistles, of the tall kind: Rome lived there,
Some hurt centurion got his grant or tenure,
Built farm with fowl and pigsties and wood-piles,
Waited for service custom between whiles.
The farmer ploughs up coins in the wet-earth-time,
He sees them on the topple of crests' gleam,
Or run down furrow; and halts and does let them lie
Like a small black island in brown immensity,
Till his wonder is ceased, and his great hand picks up
   the penny.
Red pottery easy discovered, no searching needed . . .
One wonders what farms were like, no searching
   needed,
As now the single kite hovering still
By the coppice there, level with the flat of the hill.

(K2004)

⑥ At the field corner, do not go through the gate uphill into the woods (although that is a short way back to the return route at Point 9) but turn down alongside the field edge, imagining the Roman villa spread out to your left and passing a spring that trickles into an old bath. Cross the driveway of Dryhill Farmhouse, perhaps pausing to catch a glimpse of it, before making for the gate into the lower fields.

### Dryhill Farm

The original buildings on this site were part of the Roman *villa rustica* sited here in about AD 76 and remnants of the villa stone can be found in Dryhill's cellar walls. A Roman vineyard was situated below the farmhouse and this use has been reintroduced by the present owner. Part of the present building dates from the eighteenth century.

Ivor Gurney worked as a farm labourer at Dryhill between April 1919 and mid-1920 and was given the attic (which still exists) as his bedroom. During the 1970s, when Leonard Clark's *Selected Poems of Ivor Gurney* was published (1973), the *Gloucester Citizen*

*Dryhill – the old part of the house (photo: Nigel Rowley)*

newspaper published various recollections by people who remembered Gurney. One (29 August 1973) was from Mrs Helen Herring, who recalled her time as the nine-year-old daughter of the farmer at Dryhill Farm.

> I remember so well the first cup of tea in the kitchen and my mother trying to get him to talk. But all he would do was to look out on to the wash house roof and go into raptures over the moss and broken tiles. My father swept out, remarking, 'A rum chap to help farming'.

⑦ From the gate into the fields, walk straight ahead, then veer uphill to the right to find a blackberry bush, the field corner and another gate. Looking back to Dryhill Farm, you can appreciate its sheltered foot-of-scarp and spring-line location. Through the gate, follow the bridleway across two fields. Note the fine view of Chosen Hill from the second field. Eventually, you reach the old Greenway Lane, formerly a drovers' road, now only used as a road in its upper section, while the lower part is a deeply sunken and shady track, wet and muddy in winter, *a carpet of dust* in summer (**Roads**, p. 106).

• Walk back up Greenway Lane for about 200m.

⑧ At the Cotswold Way sign, turn right, climb a short flight of steps up from the road and follow the Cotswold Way all along the high edge. There is a bridleway to the left of a fence but take the right-hand narrow path right on the edge, with relatively young beechwood to your left and later some coniferous trees (Barrow Piece plantation) amongst the beeches. Behind the conifers to the east, you may glimpse Crippetts Long Barrow, a Neolithic burial mound dating from 3500–2500BC.

⑨ When a pathway leaves to the right (linking back to Dryhill), the scarp edge path climbs again and enters mature beechwood, with some giant beech trees managed jointly by Gloucestershire Wildlife Trust and the National Trust. The beeches are magnificent at any time of year, but particularly striking on a clear day in winter when the delicate tracery of their branches is spread out against a blue-sky background. At other times, the trees assume a more threatening manner, particularly to Gurney in a low mood. Some of the most arresting imagery of Gurney's later asylum poems refers to the gloom and menace of wind-shaken trees.

*Winter beech tree on Crickley edge*

**The Coppice**

There is a coppice on Cotswold's edge the winds love;
It blasts so, and from below there one sees move
Tree branches like water darkling – and I write thus
At the year's end, in nine hell-depths, with such
   memories;

(K2004)

• Poems like this express Gurney's fear of being banished from Gloucestershire places and from the sources of his well-being. Whereas earlier poems like **East Wind** and **Crickley Cliffs**, written when Gurney could be on his high hills, reveal the familiar world of the Cotswold Hills stretching reliably away into the distance, later poems such as **The Coppice**, written in Dartford asylum, reveal only the asylum walls and the poet's misery – *in nine hell-depths, with such memories.*

• Follow the path as it nears the edge through some large beech trees, eventually emerging at a gate into the upper Crickley car park, next to the Information Centre where you started.

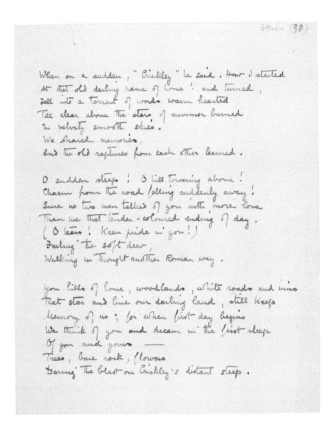

*The final three verses of Gurney's handwritten draft of **Crickley Hill**
(© The Ivor Gurney Trust)*

*'the wind is rising on those edges of Cotswold'* – the Cotswold Edge at Cleeve Common, with Huddlestone's Table in foreground

# PART FIVE: Those Edges of Cotswold

To the north of Crickley Hill the Cotswold Edge reaches its highest point on Cleeve Common. Leckhampton and Cleeve Hill are open grassland, windswept and once remote places where Gurney walked and found solace and inspiration; although, as the poem below reveals, these edges of Cotswold also feature in some of his darkest poetry. Bredon Hill is an outlier of the main scarp edge, seen by Gurney as the northerly outpost of his Gloucestershire.

**Hell's Prayer**
My God, the wind is rising! on those edges
Of Cotswold dark glory might swing my soul –
And Western Severn and North of water sedges
Mystery sounds, the wind's drums roll.
None will care to walk there. Those prefer to tell
Tales in a warm room of gossips, gettings, wages,
While I would be cursing exultant at the wind's toll
Of bell, shout of glory – swiftness of shadows.

My birth, my earning, my attained heritages,
Ninety times denied me now thrust so far in hell.

I think of the gods, all their old oaths and gages –
Gloucester has clear honour sworn without fail –
Companionship of meadows, high Cotswold ledges
Battered now tonight with huge wind-bursts and rages,
Flying moon glimpses like a shattered and flimsy sail –
In Hell I buried a score-depth, writing verse pages.

(K2004)

This poem, written at a late stage in the asylum, is a sad reminder of how much Gurney missed the high edges of Cotswold. Whilst some might prefer to gossip in warm rooms, Gurney needed to be out, running on steep slopes and shouting exultantly at the *huge wind-bursts and rages.* Instead, he is trapped in Dartford *in Hell*, writing verse pages which might never be read.

## WALK 14

# The Majesty of Leckhampton

**The Little Way** (*extract*)
On and on I knew not where, till the unknown
Majesty of Leckhampton rose Roman as shield-shape
  known
Confirming faith-of-beauty.

(GA)

Leckhampton Hill was another of Gurney's Cotswold Edge retreats which he frequented in the poet-war period. In a letter to Marion Scott (September 1919) he noted that one night, 'after going to see Emmie [Emily Hunt] at Cleeve, I walked back by Leckhampton, Shurdington, Brockworth – just missing Crickley. Meteors flashed like sudden inspirations of song down the sky. The air was too still to set firs or beeches sighing, but the grass swished; twigs crackled beneath me and the occasional stir of wild creatures in the undergrowth set off the peace.' His poetry reveals a fascination with the steep, cliff-like limestone edges, the quarrying, and the magnificent views from the summit. All these were inspiration for music and poetry. Gurney's mental health was fragile in this 1918–22 period, and some of his letters and poetry reveal depression and bitterness. At one time, he attempted a long walk back from High Wycombe, returning to Dryhill and finding his way in the early hours of the morning by recognising the *Majesty of Leckhampton*. This incident is recorded in **The Little Way**, a poem written in the asylum much later (see below).

This walk begins at the car park near Hartley House on the Cotswold plateau, before following the Cotswold Way along the Cotswold Edge, via Devil's Chimney, to Leckhampton summit. Crossing the ramparts of the Iron Age hillfort, the route continues on the high edge and then drops down to woodland and joins the Cheltenham Circular Path. Former quarries and tramways are apparent along the foot of the steep slopes until the path follows an old railway incline up to the former Leckhampton limekilns of the 1920s. A woodland path contours around the lower edge of the hill and eventually rises to join the Cotswold Way again and return to the car park.

## Route Details

DISTANCE/ TIME:
7.5km/ 4.7 miles, 2.5–3 hours

MAPS:
*OS Explorer 179, 1:25 000, Gloucester, Cheltenham & Stroud*
*OS Landranger 163, 1:50 000, Cheltenham & Cirencester*

START AND PARKING:
Start at the car park in Hartley Lane (SP 951179) near Hartley Farm (GL53 9QN), just off the A435 near the Seven Springs junction. There is also parking in the disused quarry (SP 946177). Access is also available at Point 6.

TRACKS AND PATHS:
The Cotswold Way is a well-used grassy track along the scarp edge. Steep slopes on gravel and grass and through woodland. Can be muddy and unstable in wet weather. No stiles.

*The Devil's Chimney and Cheltenham below*

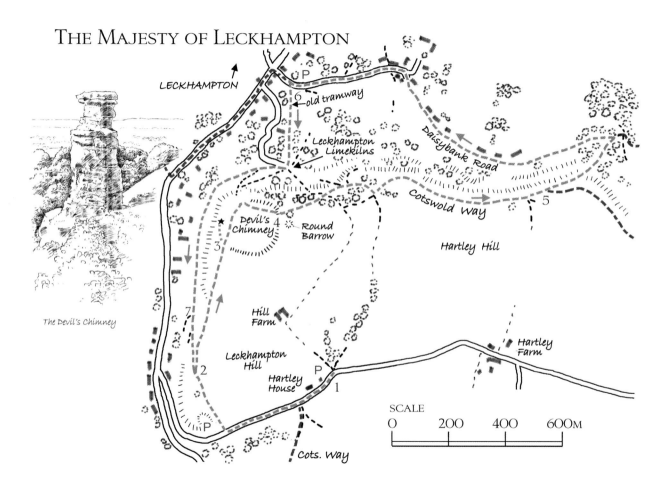

# THE MAJESTY OF LECKHAMPTON

LECKHAMPTON

P

6 — old tramway

Leckhampton Limekilns

Daisybank Road

Cotswold Way

5

Hartley Hill

Devil's Chimney

3

4

Round Barrow

The Devil's Chimney

7

Hill Farm

2

Leckhampton Hill

Hartley House

P

1

Cots. Way

P

Hartley Farm

SCALE

0       200       400       600M

184

## THE WALK

① From the car park, turn right to follow the lane down past Hartley House, eventually joining up with the Cotswold Way which comes in from your left. After 250m, the Cotswold Way turns off the lane at a sign and there are steps up to the right. Below to your left, behind the brambles, is the alternative car park occupying a disused quarry. The Cotswold Way takes you up around the edge of the quarry and out onto open grassland. There is an information board on the right of the path and, over to the left, there is a convenient bench to sit on and admire the views across to Chosen Hill and the Malvern Hills. There is a small path going down to the left but do not take this now — you will return this way later.

② From the bench, return to the path and carry on up the hill. The Cotswold Way is sometimes rough with limestone pieces and sometimes grassy. At a path junction, it is worth taking a detour to see Devil's Chimney, signed down to the left. Follow the path over rocky ledges until you reach a viewing point with a rather ugly safety fence. The Chimney is a well-known local landmark consisting of an upright pillar of limestone, probably left by eighteenth-century quarrymen as

a joke. Gurney's poem – **Leckhampton Chimney has Fallen Down** – seems strange as the chimney quite clearly still exists. However, he may either be referring to the occasional rockfall which took place, or be imagining a time when the fall of the chimney would denote irrevocable changes to his beloved Gloucestershire.

> **Leckhampton Chimney has fallen Down**
> Leckhampton chimney has fallen down,
> The birds of Crickley have cried it – it is known in the
>   town,
> The cliffs have changed. What will come next to that Line
> Watcher of West England now that landmark has fallen.
>
> Severn has changed course, it is known by Barrow;
> Malvern may heave up other lines by tomorrow,
> But Maisemore Hill stable and rounded shall stay –
> And strawberry flowers found surprise on Christmas day.
>
> Cleeve will front sunset, Birdlip shall have its road
> Flung angled and noble on its breast broad.
> Many things shall stay but the stone Chimney,
> Leckhampton's mark has fallen, like a stick or a tree.
>
> (K2004)

③ Rejoin the Cotswold Way at the path junction. Continue walking up the grassy slopes as the cliff-like edge becomes more apparent to your left, and the bumpy ridge of the Iron Age hillfort embankment are crossed. At the top of the hill is a topograph explaining the views down to Cheltenham, over to the Cotswold Edge at Cleeve and, when clear, taking in the outliers of Nottingham and Bredon Hills, and the Malvern Hills to the north-west. There is a wonderful sense of space and clarity emphasising the shape of the hill, with the high plateau top to the east gently sloping down to the south, whilst the far-flung views to the north and west call attention to the cliff edge of the scarp slope.

It is easy to understand the feeling of freedom and windswept glory that so attracted Gurney to these high edges. The poem that follows reflects both this joy (first verse) but also an intense sadness (second verse) resulting from the period of depression and mental problems Gurney was experiencing in the early 1920s. He knew that his depressive periods prevented him feeling the *crystal air-time* or hearing the *light tunes*. Like most bipolar sufferers, when he was down, *nothing is sweet to thinking*.

**When the Body might Free**

When the body might free, and there was use in walking,
In October time – crystal air-time and free words were
  talking
In my mind with light tunes and bright streams ran free,
When the earth smelt, leaves shone and air and cloud
  had glee,

Then there was salt in life but now none is known
To me who cannot go either where the white is blown
Of the grass, or scarlet willow-herb of past memory.
Nothing is sweet to thinking, nothing from life free.

(K2004)

• Leaving the topograph walk on up to a prominent embankment – a major feature of the Iron Age hillfort – with the trig point marking the top of Leckhampton Hill at 293m.

④ From the trig point, the Cotswold Way makes its way along the hilltop in a north-easterly direction until you reach a metal gate. An information board provides an outline of the hill's history, including mention of the radar station based here in the Second World War, manned by the Royal Observer Corps.

**Leckhampton** is a univallate (one line of embankment) hillfort, approximately contemporary with the Crickley hillfort, and was constructed around 650BC. The hillfort occupies 2.8 hectares (8 acres) of the hilltop with surviving ramparts to the south and east sides, and a large, ditched feature to the north. The steep hill slopes would have afforded natural lines of defence on the west and north sides. Within the fort area there is also an unusual round barrow, which may be a burial mound, within a square enclosure believed to date from the same period as the fort.

*Following the Cotswold Way*

• Do not go through the metal gate but keep following the footpath around to the left. It crosses some hummocky and often muddy ground and through a wooded copse, before heading out into the open along the scarp edge, taking advantage of a newly-graded footpath (2022). Walking the Cotswold Way along the top of the scarp edge in the twenty-first century will be a different experience from that of Gurney in the early twentieth century.

• The managed paths and information boards contrast strikingly with the wilder open sheep walks of the plateau and the steep edge scarred by limestone quarrying that Gurney would have known. In a poem of the 1920–22 period, Gurney evocatively summed up his joy at moving fast along the wilder paths of the edge. Phrases like *love of body and travel of good turf*, *breathing was loving*, *set music on glowing* take us out into the landscape directly with this young man as he is inspired and lifted by the places around him.

**Old Thought**

Autumn that name of creeper falling and tea-time
    loving,
Was once for me the thought of High Cotswold noon
    air,
And the earth smell turning brambles, and half cirrus
    moving,
Mixed with the love of body and travel of good turf
    there.

O up in height, O snatcht up, O swiftly going,
Common to beechwood, breathing was loving, the yet
Unknown Crickley Cliffs trumpeted, set music on
    glowing
In my mind. White Cotswold, wine scarlet woods and
    leaf wreckage wet.

(K2004)

During the post-war period, Gurney often walked this area when he was struggling to maintain his mental balance and to cope with the return to civilian life. In 1920, an incident recorded later in one of his asylum poems, **The Little Way**, gives us an unusual insight into both his state of mind and the importance to him of this part of the Cotswold Edge.

**The Little Way**

In the autumn of 1919, Ivor Gurney had returned to the Royal College of Music to resume his pre-war studies, but found that maintaining his old routines and living in London were not easy. He took up residence in High Wycombe with the Chapman family, with whom he had built up a close relationship before the war (when he was assistant organist at Christ Church, where Edward Chapman was churchwarden).

On 25 February, Matilda Chapman (Edward's wife) wrote to Marion Scott to express her concern about Gurney, saying he had 'left for Gloucester, on foot, the previous day'. Apparently, he wanted to go back to Dryhill Farm, a place on the Cotswold Edge that had inspired happiness and creativity (see Walk 13). Later that week, Herbert Howells also reported his concern to Marion Scott, writing in a letter of 29 February 1920:

[Ivor Gurney] walked last Tuesday from High Wycombe to a village 8 miles east of Oxford; continued on Wednesday to that city; and took a train from there to a place on the Cotswold ridge (I have forgotten the name of the village) and walked across the hills to Dryhill Farm, Crickley.

Gurney's journey started on Tuesday 24 February and, despite there being a train service from High Wycombe to Oxford, he walked from High Wycombe and travelled by foot and eventually train to return to Dryhill Farm late on the Wednesday evening (25 February).

### The Little Way

At eight o'clock, I had left my friend with appearances
Of walking just so far – taking tram and later
Train; to get home respectably and to books and a
matter of a Quartett left half-written …
   but the spirit demanding
Said 'So you did not think in your intent [interest?] of
  France'

Obedient as ever to the call leftward and south-
  eastward,
I kept my instinct past trespass. It was an all night
  chance
Of [by?] paths and of Roman ways; no hurry – but my
  body went faster
Than rules. At eleven o'clock, I was lost and in belief
  steering –
And by divine stars never before it seemed on slants
And by azure heights of heaven so ordered (Save
  Varennes'
Frost-stricken fury of beauty) Land in dim smothers.

On and on, I knew not where, till the unknown
Majesty of Leckhampton rose Roman as shield-shape
  known,
Confirming faith-of-beauty: its best way, spirit
In me – and West and South now after South alone
Moving, the dark land passing like a dream of one
Night (but Cotswold chiefest). To the spinney I had
  come

Where at last in the thick growth night unstarred
Gave gloom alone. Where I halted and lay; choosing
   as always
Tobacco for a friend, but stifled the gaudy match blaze
Hurting the dusk – lay smoked, thought of books and
   the companies
Of Roman here had travelled, rested, or blundered
   through brambles
(The camp and little most treasured farm so near.)

                          (GA)

In an article in *The Ivor Gurney Society newsletter* (2015), Phil Richardson reconstructs the journey from High Wycombe and confirms that the **Little Way** refers to the final part of this – the walk, probably from Andoversford, along the scarp edge and eventually round the top of Leckhampton Hill where the Cotswold Way now runs. The state of Gurney's mind can be deduced from the poem, which often reads more like a piece of prose, and from the fact that this walk was undertaken at night – *At eleven o'clock, I was lost and in belief steering – / And by divine stars never before it seemed on slants / And by azure heights of heaven* …. He probably left Andoversford at about 5.30pm, according to the train timetable, and he would have found this winter night-time expedition difficult and hazardous. His relief and happiness are clear when *the unknown / Majesty of Leckhampton rose Roman as shield-shape known, / Confirming faith-of-beauty.* It may seem strange that he refers to Leckhampton Hill as *unknown* but this may be his way of explaining that he did not know where he was till the shape appeared. Finally, Gurney arrived above Dryhill, the *most treasured farm* … *Where I halted and lay; choosing as always / Tobacco for a friend* …

⑤ Your daytime walk along the Leckhampton edge brings you to a path junction about 1km from the trig point. Here the Cotswold Way goes round to the right, but take the left-hand path going steeply downhill to join the signposted Cheltenham Circular Path. At this path junction, there is a main track straight ahead down the hill that eventually joins the road, and the Cheltenham Circular Path (CCP) crosses left to right. Take the smaller left-hand CCP turn into the woods.

*Looking down the scarp slope to Daisybank Road*

• Follow the CCP all along the lower hillside. At times there is a wide track serving the few houses, and a narrower grassy path the other side of a fence. It doesn't matter which you take as they all end up joining Daisybank Road which you follow to a road junction. Turn left and after about 400m notice signs of quarrying up to the left. Find the parking area at the bottom of the old tramway. Here, there is an information board and a gate.

⑥ Go through the gate and walk up the main track (the old standard gauge railway incline).

• In the early 1920s, as part of a scheme for easing unemployment after the First World War, four large limekilns, of 300 tons total capacity per day, were constructed part-way up the hill, served by tram and rail lines. The steep, straight track that you are walking was a 'standard gauge railway incline'. The very bottom of this incline, at a level lower than Daisybank Road, used to connect with further standard gauge tracks with a small steam engine going eastwards to connect to a mainline at Charlton Kings. This development was not a success and by 1927 it had closed and the plant sold. All that remains now is some stonework associated with the base of the limekilns and the ruins of an electrical plant house.

ABOVE: *The present-day ruins, with just the bases of the limekilns still visible*

LEFT: *The four limekilns in operation in 1925 (© D.E. Bick, 1997)*

• On reaching the ruined lime kilns, you will find many paths to left and right. Turn to the right but be careful to take the middle path – do not go steeply up alongside the limekiln itself, nor down towards Leckhampton. The middle path contours around through woodland for about 750m with the steep, quarried edges of Leckhampton Hill ever-present to your left, and signs of large new houses to right through the trees. The quarried area above you was referred to as Deadman's Quarry and produced the best quality building stone. At one point, Devil's Chimney appears, ghostlike, above you. I wonder if it was this view from below that inspired another poem, **Leckhampton Elbow** which talks of *the stone wonder / Set up high above Shurdington, the meadows so low. / In my mind music gathered of beauty and form*: (RW)

⑦ Where the main path meanders around to the right, take the steep uphill path to the left with steps cut into the slope. Come out on the hillside just below the bench where the walk paused at Point 2 for a view of the Severn Vale and Malverns.

• Make your way back down the hillside and along the lane to Point 1 and the car park at the start.

*Deadman's Quarry face*

*Aerial view of the Cotswold Edge, Cleeve Hill and Fort (© Historic England 2746-030)*

# Cleeve Common and Belas Knap

**Cotswold** (*extract*)
But Cotswold Wall stands up and has strength of its own,
Blue against dawn, Sunset's shield, and Time's wonder
and crown.

(RW)

Cleeve Hill is the highest point of the Cotswolds at 330m (1,082 ft), presenting a wall-like face (*has strength of its own / Blue against dawn, Sunset's shield*) to the Severn Vale below. Cleeve Hill has an impressive mountain shape and is almost moorland-like in character; but, geologically, it is very much a part of the Jurassic limestone hills of the Cotswolds. Cleeve Common is Gloucestershire's largest common, with an area of over 400 ha (1,000 acres) and it is a nationally important Site of Special Scientific Interest (SSSI) managed by a charitable trust (see: www.cleevecommon.org.uk/).

Although the core of Gurney's hill-walking centred on Crickley and Cooper's Hills, he regularly wandered further afield onto Leckhampton and Cleeve, noting the changing weather conditions, such as thunderstorms, strong winds and hill mists, as well as glorious sunshine. Descriptions of dawns and sunsets appear frequently – *Cotswold Edge shines out at morning in gold* (**Cotswold**).

This walk joins the Cotswold Edge near the summit of Cleeve, picks up the Cotswold Way and follows the steep scarp slope around in a clockwise direction, taking in spectacular views across Cheltenham, the Severn Vale, the outlying Nottingham and Langley Hills and Winchcombe. The walk along the edge passes the Iron Age Cleeve Camp, Bronze Age earthworks, Romano-British remains and the more recent scars left by quarrying. The open moorland scenery of Cleeve Common is today frequented by horse-riders, runners, golfers and dog-walkers, but in Gurney's day it probably had a more isolated feel and was mainly used for sheep grazing. Leaving the scarp edge after about 5km the route descends to the wooded edges of the Isbourne valley, past Postlip Farm and back to the small lane leading down to Winchcombe. A sharp turn up into the woods leads on a well-marked path to the Neolithic Long Barrow of Belas Knap. Field tracks take you back to the Common and the car park.

# CLEEVE COMMON AND BELAS KNAP

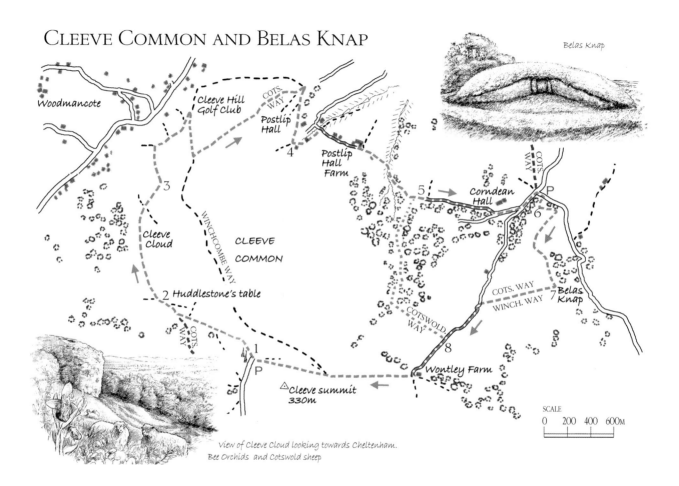

Belas Knap

Woodmancote

Cleeve Hill
Golf Club

COTS.
WAY

Postlip
Hall

4

Postlip
Hall Farm

3

WINCHCOMBE WAY

Cleeve
Cloud

CLEEVE
COMMON

5

Corndean
Hall

COTS.
WAY

P

6

2 Huddlestone's table

COTS.
WAY

1

P

COTSWOLD WAY

COTS. WAY

WINCH. WAY

7 Belas
Knap

8

△ Cleeve summit
330m

Wontley Farm

View of Cleeve Cloud looking towards Cheltenham.
Bee Orchids and Cotswold sheep

SCALE
0    200  400  600M

196

## Route Details

DISTANCE/ TIME:
11.6km (7.2 miles)/ 4–4.5 hours (shorter version 10.1km/
6 miles)

MAPS:
OS Explorer 179, 1:25 000, Gloucester, Cheltenham & Stroud,
and OL45, The Cotswolds
OS Landranger 163, 1:50 000, Cheltenham & Cirencester

START AND PARKING:
Start at the radio mast car park near Whittington, on Cleeve
Common (SO 994249; GL54 4EU). Other car parks at
Westdown (SP 009239; GL54 5TL), and the golf club off the
B4632 (SO 989272; GL52 3PW). There is a two-car layby at
Point 6 on the map, with quick access to Belas Knap.

TRACKS AND PATHS:
Well-used grassy tracks over the common, in woodland and
field tracks. Can be muddy and steep. No stiles.

## THE WALK

① Leave the car park by the gate and turn left onto the common where a wide expanse of open grassland, and usually a strong breeze, greets you. Walk down by the fence and, on a clear day, notice the distinctive shape of the Malvern Hills ahead. To your left the two outliers of Chosen Hill and Robinswood Hill become visible, and behind them the undulating line of the south Cotswold escarpment. A small path joins and soon after, at a gateway, the Cotswold Way enters the common from the left.

• Follow the Cotswold Way for the next 2km, a blowy and uplifting experience as you are at about 300m, with the limestone scarp edge sloping down to your left. At first the path is rising gradually to meet two windswept beech trees (the Twins) on the horizon ahead of you. Before climbing the hill, notice a square block of stone by a path on the edge. This is Huddlestone's Table. There is a story that this celebrates a meeting held by King Kenulf of Mercia, although it is more likely the remnant of quarrying. The Huddlestone family lived in the area in the 1520s.

*'The Twins' –
beech trees on
Cleeve Hill*

② From the twin beech trees, the Cotswold Way leads you across ditch and bank structures. These are the remains of Cleeve Hillfort.

**Cleeve** is an Iron Age hillfort dating from around 500BC and was probably built initially as a single bank and ditch, with the second ring added some two

centuries later. Stabilising work carried out in 2011 revealed that there is a stone structure forming the core of the banks – they are not just mounds of earth. This fort would have been visible for miles around and was perhaps the seat of a local chieftain. Although much of the hillfort has been destroyed by quarrying in the last 300 years, it still encloses 1.2 hectares (3 acres) and is approximately one third of a circle, as it uses the original natural edge of the scarp as one boundary.

The Cross Dyke is a long ditch and bank earthwork and is probably the oldest archaeological feature of the Common (before 700BC and pre-dating the Iron Age fort). It runs from near the top of Rising Sun Lane in the village of Cleeve Hill, diagonally up the escarpment, over the edge and it then swings left into Dry Bottom and Postlip Quarries. This linear earthwork was built as a Bronze Age territorial boundary, by scarp-foot dwellers staking their claim to part of the hilltop. Today, the parish boundary between Southam and Woodmancote still follows this historic line.

*Cleeve Hill viewpoint and topograph*

There are more earthworks to negotiate, marking the existence of another historical monument known as the Cross Dyke. Finally, reach the trig point and topograph (Point 3) at a high point on the escarpment.

③ The view from the summit (317m) is striking, even though this is not officially the highest point of Cleeve Hill (this is 13m higher and lies behind you near the radio masts). In the vale below, the settlements of Cheltenham and Gloucester seem to merge. Looking to the south-west, the line of the southern Cotswold scarp can be seen, with Leckhampton and Crickley visible and the outliers of Robinswood Hill and Chosen Hill. To the west across the vale, the prominent, treed summit of May Hill can be seen, with the Black Mountains and Welsh Hills often hazy shapes behind it. To the north is the outlier of Bredon Hill (Walk 16) in the distance, and in the foreground, Nottingham Hill can be seen as a flat-topped promontory, attached to the scarp by a thin neck of land near the Golf Club. There is a feeling of Gloucestershire being spread out below you and 'the Severn-valley clouds like banners streaming' (letter to Marion Scott, February 1917). So often in Gurney's letters and poems, he refers to the long view of Gloucestershire from the Cotswold Edge.

• After leaving the hillfort, the Cotswold Way is on the high grassland of Cleeve Cloud. Many paths snake off left-wards, down and along the rocky escarpment edge, with the village of Southam neatly set out below you. The route continues climbing ahead and slightly to the right (north north-east).

**Cotswold**

Cotswold Edge shines out at morning in gold,
It convinces as Rome convinces in the earth-stronghold
The traveller finds here and there in his walk and is sure
Of the might of her of Rome, and her right to endure.
But Cotswold Wall stands up and has strength of its own,
Blue against dawn, Sunset's shield, and Time's wonder
   and crown.
And Crickley unconscious so strong She is in Her pride,
Is master of meadows away to far Severn side –
And no man says Her nay, She is a county's wonder:
That county, Gloucestershire, wherefore many have
   crossed seas and died –
At Laventie I saw them, and at Ypres in the cannon
   thunder,
Rome would have kept silence at such courage not
   praised – Her own beside.

                                             (RW)

• Although this high Cotswold Edge inspired Gurney, it also features in some of his most disturbed and heartfelt poetry written from Dartford asylum – *the wind is rising on those dark edges of Cotswold* (**Hell's Prayer** p. 181), and *It is the year's end, the winds are blasting, and I / Write to keep madness and black torture away / A little …* (**December 30th**, K2004).

• From the topograph, don't walk straight ahead down the grassy slopes of the golf course but follow Cotswold Way marker posts down to the left, making for the golf clubhouse. This is a steep descent with many paths made by walkers through the disturbed, quarried landscape. The Cotswold Way leads you through Rolling Bank Quarry, with an information board about the geology of the area.

At **Rolling Bank Quarry**, just under the escarpment edge, you will find an information board (installed by the Gloucestershire Geology Trust).

The bedrock of the upper reaches of the Common is oolitic limestone. However, the full height of the Cotswold Escarpment is made up by layers of Early Jurassic (Liassic) clays and silts. Cleeve is the only area of the Cotswolds where the full sequence of Inferior Oolite rocks can be seen. Two layers are unique to Cleeve Hill and not visible anywhere else in Britain.

For centuries the limestone has been quarried, with different layers of rock having varying uses. Smooth-grained blocks with few imperfections, such as

Lower Freestone, made good building stone. Coarser, rubbly rocks containing many fossils, like Gryphite or Trigonia Grit, were suitable for roads and field walls. These rocks are named after the main fossil found in them: *Gryphaea* (or devil's toenail) and *Trigonia* are two distinctive species of bivalves. Fine 'Harford' sands were taken off by donkey in the eighteenth and nineteenth centuries for use in Staffordshire potteries. (Source: Gloucestershire Geology Trust).

• Almost at the clubhouse, the Cotswold Way crosses the Winchcombe Way, a well-established gravel track which takes off to the right. Follow this uphill for about 500m, past a low building. Then an obvious grassy track leads off to the left. Follow this to contour along the hillside above a deep dry valley with steep slopes reminiscent of the Pennine Dales rather than the Cotswolds. It is a pleasant walk in dry weather, but can be cold and damp when the rain arrives on the exposed hillside. Gurney recalls being out in rain and a thunderstorm on Cleeve Hill in one of his letters.

A poem of the early 1920s celebrates a *soaking* –

**The Soaking**
The rain has come, and the earth must be very glad
Of its moisture, and the made roads all dust-clad –
It lets a veil down on the lucent dark
And not of any bright ground thing shows any its
  spark.

Tomorrow's gray [sic] morning will show cow-parsley
Hung all with shining drops, and the river will be
Duller because of the all unfamiliar soddenness of
  things,
Till the skylark breaks his reluctance, hangs shaking
  and sings.

(RW)

• Eventually, at a path junction turn downhill to the right rejoining the Cotswold Way. Take another right turn at the bottom and walk along the edge of woodland. Postlip Hall (a fifteenth-century manor house, now a cooperative housing community) is hidden in the woodland. Look out for the Cotswold Way footpath sign (Point 4) leading through a gate to the left.

• Walk a little way up the valley before this next section of walk, to find the 'Washpool' – a deep, keyhole-shaped trough with stone sides, built in 1897. Recently renovated (2019) it was for centuries the gathering place for local sheep to be dipped, using water from the pool and spring immediately above it in 'Watery Bottom'.

*The washpool in Watery Bottom*

④ Follow the Cotswold Way along beside a high stone wall with woodland on your left and pasture on your right (usually horses graze here). Pass an unusual brick-arched spring and water trough before entering a farmyard. Go straight through the farmyard – don't take the Isbourne Way signed up to the right. The path goes straight on into a field alongside another stone wall and eventually comes out on a small lane. Walk up the lane to the right until you reach Postlip Hall Farm where a small field path can be used to avoid going through the farmyard. After the farmyard, follow a track downhill and take the Cotswold Way footpath left and down a field to a bridge over the stream.

• In the summer, this is a soothing place to pause in the woodland shade, with the sound of water accompanying you. Across the bridge, there is a steep and sometimes slippery climb with woodland enclosing you, until you arrive at a grassy area with a handy wooden log to sit on. Carry on across a field and out of a gate.

⑤ From Point 5, you have a choice of a slightly shorter but very steep climb via the Cotswold Way back up to the Cleeve Common at Point 8, or a one-mile longer route with the climb spread out and a historic monument to visit on the way back.

• For the **shorter route**, stay on the Cotswold Way and walk past the stables, through a gate and alongside the fence of a residential property. In the woods the path climbs gently to a gateway then climbs very steeply for nearly 1km before you reach a field of pasture. Cross the field to reach a kissing gate and join a main gravelly track, where the Cotswold Way turns left but you turn right to join the Winchcombe Way. (For a short section, the Cotswold and Winchcombe Ways have joined together).

• For the main and **longer route**, ignore the Cotswold Way sign from Point 5 and walk on down the lane to the right. This is now an easy walk for about 1km down the lane with woodland on one side and sheep grazing in large fields to your left. At one point, you will pass the entrance to Corndean Hall. Just before you reach a road junction, there is a small path signposted into the woodlands to your right. Follow this until you reach a sharp right turn uphill. Below you on the road is the layby and extra parking space at Point 6. (Note that the Cotswold Way and Winchcombe Way have briefly joined up).

• After the windswept high plateau, the woodland walk will probably be a quieter experience. A poem written in 1920, also called **Quiet Talk** or the **Trees are Breathing**, sees Gurney pondering the feeling of walking amongst quiet trees and wondering about the changing moods of the woodland. This poem can be read whichever route you are following:

**Late September**
The trees are breathing quietly today
Of coming Autumn and the Summer over;
Pause of high Summer when the year's at stay
And the wind's sick, that moves now like a lover.

On valley ridges where the beeches cluster,
Or changing ashes set by slopes of plough,
He goes; now sure of heart now in a fluster,
Of teasing purpose. Night shall find him grow

To dark strength and relentless-spoiling will.
First he loves baffle* streams and dull the bright;
Cower and threaten both about the hill –
Before their death trees blast in full delight.        (80P)

* reading this as 'to baffle' clarifies the way that Gurney is alluding to wind with both meanings of baffle: to bewilder and to restrain the flow or movement of, in this case, water.

⑥ From the layby near Point 6, climb up the steep but short woodland track to a gate. Go through it and into a field. Here the official route is along the bottom of the field to the left and then up the slope ahead by the fence.

• On a sunny day it is an enjoyable climb, if taken slowly and pausing to enjoy the view back across woodland. At the top of the field follow the signs left, maybe through another gate (dependent on stock grazing) and into an area of woodland where the track is stony and often muddy. At a stone stile turn right into the Belas Knap enclosure.

⑦ Spend a few minutes exploring Belas Knap.

• Leave Belas Knap by the exit into the field to the west of the site and follow the field boundary to join a track, which serves as both the Cotswold Way and the Winchcombe Way. After about 0.5km you will reach the kissing gate (right) which marks the Cotswold Way leaving down the field and woodland track (the shortcut route coming up from Postlip).

⑧ Carry straight on and soon downhill to reach the deserted Wontley Farm buildings at a junction. Turn right by the old barn and take the path uphill through fields and under a high voltage cable. Go through a gate back on to the common land. Do not take the immediate left alongside the wall but the next path slightly to the left and straight up the hill ahead. As you top the hill you will see the radio masts ahead. You can make a detour to reach the actual summit of Cleeve at the trig point or make for the radio masts and finish the walk at the car park.

### Belas Knap

Belas Knap is a fine example of a Neolithic long barrow, probably constructed around 3000BC. The impressive entrance is a dummy and the burial chambers are entered from the sides of the barrow – when closed and covered by earth they would have been invisible from the outside.

It was used for successive burials until eventually the burial chambers were deliberately blocked. Excavated in 1863–65 and again in 1928, the remains of 31 people were found in the chambers. Romano-British pottery found inside one of the burial chambers shows that it was open in Roman times. The false portal may have been built to deter robbers, or it might have functioned as a 'spirit door' to allow the dead to come and partake of offerings brought to the tomb by their descendants. Belas Knap is in good condition as a result of several restorations.

*Belas Knap – the false entrance*
*(© Philip Halling cc-by-sa/2.0)*

(For further information, see: www.english-heritage.org.uk/visit/places/belas-knap-long-barrow/history/).

# Far Bredon

**The County's Bastion** (*extract*)
What looks far Bredon had, words to make said
Nothing are wanting; but will not square to place
Fall – the poet is hurt – of tears are his bread –
And takes his words, as pangs, as untold mischance.

(K2004)

My thoughts of England are first and foremost
of the line of Cotswold ending with Bredon Hill,
near Tewkesbury, and seen with him.* Or the blue
Malverns seen at a queer angle, from the hayfield,
talking when war seemed imminent, and the whole air
seemed charged with fatal beauty.

(Letter to Marion Scott 23 February 1917<br>*the 'him' is Will Harvey, then in a prison camp)

This walk takes place on Bredon Hill, an outlier of the main Cotswold escarpment, which stands at the northern edge of Ivor Gurney's Gloucestershire and acts as a *bastion* (**The County's Bastion**) between Gloucestershire and Worcestershire. The hill is actually in Worcestershire so that the significance of this walk lies not in the site itself but more in its symbolic value as both a vision of the beauty of Gurney's county (*my county*) seen from afar, and a guardian of that beauty.

Gurney's walking in this area mainly took place in the post-war period when he was trying to negotiate his return to civilian life amidst growing signs of mental instability. The poems range between those that revel in the countryside and those that reflect his increasing depression. Sometimes, as in **The County's Bastion**, both emotions are found in the same poem – the beautiful view of *far Bredon*, the *tears* and *hurt* of the poet.

From the village of Bredon's Norton, the walk contours round the north-west side of Bredon Hill, climbs to the top of it and back down again, providing in small scale the full experience of Cotswold landscapes – the scarp edge, the dip slope, the wooded copses and wild flowers. From the top of Bredon Hill there are panoramic views to the Malverns, the Cotswold Edge, May Hill and the small hills of the Severn Vale.

*'What looks far Bredon had' – Bredon Hill from the south*

## Route Details

DISTANCE/ TIME:
10.3km (6.4 miles)/ 3.5–4 hours

MAPS:
*OS Explorer 205, 1:25 000, Stratford-upon-Avon & Evesham*
*OS Landranger 150, 1:50 000, Worcester & The Malverns*

START AND PARKING:
Start in Manor Lane, near to the red telephone box
(SO 932391) where a small number of parking spaces are
available on the side of the road (nearest postcode, Village
Hall: GL20 7EZ). Alternative parking may be found along
Lampitt Lane near Point 2.

TRACKS AND PATHS:
Lanes, gravel tracks, woodland and grassy paths. Some
sections are steep and can be muddy. There are only two
stiles, both easily negotiated or with an alternative gate.

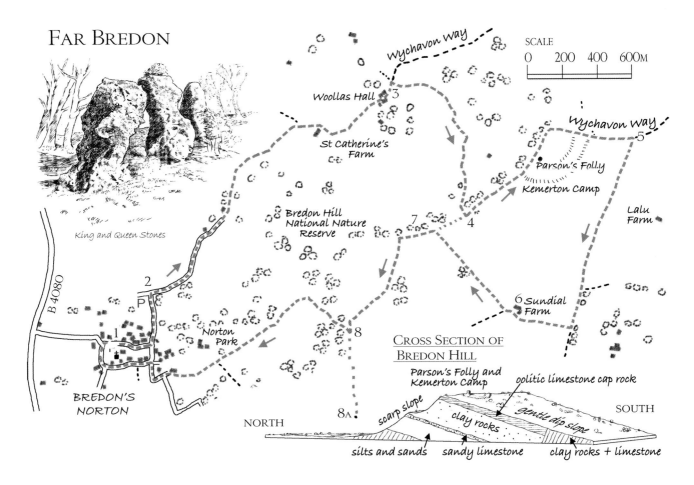

# FAR BREDON

King and Queen Stones

Wychavon Way

SCALE

0  200  400  600M

Woollas Hall  3

Wychavon Way

St Catherine's
Farm

Parson's Folly

Kemerton Camp

Lalu
Farm

Bredon Hill
National Nature
Reserve

7

4

5

B 4080

2

P

Norton
Park

6 Sundial
Farm

1

8

BREDON'S
NORTON

8A

NORTH

## CROSS SECTION OF
BREDON HILL

Parson's Folly and
Kemerton Camp

oolitic limestone cap rock

scarp slope

clay rocks

gentle dip slope

SOUTH

silts and sands    sandy limestone

clay rocks + limestone

# The Walk

① Before starting the walk at the red telephone box (SO 932390), read the introductory poem.

### The County's Bastion

What looks far Bredon had, words to make said
Nothing are wanting; but will not square to place
Fall – the poet is hurt – of tears are his bread –
And takes his words, as pangs, as untold
   mischance.

But azure and noble, like the thought of Rome –
Show under clear after dawn – Soft like love's
   thought
Bredon after night working showed from the
   home
I had, where Rome loved me – and strict to
   work brought.

Bredon, and Nottingham Hill, Cleeve, Crickley
   and those
Sudden with new beauty, day after unlooked-
   for day.
The poet might weep to have such thoughts,
   but well knows
Earth's poetry calls his pen; nothing of his own
   of poetry.
Save God he follow, in simple spirit, till his lamp
   light goes.

                     (K2004)

This poem was written in the asylum in the mid-1920s and shows many of the idiosyncrasies and difficulties that characterise Gurney's later poems – the second verse has been described as 'not quite nonsense' by Andrew Hodgson in *The Poetry of Clare, Hopkins, Thomas, and Gurney* (2019) – but the tangle of words does not invalidate his very personal relationship with Gloucestershire and the significance of Bredon Hill, all expressed here.

Gurney is seeing Bredon from afar – *What looks far Bredon had* – and feeling *hurt* that he cannot express these feelings that lie in the landscape as well as a poet should: his words *will not square to place,* and are like *pangs* of *untold mischance* (lost opportunity because he is in the asylum using memory rather than direct experience?). The second verse remembers where Gurney was when he used to watch *far Bredon* – at Cold Slad in his cottage under the nose of Crickley Hill (*the home I had*), which Gurney believed had been the site of a Roman military outpost. The *night working* refers to his tendency to sit up at night and write music and poetry, often till the dawn arrived, when he began to catch glimpses of the far hills (*Show under clear after dawn*). Finally, the last verse is putting Bredon in context as part of the line of hills that defined this northern part of Gurney's county – *Bredon, and Nottingham Hill, Cleeve and Crickley. Sudden with new beauty* explains his wonder at seeing these sights *day after unlooked-for day* and reiterates his claim that the landscapes of Gloucestershire are calling him to write

and fearing that he may not fulfil this expectation – *the poet might weep to have such thoughts.*

Hodgson suggests – 'it [**The County's Bastion**] is a poem whose oddness is at once its making and its near undoing.'

• Walk up the lane (east) from the telephone box and turn left at the T-junction, marked 'No Through Road' (Lampitt Lane). The landscaped grounds of Norton Park House (1839) can be seen to the right and soon the lane veers right when a footpath takes off to the left (there is a possible parking place here).

② Follow the lane on along the lower edge of Bredon Hill. At a cattle grid about 0.5km along the lane, this turns into a track with footpath access and fields on either side. You are entering Bredon Hill National Nature Reserve.

### Bredon Hill Nature Reserve

This is a 45-hectare (111-acre) site occupying the north-western slopes of Bredon Hill and comprising mainly rough grassland, shrubs and some widely-spaced trees, many of which are more than 300 years old and direct descendants of the original 'wildwood'. The trees are home to a vast array of invertebrates that depend on decaying wood in ancient trees – this is one of the top five British sites for these creatures. According to the website for Worcestershire's National Reserves, 'the unimproved grassland is herb-rich with salad burnet, wild thyme, common rock rose, pyramidal orchid and dwarf thistle. Locally uncommon plants found here include chalk milkwort, horseshoe vetch and bee orchid'.

• The path is gently rising. Ahead is the county of Worcestershire and over to the left you will see the Malvern Hills. Up to the right are the slopes of Bredon Hill itself. Looking back to the south-west, on a clear day you can pick out the shape of Barrow Hill near Ashleworth (see Walk 19).

**Cotswold Geology** – the illustration next to the map is a cross section, north–south through Bredon Hill, reminding us that the whole walk is like a traverse of the Cotswolds in miniature (see Introduction). Bredon Hill is capped by the Inferior Oolite limestone. It lies over layers of the Liassic clays, siltstones and occasional bands of marlstone (sandy limestone), all of which are tilted to the south-east, giving rise to the scarp and dip characteristics of Bredon's scenery. The walk begins by skirting round the clay base of the scarp (Points 2 to 3), then rising onto the marlstone platform and up the steep limestone scarp slope (Points 3 to 4), and eventually to the summit of Bredon. From Point 5 of the walk, you are travelling briefly down the dip slope before gaining the ridge again at Point 7, and eventually walking back down to the village.

• St Catherine's Farm, now a private house, is reached after about 2km from the start and here the track turns slightly right and uphill, eventually gaining the seventeenth-century building, Woollas Hall, with wonderful views over the Vale of Evesham. It was erected by John Hanford in 1611, but has recently been converted into several self-contained residences, as have the outbuildings and the coach house.

③ Walk through the Woollas Hall complex to the entrance road. Turn right and over a stile to join the Wychavon Way, rising first gradually then more steeply uphill towards the summit of Bredon Hill. Parson's Folly tower is visible during most of the climb. Your path lies through rough pasture often with sheep grazing, and to the left the ground may be muddy and wet in the autumn and winter as springs and small steams appear on the side of the hill. The hummocky appearance of the slope is a phenomenon of scarp slopes where limestone rock lies over the less stable clays and sands – as Gurney noted in his poem **East Wind** (Walk 13): *Naked landslips show, away downhill mist-shades cover / The land.*

• Before the last steep section onto the summit ridge, the path takes you away to the right. Go through an iron gate and climb to meet the path from Westmancote and Bredon's

*The hummocky slope up to Bredon Hill ridge and Parson's Folly*

Norton coming up from the right. (Note that this is a shorter return route if you wish to use it after visiting the summit.) For the full walk, turn left to follow the Wychavon Way along the ridge.

④ The view from the ridge is breathtaking. Over the wall in front of you are Worcestershire, Herefordshire and the Malverns. Behind you, across the gently sloping fields of the dip slope, is the long line of the Cotswolds. In a letter to Marion Scott (18 February 1918) Gurney describes how he climbed Bredon during his leave: 'I had three whole days at home' (here Gurney makes a list of Gloucestershire places visited), and then refers to 'a view from Bredon Hill to the hills above Bath. To Malverns, Herefordshire, Bristol Channel, May Hill. Three days but what a time!'

### The Touchstone – Watching Malvern

What Malvern is the day is, and its touchstone –
Gray [sic] velvet, or moon-marked; rich, or bare as bone;
One looks toward Malvern and is made one with the
   whole;
The world swings round him as the Bear to the Pole.

Men have crossed seas to know how Paul's tops Fleet;
That as music has rapt them in the mere street;
While none or few care how the curved giants stand,
(Those upheaved strengths!) on the meadow and
   plough-land.

(K2004)

*The Banbury Stone with the Malverns in the distance*
*(© Philip Halling cc-by-sa/2.0)*

• Walk on along the path to Parson's Folly tower and the top of Bredon at 299m (981ft).

• Located north of Parson's Folly is a topograph, worth looking at to appreciate the distance to other features of Gurney's Gloucestershire. Cleeve Hill, for example (mentioned in **The County's Bastion**) is nine miles away.

### Parson's Folly and Kemerton Camp

Parson's Folly is a small stone tower, built in the mid eighteenth century for John Parsons, MP (1732–1805), squire of Kemerton Court, and was intended as a summer house. It was reputedly last lived in by a hermit who was eventually moved after the Second World War to make way for renovation.

The hilltop is also known for the Banbury Stone (also known as the Elephant Stone), a large rock on the summit in a dip to the north of the tower. It is an example of a geological feature called a 'gull'. In this part of the Cotswolds where the limestones of the Inferior Oolite are sloping (in this case south-eastwards) and overlie weaker Liassic clay and mudstones, fractures form parallel to a valley side and may be partially or wholly filled with unconsolidated material such as earth or rock fragments, the whole mass being cemented together by percolating lime-rich water. Once this hard rock plug has formed it is often harder than the surrounding rock and eventually is revealed by erosion and stands upright. Gulls can range in size from millimetres in width to tens of metres. They are relatively common in the Cotswolds – indeed there are two more on Bredon Hill (the King and Queen Stones) which can be viewed on the way down the hill (Point 8A).

Another striking feature likely to have taken Gurney's eye is Kemerton Camp, the Iron Age hillfort on the top of Bredon Hill. With a steep escarpment dropping away on the north side of the Hill, it has two sets of ramparts and ditches to the south. The inner ramparts possibly date to 300BC. In Walk 8 (Uley) an extract from Gurney's poem, **Unfamiliar Camp**, is included. It could easily refer to the camp on Bredon (*Some day (I know) they will dig up the ramparts perhaps / To find money hidden or broken swords or spear tips*), since it was only in the 1930s, when Gurney was in Dartford asylum, that excavations at Kemerton Camp uncovered the burial place of some 50 slaughtered men, along with a great number of weapons near the entrance to the inner ramparts of the fort.

• From the topograph, rejoin the Wychavon Way as it bends slightly to the east following the wall along the scarp edge and breaking through the embankments of the hillfort. In early July when this walk was planned, there were flowers everywhere – harebells, coltsfoot, clover, wild thyme, viper's bugloss to mention a few – and a constant hum of bees.

In his poem **Bredon Hill**, another well-known poet, A.E. Housman, recalls how a young man surveyed the view of the *coloured counties* from this hill-top and lay with his love *among the springing thyme*.

*The 'springing thyme' on Bredon*

⑤ As you approach a wooden gate leading into a small wood, leave the Wychavon Way and turn right on a bridleway going down the dip slope by a stone wall. The views of the Cotswolds will be getting clearer and Lalu Farm is away to left, although ignore the path towards it. Walk past a left turn along a bridleway (on the OS map named as the Belt). At the next hedge, take a right turn at a footpath sign to reach Sundial Farm.

*The footpath to Sundial Farm*

⑥ A disused barn is all that remains of Sundial Farm, although this is a fine mid eighteenth-century Grade-II Listed building with some mid twentieth-century alterations. The walls are of Inferior Oolite limestone containing occasional fossils. Notably, Sundial Farm has a stone sundial that shows the hours 7am to 6pm divided into half-hours. Across the top a motto reads *Nunquam Reditura* (Never to Return) – a phrase that recalls a poem written just before Gurney was committed to Barnwood asylum. **The Not-Returning** is a heartfelt cry from someone whose creativity and joyful connection with the countryside is being threatened by his increasingly unstable mental state –

### The Not-Returning

Never comes now the through-and-through clear
Tiredness of body on crisp straw down laid,
Nor the tired thing said
Content before the clean sleep close the eyes,
Or ever resistless rise
Pictures of far country Westward, Westward out sight
  of the eyes.

Never more delight comes of the roof dark lit
With under-candle flicker nor rich gloom on it,
The limned faces, and moving hands shuffling the cards.
The clear conscience, the free mind moving towards
Poetry, friends, music, the old earthly rewards.
No more they come. No more.
Only the restless searching, the bitter labour,
The going out to watch stars, stumbling blind through
  the difficult door.

(K2004)

• Pass the barn and take a footpath leading off to the right. Don't go on down the main track. Walking along the gently rising path, look behind you to see typical Cotswold dip slope scenery with its large fields, stone walls and clumps of beech and blackthorn providing cover for pheasants. After the drama of the scarp edge, the dip slope is more restful. Gurney's poem **Pilgrimage** begins with the autumn browns, golds and greys of stubble fields and beech copses, and sings the praises of many such *places dear to no man known but me.*

*Sundial Farm on Bredon Hill (© Philip Halling cc-by-sa/2.0)*

### Pilgrimage

I will go rest my eyes upon
Soft grays [sic] and browns and stubble gold
When clouds have hidden Autumn-sun
And the free wind blows cold, –
To eat with labouring men under the hedges
Hear many a rough tale told.

For I am tired of towns and smoke
For ever thickening the pure air
Too hard for me the heavy yoke
Too hard and heavy to bear.
Out in the countryside the woodsmoke rises
Pale blue into the air.

Maybe to walk the woods and hills
Or out by Severn side,
Or stand by little water mills
To watch green water glide
To break in foam, what matter wither,
So the wind be my guide.

There are a hundred places dear
To no man known but me,
With rough travel without fear
I shall haste soon to see
Those fields of battle, good inns, old houses
The stuff and life of me.

Alone I shall go without a friend
That need none but the brown
Earth, shelter at the day's end
Bread, water, dead leaves strown
Loose on the white road, the free wind blowing
By field and empty down.

(CPW)

⑦ When the footpath reaches the top of the scarp slope again, turn left. (A few metres up to the right is Point 4 at which you arrived on the way up the scarp slope.) Walk to the left down through the woods which are often windswept when the winds blow hard across the scarp edge. In the asylum in the mid-1920s, Gurney wrote about his outings on the wooded edges of Cotswold slopes with a mix of exultation (*cursing exultant at the wind's toll*, **Hell's Prayer**) and despair (*in nine hell-depths with such memories*, **The Coppice**, Walk 13) and perhaps, as in **December 30th**, inspired by the weather at the time: *It is the year's end, the winds are blasting, and I / Write to keep madness and black torture away.*

• Follow the path down, bearing left at the edge of the wood and round the boundary of a field. At a gate, continue down the path past signs of quarrying. Here at Point 8 one path goes straight on towards Westmancote while the route back to Bredon's Norton goes right.

⑧ Taking the Westmancote path for a short way will allow you to visit the King and Queen Stones (off the path to the right in woodland, Point 8A) – examples of 'gulls', as described above.

• Leaving the Stones, return to the junction (Point 8) and turn left to go down the slope through patches of woodland and the meadows of Norton Park. At a metal gate level with an old walled garden, veer right to a gate in the fence. Walk through a paddock and out onto the lanes at the southern end of Bredon's Norton. Make your way back to your starting point.

# Part Six: Severn Meadows

The Severn Meadows from Tewkesbury to Gloucester is an enchanted world of settled villages, hidden manor houses, ancient churches, riverside paths, narrow lanes and sudden hilly heights. Gurney walked and cycled its lanes and paths as a youth before 1914. During his time in the trenches, he often referred to this area and to its connections in his mind with *the spirit of England*. On his return to Gloucestershire in 1918, his walking was often solitary and the Severn Meadows became a place of memory and longing for past joys and friendships.

**Strange Service**
Little did I dream, England, that you bore me
Under the Cotswold Hills beside the water meadows,
To do you dreadful service, here, beyond your borders
And your enfolding seas.

*The Severn Meadows at sunset – view across the Severn at Wainlode*

I was a dreamer ever, and bound to your dear service,
Meditating deep, I thought on your secret beauty,
As through a child's face one may see the clear spirit
Miraculously shining.

Your hills, not only hills, but friends of mine and kindly,
Your tiny knolls and orchards hidden beside the river
Muddy and strongly-flowing, with shy and tiny
    streamlets
Safe in its bosom.

Now these are memories only, and your skies and
    rushy sky-pools
Fragile mirrors easily broken by moving airs …
In my deep heart for ever goes on your daily being,
And uses consecrate.

Think on me too, O Mother, who wrest my soul to
    serve you
In strange and fearful ways beyond your encircling
    waters;
None but you can know my heart, its tears and sacrifice;
None but you repay.

(K2004)

The poem, **Strange Service**, was written at Tilleloy, northern France and sent to Marion Scott in a letter on 27 July 1916. Gurney explained, 'There is nothing but burbling in my mind, nothing but an empty ache for Maisemore and Framilode and such'. The third stanza, speaking of *your hills … tiny knolls and orchards* and the river *muddy and strongly flowing*, is referring to the terraced landscapes of the Severn Valley (see Walk 3).

**Strange Service** probably represents the beginning of Gurney's disillusionment with the war, as evidenced in the first stanza: *Little did I dream England, that you bore me / Under the Cotswold hills beside the water meadows, / To do you dreadful service, here, beyond your borders / And your enfolding seas.* It also reveals that Gurney knew he was relying on memory, as fragile as the reflections of waterside reeds on the surface of the Severn, to keep Gloucestershire places fresh in his mind – *Now these are memories only, and your skies and rushy sky-pools / Fragile mirrors easily broken by moving airs …*

# Deerhurst: lonely village

'Yesterday I went to Deerhurst for my first time'
Letter to Marion Scott, May/ June 1922

In May 1922, Ivor Gurney visited the riverside village of Deerhurst for the first time. He was living with his aunt Marie in Longford on the north-western edge of Gloucester (Walk 20), finding it increasingly difficult to reach a stable and satisfying way of life. His letters to Marion Scott swing between optimism about his writing and anxiety about his failure to find a job or security. He hated the idea of living on charity, receiving money from friends and relying on the kindness of his aunt Marie. One advantage of Longford was that Gurney could quickly walk out across the river meadows to Sandhurst, Wainlode and Norton, or cycle further to visit Tewkesbury – and, in this case, Deerhurst.

Deerhurst is a tiny village on a low terrace of land next to the River Severn. It lies within the parish of Apperley and Deerhurst, and is only a couple of miles south of Tewkesbury. When Gurney first saw it he found it 'extraordinary to come across that lonely village by the Severn' with its 'few cottages, a manor house and a sort of queen ruler of a church over all' (Letter to Marion Scott, June 1922). The fine Saxon church of St Mary is only one of two significant buildings on this site; the other is the chapel known as Odda's Chapel. In his letter to Marion Scott, Gurney mentions that the Deerhurst area was the site of the Isle of Olney, 'which Oman [historian, Charles Oman] says was the Canute Edmund Ironside affair not the Alney of Gloucester'. Here Gurney is referring to the suggestion that the historic treaty between Edmund Ironside and King Cnut, that divided England between them in 1016, was not signed at Gloucester but at Deerhurst. Author Simon Jenkins (*England's Thousand Best Churches*) seems to agree – but notes that 'The unfortunate Edmund died within the year and Cnut took over the entire kingdom.'

The place-name Deerhurst is derived from Old English and means 'deer-wood'. It was spelt *Deorhyrst* in AD 804, *Dorhirst* in about 1050 and *Derherste* in the Domesday Book in 1086.

The walk begins at the car park near Odda's Chapel and takes a route past St Mary's Church, Deerhurst and the Priory farmhouse before rejoining the country lane to Apperley. From here you take the field footpath across gently rising ground towards Apperley village. Leaving the village via Gabb Lane, the River Severn is reached at Coalhouse Inn before a 2.25km walk back along the Severn Way to Deerhurst. Note that Deerhurst is prone to frequent flooding in the winter months so this walk may best be done in summer or early autumn.

### Route Details

DISTANCE/ TIME:
6.5km (4.1 miles)/ 2.5–3 hours.

MAPS:
OS Explorer 179, 1:25 000, Gloucester, Cheltenham & Stroud
OS Landranger 150, 1:50 000, Worcester & The Malverns

START AND PARKING:
Start in the small car park next to Odda's chapel in the village of Deerhurst (SO 869299; GL19 4BX). Parking may also be available in the lane leading to the church.

TRACKS AND PATHS:
Lanes and grassy paths. Some sections of the Severn Way may be muddy. There are four stiles, but usually with an alternative gate.

*St Mary's church, Deerhurst – 'a sort of queen ruler of a church'*
*(© Philip Halling cc-by-sa/2.0)*

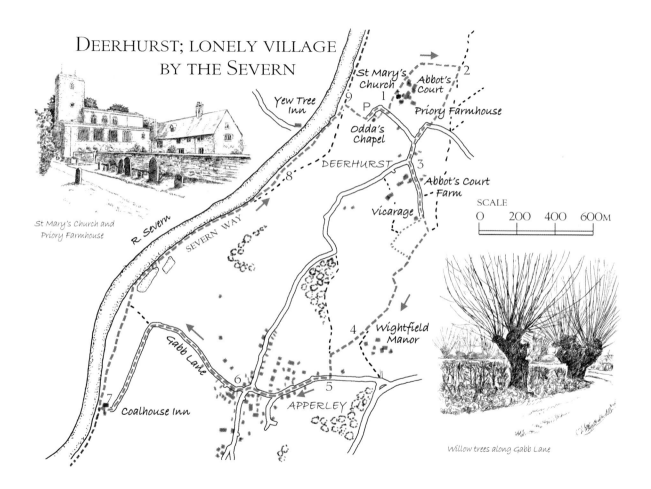

# DEERHURST; LONELY VILLAGE BY THE SEVERN

Yew Tree Inn

St Mary's Church

Abbot's Court

9

1

2

P

Priory Farmhouse

Odda's Chapel

DEERHURST

8

3

Abbot's Court Farm

Vicarage

R. Severn

SEVERN WAY

4

Wightfield Manor

Gabb Lane

6

5

7

APPERLEY

Coalhouse Inn

*St Mary's Church and Priory Farmhouse*

### SCALE

0    200    400    600M

*Willow trees along Gabb Lane*

## THE WALK

① The walk begins at the car park next to Odda's Chapel (SO 869299).

### Odda's Chapel

The Chapel is a Grade-I Listed building cared for by English Heritage. It is named after Earl Odda, a kinsman of Edward the Confessor and the person who had the chapel built in memory of his brother Aelfric, ruler of the Saxon kingdom of *Hwicce* before the Norman Conquest. Originally the chapel had been built to serve Aelfric's monastery in the eleventh century but in the years that followed the chapel was deconsecrated and subsumed within what had been the Abbot's house next door. After the monastery's dissolution in 1540, the Abbot's house became a farmhouse and the chapel was forgotten until rediscovered during renovations in 1885. Viewing the buildings from outside makes clear how the Abbot's courthouse has been built right up against the chapel which occupies the western end of

*Odda's Chapel viewed from the river*
*(© Philip Halling cc-by-sa/2.0)*

what was formerly a timber-framed farmhouse. Inside, the nave of the chapel is small and rectangular and had been used as a kitchen, while the chancel, an even smaller rectangle, had been divided by an intermediate floor. The Reverend George Butterworth, whose picture features on the information board, was the person who, in 1885, realised the significance of the oddly-shaped windows and uncovered the Anglo-Saxon chapel. An inscribed altar slab found near the building in 1675 and dedicated to Aelfric by Earl Odda, enabled the chapel to be dated accurately to 1056. The original slab is now in the Ashmolean Museum in Oxford and a replica is displayed in Odda's Chapel. The original slab reads:

> Earl Odda ordered this royal hall to be built and dedicated in honour of the Holy Trinity for the soul of his brother Aelfric, taken up [into heaven] from this place. Ealdred was the bishop who dedicated the building on the second day before Ides of April in the fourteenth year of the reign of Edward, king of the English.

• From the chapel car park, follow the small road on round to visit the church. On the way notice the large green flood-gates that protect both the church and the houses in the village, as this area lies only about 10–15m above the river, and is prone to flooding.

## St Mary's Church, Deerhurst

*The Buildings of England* series edited by Pevsner (Verey, 1970) refers to this church as 'an Anglo-Saxon monument of the first order' and it is also a Grade-I Listed building. What we see today is a mix of many different versions of the church, with the earliest being the rectangular church that was part of the monastery known to be standing here in AD 804. During the ninth century, the semi-circular apse was rebuilt and decorated with pilaster strips, two side chapels were added and the walls were raised higher. The tower was added in the tenth century when the monastery was re-founded as a Benedictine priory. Further amendments were made in the twelfth century, including the piercing of the Saxon side walls by three arches on each side to allow the addition of north and south aisles. A significant restoration took place in 1861-63.

This history partly explains why there is evidence of so many arches and doorways, many now bricked up. An interesting feature is the tenth-century angel to be found on the ruined apse at the southern corner of the building between structural pilaster strips.

Attached to the church on its southern side is the Priory Farmhouse. Look closely and you can see that the line of corbels on the church continues along the farmhouse, because they once supported the cloister roof. The farmhouse itself was probably the monks' dormitory.

Gurney's poem entitled **Deerhurst Church** and probably written in 1922 after his visit, refers to the tower, a well-known landmark in this part of the Severn Valley, and reflects his 'sense of the Saxons' still haunting the landscape.

**Deerhurst Church** (*extract*)

There is something wrong there, with that the gracefullest
Of strong things Severn Knows and had long loved best,
A tall thing clean and poised like any boy walker
Above where the swamp dwellings and old fastnesses were,
Such reeds and broad stretches recall inevitably
The otter hunter and wild heron stalker
Gone whole day in the chase, and the flat boats, and glee
Of Saxon children the bright bream or lank eel to see.

(RW)

Later in the poem he explains that the *something wrong* is the surprise of finding it here, *this upright unexpected white shell of stone – save few cottages – in the water meadow alone.*

It is interesting that Gurney's first view of Deerhurst focused not on the chapel but on the elegance and significance of the Norman church tower – and this rather than on the rectangular Saxon part of the church. This is probably because, although the chapel had been discovered, it wasn't fully disentangled from the farmhouse until 1965.

'The Saxon chapel is nothing but the Norman and later church was very interesting with a tall oblong tower, graceful and strong and some of the finest carved doorways you could wish to see. The country is too full of foliage now – the Severn Plain is better severe.' (1922) As always, Gurney liked to see the whole picture of the buildings in the landscape, hence his comment about the foliage.

• After viewing the church, follow the footpath on past the church door heading north, with newer farm buildings on the right, and out into the fields. Follow the path veering right, leading to a raised trackway dividing the fields, until you reach a gateway and a 90 degree turn to the right.

② Walk on this raised path with grazing either side. Away to the east on a clear day can be seen the long *blue line* of Cotswold, a feature often mentioned by Gurney in his poetry, as if it was the talisman of his identity, a confirmation that all was right with the world.

• Eventually, the field path joins the road at a stile. Here, turn right and follow the road round a bend and back into Deerhurst, noting occasional views of the church tower and passing the entrance back to your parking place.

③ At a road junction take the left turn signed as a 'no through road' and walk up it until you reach the red-brick Victorian vicarage on the right. Notice the tall red chimneys, the kind of feature that Gurney might have noted as one of the *strange things one comes across on walks* (**Cotswold Ways**).

• Do not turn down by the vicarage (although there is an alternative route this way) but go straight ahead up the slight hill to two gates, on the right-hand side of which is a stile. Cross the stile and take the obvious pathway across the field to meet a field boundary which the path now follows. You are walking on the top of the 46m (150ft) river terrace, gradually moving downhill through the fields to Apperley, lying at a slightly lower height on the same terrace. To the west lies the Severn just out of sight below the low ridge, but away to the north and east is the familiar line of the Cotswolds.

The poem **Friendly are Meadows** was written by Gurney in 1922 and seems to fit this moment very appropriately. We know that Gurney had visited Deerhurst in 1922 and so it is not unlikely that he should walk through the meadows afterwards with his head full of church architecture and stone curves, noticing willows and stiles. The poem even refers to *a sense of strings music begun* and *Quartetts dreamed of* *perfection achieved masterless*, when, in the letter written to tell Marion Scott of his visit to Deerhurst, Gurney also told her about his String Quartet being still unfinished and *without expression marks*. The poem also refers to *Brave elms and stiles, willows by dyked water-run* – all of which, apart from the missing elms, are characteristic of the area today.

*'friendly are meadows' – a solitary tree on the walk to Apperley*

**Friendly are Meadows** (*extract*)
Friendly are meadows when the sun's gone down in
And no bright colour spoils the broad green of gray, [sic]
And one's eyes rest looking to Cotswold away, the
   northline away,
Under cloud ceilings whorled, and most largely
   fashioned
With seventeenth century curves of the tombstone way –
A day of softnesses, of comfort of no false din.
Sorrel makes rusty rest for thy eyes and the worn path
Brave elms and stiles, willows by dyked water-run
North-France general look, and a sort of bath
Of freshness – a light wrap of comfortableness
Over one's being, a sense of strings music begun –
   A slow gradual symphony of worthiness –
Quartetts dreamed of perfection achieved masterless,
As by Robecq I dreamed them, and to Estaires gone.

(RW)

• The field path steers around Wightfield Manor, partially hidden by trees. This moated manor house was mentioned in the Domesday book as being granted to the Abbey of Westminster by Edward the Confessor, but the main building dates from the sixteenth century, when rebuilding used stone from the Deerhurst monastery buildings after its dissolution in c.1547. The manor is privately owned so cannot be visited, although more of the building can be seen from the road.

④ At a fork by a large grey barn, take the right-hand turn and, as the path joins a hedgerow, a stile will be found on the left. Cross this into the Apperley recreation ground and walk across the playing field to the car park next to the village hall. Apperley is one of the Severnside villages on the middle terrace at about 30–45m (100–150ft).

⑤ Leaving the village hall car park, turn right and walk up the village street. Apperley is quite a large village which has seen a lot of new housing since the 1960s, although the older part of the village peeps through the later additions, showing the typical red-brick or timber-framed cottages that were a feature of this area. Apperley boasts a good example of a cruck cottage (with curved timbers forming a cruck-truss in the gable end), which can be seen on the Deerhurst road a short way down the road on the left, if you have time to make a diversion. Otherwise continue walking up into the village to the crossroads opposite a timber-framed house called Box Hill Farm.

*A timber-framed cottage in Apperley*

⑥ Take the lane signposted as Gabb Lane and Coalhouse Wharf. Your journey down the lane will reveal how the village of Apperley is so well-sited above the river floodplain. For the first half-mile the lane is running down the slope of the 45m (150ft) terrace, leaving Apperley high and dry above the floodplain. Near the bottom of the slope the lane turns left and there is a footpath sign for a path to the river. Do not take this but continue along the lane bordered by willows. There are several paths signposted up the steep slope of the terrace back towards Apperley but you still cannot see the River Severn which remains hidden behind a protective dyke. Eventually, about half a mile from the bend, the lane does a sharp right past some outbuildings and turns into the car park of the Coalhouse Inn (formerly known as The White Lion), with a caravan site on the left.

The Coalhouse Inn served as a coal wharf in the nineteenth and early twentieth centuries when the barges came upriver to unload coal for Apperley and local villages. Gurney was aware of this trade and often called at the inns serving the bargees who managed the boats carrying coal. The Boat Inn at Ashleworth (Walk 19) is another example. He liked the feeling of companionship with the ordinary working men of Gloucestershire, particularly in the post-war period when perhaps he was finding the lack of army structure difficult. *The waggoners, bargemen and cowdrivers I will get to know*, he wrote in the poem, **Ashleworth** (80P).

*The Coalhouse Inn, formerly the White Lion* (© Dreghorn, 1967)

• Pause for a moment to look at the location of the Coalhouse Inn (not surprisingly still prone to flooding), and at the river sweeping dangerously close to the road and buildings during spring and autumn rains. This is frequently a muddy track. In a poem called **Crucifx Corner**, written at about the same time as **Friendly are Meadows**, Gurney recalls a water station near Aveluy in the Department of Somme, France. Stationed at Albert in autumn 1916 to March 1917, he remembers the water carts coming every day to fill their tanks with muddy, chlorinated water from the Ancre, a river which runs through Albert and then south-east eventually to join the River Somme near Corbie. The activity reminded him of *the Severn Meadows* – perhaps a location such as Coalhouse Wharf with its mixture of busy working routines and low-lying marshy land.

**Crucifix Corner** (*extract*)
There was a water dump there and regimental
Carts came every day to line up and fill full
Those rolling tanks with chlorinated clay mixture
And curse the mud with vain veritable vexture.
Aveluy across the valley, billets, shacks, ruins.
With time and time a crump there to mark doings.
On New Year's Eve the marsh gloomed tremulous
With rosy mist still holding so marvellous
Sunglow; the air smelt home; the time breathed home –
Noel not put away; New Year's Eve not yet come.
All things said 'Severn', the air was of those dusk
  meadows –
Transport rattled somewhere in southern shadows,
Stars that were not strange ruled the lit tranquil sky,
Arched far and high.

(K2004)

• Look away to the north-west and you should, weather permitting, be able to see the profile of the Malvern Hills clearly marking the horizon.

⑦ Go through a gate next to the Coalhouse Inn. The walk now runs northward, following the Severn Way for about 2.5km back to Deerhurst. This is a gentle walk keeping to the slightly higher ground of the lower terrace and the protective dyke. At first there is low pastureland on the inland side, then later there are backwater ponds and some scrubby woodland, until the meadows south of Deerhurst open out again. Always there is the rising ground of the river terrace to the east and the presence of the River Severn, sometimes obvious with its dark waters swirling, sometimes hidden with only a glint of water behind bushes and reeds, as the poem **Water Colours** suggests:

**Water Colours**
The trembling water glimpsed through dark tangle
Of late-month April's delicatest thorn,
One moment put the cuckoo flower to scorn
Where its head hangs by sedges, Severn bank-full.
But dark water has a hundred fires on it:
As the sky changes it changes and ranges through
Sky colours and thorn colours, and more would do,
Were not the blossom truth so quick on it
And beauty brief in action as first dew.

(K2004)

⑧ Eventually, the Malverns appear again away to the north-west. In the foreground, you will see the buildings of Chaceley Stock and the boats moored next to the Yew Tree Inn. There used to be a ferry service to link the east bank here with the Inn. Finally, the buildings of Deerhurst become visible and a view across the meadows towards Tewkesbury and its abbey. Was it somewhere here that Gurney thought, *Some Dane looking out from the water settlements, / If settlements there were, must have thought as I, / Square stone should fill that bit of lower sky.* (**Tewkesbury**, K)

⑨ A footpath signposted to Odda's Chapel leads off the Severn Way to the right and takes you back to the car park beside the chapel.

*'Water colours' – an autumnal riverside scene on the Severn Way*

# Wainlode: by Severn

**By Severn** (*extract*)
If England, her spirit lives anywhere
It is by Severn, by hawthorns and those grand willows.

(K2004)

The riverside between Sandhurst and the outskirts of Gloucester at Longford provided a quick escape from the city for Gurney. Leaving his childhood home in Barton Street, the cathedral or his aunt's house in Longford, he could quickly follow Sandhurst Lane northward and up the gentle hill to the village of Sandhurst, then down to the river meadows and footpaths, and to Rodway Lane with its ferry connection to Ashleworth. The hamlet of Wainlode with its well-known cliffs of red, grey and green earth overlooking the Severn and forming a curved embayment near to the Red Lion Inn, was identified as a special place by Gurney. Fascinated by the shape of the cliff, the colours in its rock layers and its

almost mystical serenity seen on a summer evening with the sun setting to the west, Gurney imagined Wainlode as a symbol of English identity in the poem **By Severn** (written 1920–22).

In the late 1950s, when I visited Wainlode as a child on sunny weekends, the area would be crowded with people, and alive with the sound of shouting as children and young people swam in the river and scrambled on the red Wainlode cliffs. In Gurney's day it might have been quieter but was undoubtedly in use as a bathing place. Now signs make clear that bathing is forbidden and the whole site bears a more managed appearance.

This walk begins at the Red Lion pub near to the river cliff of Wainlode. The route takes you first along the Severn Way following wooded paths above the water, and then walking through flat, grassy meadows. At the former ferry crossing to Ashleworth, you climb Rodway Lane and follow lanes back to Sandhurst village with its church, farms and settled village landscape. The return journey rises steeply up the river terraces of Sandhurst Hill and Norton Hill, with surprisingly good views across the Vale of Gloucester and the Cotswold Edge, before dropping back down the slope to the Red Lion.

*Wainlode red cliff and beach (2010)*

## Route Details

Distance/ Time:
9.6km/ 6 miles, 3–3.5 hours

Maps:
*OS Explorer 179, 1:25 000, Gloucester, Cheltenham & Stroud*
*OS Landranger 162, 1:50 000, Gloucester & Forest of Dean*

Start and Parking:
Start at The Red Lion Inn, Wainlode (SO 848259, GL2 9LW), after turning off the A38 near the village of Norton north of Gloucester. Park outside the pub if you are going to take refreshment there. Or park further northward alongside the road; or, in summer, in the meadow-side parking made available.

Tracks and Paths:
Grassy, woodland and field tracks. It can be muddy and there are some steep sections. Two stiles.

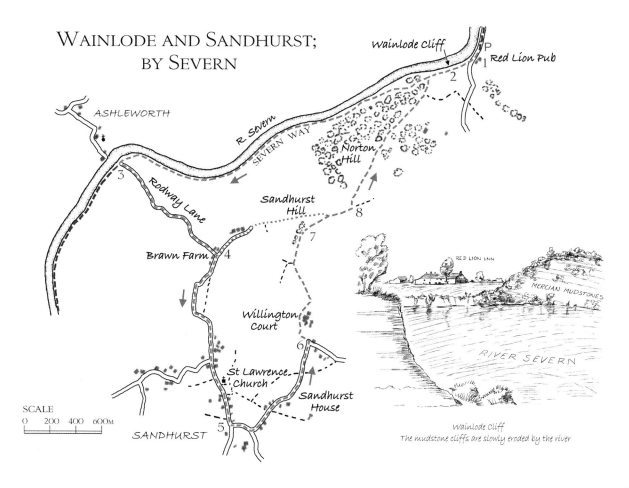

# WAINLODE AND SANDHURST;
# BY SEVERN

ASHLEWORTH

Wainlode Cliff

P

Red Lion Pub

1

2

R. Severn

SEVERN WAY

Norton Hill

3

Rodway Lane

Sandhurst Hill

8

7

Brawn Farm

4

Willington Court

6

St Lawrence Church

Sandhurst House

SCALE

0  200  400  600M

SANDHURST

5

RED LION INN

MERCIAN MUDSTONES

RIVER SEVERN

Wainlode Cliff
The mudstone cliffs are slowly eroded by the river

## THE WALK

① Your walk takes you up the marked footpath (the Severn Way) opposite the Red Lion and through a gateway to the left as you face the river. However, before you start, walk across the grass past the pub's outdoor tables and along the bank to the sign about fishing rights. Ahead of you, the cliff, and the curved, reddish-coloured riverbank below it, will start to become apparent, although covered with a tangle of scrub and woodland. You may see this better if you walk to the end of the bank and go down the steps to the riverside itself. However, this is muddy in most seasons and very slippery after rain. There are also brambles and weeds to trip you up so all but the most intrepid visitor should stay on the upper bank. With this slightly longer view you are aware of Sandhurst Hill rising steeply above the cliff face and river, and of the deep waters of the River Severn passing beneath you. On the opposite bank Gurney's Barrow Hill (see Walk 19) is a clear landmark to the west.

### Wainlode's Cliff

The geologist, William Dreghorn (1967) drew attention to the red and green-grey layers of rock that are clues to the formation of Wainlode's cliff and embayment. Wainlode is at the junction of two different geological periods – the Triassic and the Jurassic. As a rule, in this part of Gloucestershire, the Triassic rocks lie to the west of the Severn and the Jurassic rocks to the east. In the older Triassic period (about 200–250 million years ago) hot, dry desert conditions prevailed, and the muds and sandy deposits that were laid down in occasional lakes contained iron-rich ferric minerals, giving the red colour rock (Keuper marls on Dreghorn's diagram, now known as Mercian mudstones) that are noticeable here and all along the Severn meadows on the western bank, and here at Wainlode on the east as well. Later, as the climate changed to become more humid in the later Triassic (known as the Rhaetic or Rhaetian period), the muds and silts laid down (Tea Green marls on the diagrams, now called Blue Anchor Formations) contained the green-coloured ferrous minerals, signifying that less oxygen was available as the amount of water increased and the sea gradually invaded the land. Finally, the sea invaded completely, firstly remaining shallow and filled with a range of fish, shellfish and reptiles, but later becoming deeper in the next geological period (the Jurassic, 145–200 million years ago) and forming the Liassic sea in which the clays and occasional limestone ridges of the Vale of Gloucester to the east were formed.

This geological history is seen in the cliff at Wainlode, although now covered by shrubs. The lower layers are the red rocks of the Triassic desert. Higher up are the greenish layers representing the onset of wetter conditions, while above that are the thin, shaley, black layers signifying the shallow coastal waters of the Rhaetic sea, full of the bones of fish and reptiles (bone beds). Finally, high up the cliff and forming the slopes of Sandhurst Hill, are bands of sandy limestone with marine fossils, grey shales and a blue limestone band which is the evidence of the base of the Jurassic formation (rocks formed under warm shallow seas 200–150 million years ago) known as Lower Lias.

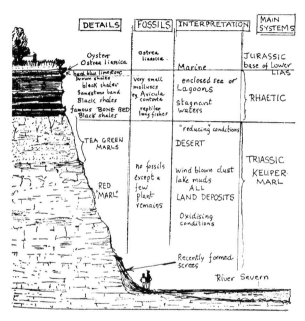

*Simplified section of Wainlode's cliff*
*(© Dreghorn, 1967)*

**By Severn**

If England, her spirit lives anywhere
It is by Severn, by hawthorns and grand willows.
Earth heaves up twice a hundred feet in air,
And ruddy clay-falls scooped out to the weedy shallows.
There in the brakes of May, Spring has her chambers,
Robing-rooms of hawthorn, cowslip, cuckoo flower –
Wonder complete changes for each square joy's hour,
Past thought miracles are there and beyond numbers.

If for the drab atmospheres and managed lighting,
In London town, Oriana's playwrights had
Wainlode her theatre and coppice clad
Hill for her ground of sauntering and idle waiting,
Why, then I think, our chiefest glory of pride,
(The Elizabethans of Thames, South and Northern side)
Would nothing of its meeding be denied,
And her sons' praises from England's mouth again be
   outcried.

                                      (K2004)

### By Severn and Wainlode's Cliff

Some poetry critics talk in general terms about this poem referring to the River Severn, as if it doesn't matter where exactly this place is, but it does matter. The natural amphitheatre that lies beneath Wainlode Cliff, with the 46m (150ft) rise of Sandhurst Hill (*coppice clad Hill*) and the 85m (283ft) eminence of Norton Hill behind it, are exactly what Gurney had in mind when he wrote, *Earth heaves up twice a hundred feet in air*, whilst *ruddy clay falls scooped out to the weedy shallows* refers to the red mud of the slope and amphitheatre.

Dreghorn talks of fine, red cliffs by the Red Lion Inn, in front of which green meadows stretch down to the river's edge, being used as Gloucester's 'Lido'. Although Dreghorn's description of the river as a bathing area is no longer correct, it would have held true in Gurney's day and he would have seen the area busy with people – and probably swum here as a boy. He certainly walked along the riverbanks at Wainlode and Ashleworth, and knew the red cliffs well.

TOP: *Wainlode, 'Gloucester's lido', June 1959* (© *Caroline Johnson*). BOTTOM: Red Lion, Wainlode

'Visitors to Wainlode Cliffs can actually hear and see erosion [of the red cliff deposits] taking place', writes Dreghorn, speaking of the 1960s, 'particularly on summer evenings after a fine day when the sun has been shining on the cliffs. As the temperature drops in the evening there is expansion and contraction of the cliff surface and little pieces of rock come tumbling down'. (Note that the growth of vegetation means that these rock falls are less likely to take place today in 2020s). When Gurney mentions the red cliffs (*ruddy clay*) he refers to *falls*, possibly referring both to the steepness and to the pieces that fall to the river beach. What is more, he likens the natural stage set of this site to the theatres of *London town* in the Elizabethan era, claiming that the Elizabethan playwrights (*Oriana's playwrights*) would glory in this natural theatre. This is a real place – the Wainlode Cliff recognised by the geomorphologist, Dreghorn, with its peculiarities of rock type and formation; but it is also a creation of the poet's mind, in which Gurney, the walker, has crossed time and space to elicit a richly-layered 'spirit' of England.

② Return to the Severn Way sign next to the road and ascend the steep hill up the side of Wainlode Cliff. The river is below to your right. After a metal gateway the path levels out and narrows between a hedgerow and a fence. Go through another gateway and almost immediately the path divides. Ignore the path rising to the left and take the right-hand way signposted into the woods. This path is often muddy and dark on a misty day, but when the sun is shining you catch glimpses of the River Severn below. There are a couple of wooden bridges crossing wetter parts of the path and then the way opens out into grassy pasture with the hill rising steeply behind. After about a 1.5km from the start of the walk, you cross a stile into grassy meadowland.

• Now there is a long stretch of Severn pastureland, in which you may find sheep or cattle grazing. It is a beautiful walk in all seasons, but particularly attractive in autumn when the occasional oak tree or the line of ash and willow on the field edges give rich colour to the scene. There are frequently autumn mists lying over the river so that ghostly shapes of trees or swans appear out of the gloom, and occasional glimpses of the other bank are like a floating landscape.

Gurney turned again and again to such places – his Severn Meadows – in his poetry and his letters of longing. 'The best roads in England, the finest cider, the richest blossom in the most magical orchards, beauty in security', he wrote in a letter to Marion Scott (22 March 1916) from his army training camp on Salisbury Plain, 'are not these of my county, my home?'

• After crossing four fields, about 5km (3 miles) from the start, you will come upon a gate on your left with a small lake just beyond it. This is the entrance to Rodway Lane and is signed as a restricted byway.

③ Rodway Lane used to reach right down to the riverbank where the ferry service to Ashleworth Quay operated. You can just about make out the line of the lane and if you peer through the trees at this point, Ashleworth Quay and the Boat Inn can be seen on the opposite bank.

• Imagine Gurney walking up from Gloucester through the village of Sandhurst and taking Rodway Lane down to the river to catch the ferry: *And I who had passed from the city once all Roman, / By ways of Dane, by a church named of Saxon, / Looked over to Ferry, hailed and shouted on / Till the boat came –* as he tells us in **Harper's Ferry**, a rather rambling poem written in the asylum in 1925 (for a longer extract, see Walk 19, p. 248). The city *all Roman* is Gloucester; the *Church named of Saxon* is St Lawrence at Sandhurst.

• Now go through the gate and follow Rodway Lane, first up a gentle hill and then, after a left-hand bend, up a much steeper hill to reach a gate and track to Brawn Farm and its outlying buildings (now converted to smart apartments).

④ Beyond the farm buildings the track reaches a T-junction with Sandhurst Lane. The left turn takes you up Sandhurst and Norton Hills and can be a shorter route back to Wainlode, but this walk takes the right turn, following the lane down into Sandhurst village, where old and new farm buildings jostle with more modern infilling. Pass the village green and find the church and former village school building, now a private house. St Lawrence Church was originally an outpost of St Oswald's Priory, Gloucester. The present building is partly fourteenth-century but was mainly rebuilt in 1858. Follow the road beyond the church for about 0.5km.

⑤ At a junction, take the left turn marked Twigworth. (6km/ 3.7 miles from start). Over to the left, you should catch glimpses of Barrow Hill, one of Gurney's favourite places near Ashleworth. In a few hundred metres turn left again, signed Twigworth (Gloucester is straight on) and walk through some modern housing. Pass red-brick Sandhurst House on the right and walk along the road to a sharp right bend about 1km outside the village centre. Here you will see a timber-framed farmhouse, Willington Court, and Sandhurst Hill rising behind it.

⑥ Turn left at the footpath sign at Willington Court. Follow the path slightly to the left of the main entrance to the house as it steers you around the back of the outbuildings. Do not stray too far to the right behind the outbuildings or you will reach the private Willington airstrip, still occasionally in use. Turn diagonally across the field to climb towards the base of the wood that ascends Sandhurst Hill. At the top of the field at a hedgerow, the path meets another coming in from the left. Ignore this and carry on straight up the steep, grassy and tree-lined track ahead, following the edge of the wood. As the path levels out, a wonderful view opens out to the east and north-east.

• In France, Gurney was often drawn to landscapes that bore similarities with his native Gloucestershire. A poem written in 1924 and looking back to Gurney's time stationed in Laventie, northern France, claimed that *The low ridge of Laventie / Looked like Wainlode's / Coming up from Sandhust's / Orchard-guarded roads.* (**Laventie Ridge**, RW)

⑦ Pause at the well-located seat (dedicated to Keith Lyons). Laid out before you on a clear day is the alluring line of the Cotswold Edge, ranging from Cleeve and Leckhampton through Crickley, Cooper's, Painswick Beacon and Haresfield Beacon, and maybe even to Cam Long Down above Dursley if the light is right. In front of the Edge the outliers of Chosen Hill and Robinswood Hill stand out. Bredon Hill is almost hidden behind foliage. In the foreground slightly to your right are the towers of Gloucester Cathedral. One could imagine that this was the view that inspired Gurney to write **Yesterday Lost**:

> **Yesterday Lost**
> What things I have missed today, I know very well,
> But the seeing of them each new time is miracle.
> Nothing between Bredon and Dursley has
> Any day yesterday's precise unpraiséd grace.
> The changed light, or curve changed mistily,
> Coppice, now bold cut, yesterday's mystery.
> A sense of mornings, once seen, for ever gone,
> Its own for ever: alive, dead, and my possession. (K2004)

In this poem, Gurney marvels at the changed light, or *curve changed mistily.* If you are lucky you will see the view on a clear sunlit day. At other times, the slopes are shrouded in mist and clouds so that, as Gurney explains, a coppice that on one occasion is prominently displayed, has on another mysteriously disappeared. The poem has greater poignancy because it was written in the 1920–22 period, just before Gurney entered Barnwood asylum never to have the freedom of his Cotswolds

*'Yesterday Lost' – the view from Sandhurst Hill*

again. It reads as if he is foreseeing his banishment and the need to hold the memories close (*once seen, forever gone, Its own for ever: alive, dead and my possession.*).

• From the 'Keith Lyons' seat, walk on up the grassy slope and through a gate in a hedge to find a new panorama of views to the west, as you join the track coming up from Brawn Farm. Your route takes you to the right but, before you go, look north-west to see the river flowing below you and, away in the distance, the low hills of west Gloucestershire and the distinctive profile of the Malvern Hills.

⑧ Continue to the summit trig point on Sandhurst Hill and another chance to enjoy the views, this time to the east (the Cotswolds and outliers) and less clearly to the west (west Gloucestershire hills and the Malvern backcloth).

• Walk on northwards, ignoring the right-hand path to Bishop's Norton. The path takes you through woodland and steeply downhill through pasture, passing the metal gate into the woods. Follow the narrow path alongside a fence back to the final metal gate. Notice the river below you and the opposite bank framed in thorn bushes and bramble. A relatively steep descent returns you to the tables of the Red Lion.

*Evening at Wainlode with Barrow Hill in the distance*

# Above Ashleworth

**Ashleworth** (*extract*)
I would see the gray [sic] church spired again
And then die.
Other things are weariness; I am tired of them altogether.
There I am I.

(80P)

This walk will take you around Ashleworth, a village deeply set in Gurney's Severn Meadows. With its striking tithe barn, manor house and *gray* [sic] *church*, assembled near the waterside at Ashleworth Quay, this was a favourite destination for Gurney's riverside walks. A particular attraction was the amazing view from the top of Barrow Hill. Gurney often walked and cycled in this area, heading out from Gloucester whenever he could get away, to find peace and creative inspiration. Before the war, he was a regular visitor at the Boat Inn, and was known to the barge men, fishermen and farmers who frequented the bar.

Ashleworth and the Severn Meadows became an *ideal place* to which he longed to return when in exile in France. Although he did return to walk there post-war, he was already suffering from depression and the return of his mental illness, so the incidences of such joyful walking were interspersed with expressions of melancholy. The introductory poem, **Ashleworth**, is one of many Severn Meadows poems written just before Gurney was committed to the asylum. Many of them appear in the book *80 Poems or So,* assembled by Gurney but not published until long after his death. They reveal Gurney as a restless walker, roaming through the Severn Meadows and on the Cotswold Edge, desperately seeking the remedy for his depression and the chance to *live deep there and slow*.

The walk begins by the River Severn at Ashleworth Quay, heading through the edge of the village past the tithe barn, church and big house before climbing up Barrow Hill – the hill featuring in another poem **Above Ashleworth**. The return journey takes in Foscombe Hill, with its woodland and grand Gothic house, then follows footpaths and lanes leading back to Ashleworth village and the riverside.

TOP: *The church and tithe barn at Ashleworth*
BOTTOM: *View of Barrow Hill, Ashleworth, from the lane*

## Route Details

DISTANCE/ TIME:
7.6km / 4.7 miles 3–3.5hrs

MAPS:
*OS Explorer 179, 1:25 000, Gloucester, Cheltenham & Stroud*
*OS Landranger 162, 1:50 000, Gloucester & Forest of Dean*
Ashleworth Parish Council also publishes a leaflet of walks in this area, available from the church.

START AND PARKING:
The walk starts at Ashleworth Quay next to the Boat Inn (SO 818251, GL19 4HZ) which, since the 2020 floods, is now closed (2022). It may be possible to park next to the Boat Inn or on the grass verges near the tithe barn. Otherwise, park safely elsewhere in the village.

TRACKS AND PATHS:
Field paths and lanes; occasional steep slopes and muddy gateways. There is one steep stile (Point 3), with alternative route possible.

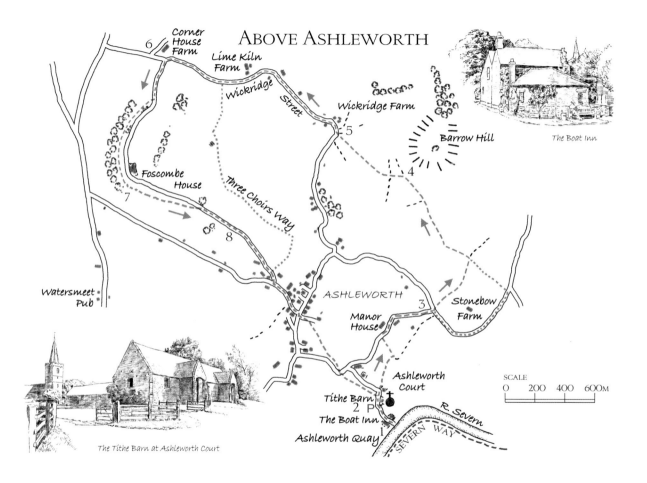

# ABOVE ASHLEWORTH

Corner House Farm

6

Lime Kiln Farm

Wickridge Street

Wickridge Farm

5

Barrow Hill

*The Boat Inn*

Foscombe House

7

Three Choirs Way

8

4

Watersmeet Pub

ASHLEWORTH

Manor House

3

Stonebow Farm

Ashleworth Court

Tithe Barn

2 P

The Boat Inn

Ashleworth Quay

1

R. Severn

SEVERN WAY

*The Tithe Barn at Ashleworth Court*

SCALE

0    200    400    600M

## THE WALK

① The route begins at Ashleworth Quay next to the Boat Inn. It is an old ferry point and coal quay, active in the eighteenth and nineteenth centuries, dealing with boats carrying coal from the Forest of Dean coalfield. When Ivor Gurney walked here, both the quay and the Boat Inn would have been busy with boats and watermen of all kinds. Until 2003, the pub landlords were descendants of the original ferryman (a man named Jelfs) who was granted rights to the crossing here in perpetuity by the future King Charles II, as payment for services ferrying him across the river after the Battle of Worcester in 1651.

• If you look straight across the river, you will see the landing point on the other bank at Rodway Lane (see Walk 18). Nowadays there is an air of peace and harmony, the river flowing smoothly, its pathway framed by willow and ash hanging over the water. On this side of the river, a pathway runs beside the water's edge through meadows, often flooded in winter, but in the late spring sporting an array of wild flowers next to the path. The Boat Inn looks like an old red-brick cottage rather than a public house, perched on a knoll a few yards from the river, with seating on the grassy bank outside. In 2020 the landlord was photographed standing waist-deep in water at his pub door and as a result the pub is still closed (2023).

*The Boat Inn at Ashleworth before the 2020 floods*

*The Boat Inn during the 2020 floods*

(*photograph © Gloucestershire Live*)

**Harper's Ferry** is the name of an American civil war battle site, and the poem below is part of a group of 'American poems' in which Gurney (then in Dartford asylum) struggled to make sense of his mental illness and changed world. He makes many connections between his own life and names that he discovered in an atlas of the American Civil War. Imagine, as Gurney did in this poem, him arriving by ferry after walking or cycling from Gloucester – it is not just a river landscape that he is describing but a place alive with the ghosts of those who have gone this way before him (Britons, Romans, Danes). The *church named of Saxon* is St Lawrence's at Sandhurst.

### Harper's Ferry

Since Roman had gone there, Dane also gone
Surely it was before the old path of Briton –
Many had gone before me, with music had
   foregone.
And I who had passed from the city once all
   Roman,
By ways of Dane, by a church named of Saxon,
Looked over to Ferry, hailed and shouted on
Till the boat came – and where Harpers had
   often ferried;
I also was rowed on Severn, Severn me bore and
   carried;
(who had writ verse at Dane Rouen, music near
   Roman Vermand,)
To see the tithe barn so noble, the church by
   time scarred;
But praise both of Divinity and the making hand.
Ashelworth,* name as musical as any in the wide
   Severn-land.

(GA 1925)

* Gurney's spelling

• Turn your back on the river and walk up the lane away from the quay.

② Almost immediately you come to the fifteenth-century tithe barn, followed by the large house, Ashleworth Court and, behind it the church of St Andrew and St Bartholomew.

• When the road bends left, take the footpath straight on, walking down the edge of the field. On the other side of the hedge is the village graveyard where former Boat Inn publicans are buried. Go through a gate ahead and turn left, walking across the field to reach the lane. Walk to the right down the lane and note Ashleworth Manor, a handsome building with an E-shaped plan-form, said to have been built in 1460 as a summer residence for Abbot Newberry of St Augustine's Abbey, Bristol. Walking on, views of Barrow Hill (78m), will begin to appear ahead, while looking east you may catch a glimpse of Norton Hill, its twin on the other bank. Both hills are remnants of the highest river terraces of the Severn. On reaching a T-junction, cross the road to access the signposted footpath by a high stile in the hedge.

## Severn buildings

'There are on the Severn many groups of buildings which linger in the memory', wrote J.H.B. Peel in 1968 in his book *Portrait of the Severn*, but 'this group certainly stands high among my favourites.' The church provides a cross-section of architecture from Norman to Victorian, although there are also some traces of the original Saxon church – a Saxon doorway blocked up, some herringbone brickwork. The house is a beautiful timber-framed, fortified Tudor dwelling and was originally thatched; and the tithe barn is massive (38m/ 125ft long and 7.6m/ 25ft wide). The structure was originally built by the canons of St Augustine's Abbey, Bristol. If you look inside, you will appreciate what a huge space this is, with its timber arches, two threshing floors and double doorways. It is now part of a working farm managed by the National Trust. The buildings are all built of the local blue Lias stone. (For further information: www.nationaltrust.org.uk/visit/gloucestershire-cotswolds/ashleworth-tithe-barn).

• If the stile seems too difficult, an alternative is to follow the Haw Bridge road for 0.5km round to the right, eventually turning left on a bridleway (rejoin the walk from **A** below).

③ From the stile, follow the footpath across three or four fields (the number varies according to temporary fences), usually containing grazing sheep, cattle or horses. You are heading towards the lower slopes of Barrow Hill with Stonebow Farm over to the right. At a small bridge over a ditch, your path crosses a bridleway contouring along the lower hill slope (**A**, alternative route joins). Join the bridleway going left and walk along this potentially muddy path. The path improves underfoot as it rises north-westward, eventually leaving behind the hedgerows and shrubs, and entering pastureland. After passing through a couple of gates (about 0.75km from the bridge), you will go through another gate into the lower corner of the field which contains Barrow Hill summit. The public footpath continues contouring at this height, but the summit is a short distance up to the right.

④ In the past it was possible to climb to the summit, with its clump of horse chestnut trees, and to enjoy a magnificent 360-degree view across Gurney's Gloucestershire, including

*'Oh does some blind fool now stand on my hill' –*
*The top of Barrow Hill with its clump of trees*

Bredon Hill to the north, the Malverns over to the north-west and the north Cotswolds to the east. Now the landowner has fenced off the summit, restricting access. However, from the public footpath you should be able to see Ashleworth nestling below you to the south – and, on a sunny day, the light glints off the towers of Gloucester Cathedral in the distance. Facing south-east and looking in the foreground, you may see Wainlode Cliff with Sandhurst and Norton Hills behind it, and further away still *the Cotswolds stand out Eastward as if never / A curve of them the hand of Time might change*, as Gurney described it in his poem **Above Ashleworth**.

## Above Ashleworth

O does some blind fool now stand on my hill
To see how Ashleworth nestles by the river?
Where eyes and heart and soul may drink their fill.

The Cotswolds stand out Eastward as if never
A curve of them the hand of time might change;
Beauty sleeps most confidently for ever.

The blind fool stands, his dull eyes free to range
Endlessly almost, and finds no word to say:
Not that the sense of wonder is too strange

Too great for speech. Naught touches him; the day
Blows its glad trumpets, breathes rich-odoured breath;
Glory after glory passes away.

(And I'm in France!) He looks and sees beneath
The clouds in steady Severn silver and grey
But dead he is and comfortable in Death.                    (K2004)

For Gurney, Barrow Hill seems to have been a special refuge, a place to which he came frequently for physical exercise and to be inspired by the scenery. Ideally **Above Ashleworth** should be read as you stand on the hilltop, but read it here below the summit.

When in France, Gurney was able to return to this beloved place in his memory. However, as the poem explains, he can no longer participate in the glory of the place (*naught touches him*) because he is exiled in France – and so, in this sense, he is blind and dumb; Gurney himself is the *blind fool*.

The poem was written in Seaton Delavel Army Command Depot, where Gurney was signed up for a Signallers Course from November 1917, but it was included in a letter to Marion Scott from the hospital ward at Brancepeth Castle on 12 March 1918, where Gurney was being treated for 'stomach problems caused by gas'.

• Walk on along the bridleway and leave the field at the south-west corner through a gateway. You may glimpse May Hill with its treed summit and, in the distance, the hills of the Forest of Dean or the Welsh mountains. Follow the hedgerow down to another gate and go into the next large field of rough pasture. The path runs first downhill but then bears to the right through (or around) some shrubs before taking a diagonal line to exit through a gate at the corner of the field. You should come out on a lane beside Wickridge Farm.

(5) Walk up the quiet country lane through the hamlet of Wickridge Street.

• The first stanza of Gurney's poem **Riez Bailleul** was written at the first place that the 2/5 Gloucesters were stationed at in France. He was only a few weeks away from England but was already hanging on to images of these Severn lanes of home as he waited to go *up to the line*. The second stanza is more difficult to follow but almost certainly refers to Will Harvey's Minsterworth house (see Walk 5) where he and Will would sit in the *firelight dancy* on the sofa and talk about music and poetry:

*'The Severn lanes and roads where the small ash leaves lie' – The lane at Wickridge Street*

**Riez Bailleul** (*extract*)
Riez Bailleul in blue tea-time
Called back the Severn lanes, the roads
Where the small ash leaves lie, and floods
Of hawthorn leaves turned with night's rime,
No Severn though nor great valley clouds.

Now in the thought comparisons
Go with those here-and-theres, and fancy
Sees on the china firelight dancy,
The wall lit where the sofa runs.
A dear light like Sirius or spring sun's.

But the trench thoughts will not go, tomorrow
Up to the line …

(K2004)

• After Wickridge Farm, pass Berrow Farmhouse on the left behind a high, evergreen hedge and, in a little while, Yew Tree Farm (formerly Scarifour Farm) and Limekiln Farm, presumably on the site of an old limekiln. In **Kilns**, Gurney wrote that, *Severn has kilns set all along her banks / Where the thin reeds grow and rushes in ranks*. Uphill from Limekiln Farm you will meet the Three Choirs Way which can be followed, as it turns down a track to the left, for a shorter return journey. Otherwise, carry on along the lane and about 1km from Wickridge Farm, you will reach Corner House Farm. A few steps beyond, turn left through iron gates into what looks like a private drive but is signposted Whitmore Way.

⑥ Walk along the drive. In the spring you will be surrounded by bluebells, wild garlic and cowslips in the hedgerows, while away to your left you will catch sight of Barrow Hill again. Your path turns half-right to avoid Foscombe House but, as you walk, you will catch glimpses of the Victorian Gothic house. Built by Thomas Fulljames (who at the time was resident architect to Gloucester Cathedral), Foscombe House is built of local blue Lias stone with a slate roof, turrets and a castellated tower. To your right, a view opens out to the south – to the small but prominent Catsbury Hill in the foreground and the higher wooded slopes of Woolridge Hill behind it. Gurney's poem **On Foscombe Hill** does not celebrate the view but focuses, as he often does, on the commonplace – in this case the small stream (*talking water*) that rises in a spring near the house and runs in an easterly direction down into Ashleworth and eventually the Severn.

## On Foscombe Hill

O exquisite
And talking water, are you not more glad
To be sole daughter and one comfort bright
Of this small hill lone-guarding its delight,
Than unconsidered to be
Some waif of Cotswold or the Malvern height?
Your name a speck of glory in so many.
You are the silver of a dreaming mound
That likes the quiet way of thought and sound,
Moists tussocks with a sunken influence,
Collects and runs one way down to farm yard
Sheds, house, standing up there by soft sward,
Green of thorn, green of sorrel and age-old heath,
Of South-West's lovely breath.

(K2004)

⑦ After passing around the back of Foscombe House, continue along the main path leading downhill. The driveway to the house is behind the hedge-line you are following. At one point, there is a sign for a footpath which crosses it to reach the Three Choirs Way. Ignore this and go straight on downhill. Eventually, your way merges with the road as it leaves the grounds of Foscombe House.

⑧ Walk down Foscombe Lane, to be joined eventually by the Three Choirs Way as it meets the road near Ashleworth Sports Club. Pass some new housing development and arrive opposite the village Post Office and Shop. To the right of the Post Office turn down a footpath into the driveway of the Doctor's house then right again down a well-marked footpath.

• Follow this path winding its way through a plantation of trees and pastureland, eventually reaching a gate onto a road (note that there are several routes across this area – it doesn't matter which you take as long as you come out on the road). Either follow the road back to the tithe barn or cross over and take a footpath leading across the field, aiming directly at the church tower. This field is often deep in crops and difficult to negotiate, but at other times it is a useful shortcut. Return to the tithe barn and so make your way back to the start at Ashleworth Quay.

## Ashleworth

I would see the gray [sic] church spired again
And then die.
Other things are weariness; I am tired of them
    altogether.
There I am I.

And nothing but the river's mournfulness,
Or clouds wet to spoil
Attempts so feeble yet brave for happiness,
Cheating Time's guile.

The clouds' peace with the water peace there mixes,
Pastures a third.
And one may read books there, Poetry fine flower,
Flame in the word.

The waggoners and bargemen and cow-drivers
I will get to know,
And talk to them, and draw peace and strength from
    them,
Live deep there and slow.

(80p)

*'I would see the gray church spired again' –*
*The path back across the fields to Ashleworth Church*

# Behold me walking:
# Longford and Twigworth

**Going Out at Dawn** (*extract*)
Yet here at five, an hour before day way* alive …
Behold me walking to where great elm trees drip
Melancholy slow streams of rainwater, on the too wet
Traveller, to pass them, watching, and then return.
Writing Sonata or Quartett with a candle dip.

(K2004)

* written as 'way' in Kavanagh 2004

Longford and Twigworth are both important sites in Ivor Gurney's life, and we know that he walked between them and along the riverside nearby at all hours of the day and night. However, because both villages are on the outskirts of Gloucester on the busy A38 road, and so much redevelopment and building has occurred in the last one hundred years, it is suggested that visits to both villages are undertaken separately from the riverside walk. Longford is the village at which Gurney stayed with his aunt in 1921–22 when he was finding life difficult in the post-war period; and, as the poem **Going out at Dawn** suggests, he used her house as a base for walking and writing. Twigworth was the home of Alfred Cheesman, his mentor from his childhood days and, from 1912, vicar at St Matthews, Twigworth. Ivor Gurney was buried in Twigworth in 1937.

The walk begins on Base Lane, Sandhurst and follows Sandhurst Lane to the northern edge of Longford parish at Broadboard Bridge. Sandhurst Lane would have been the way Gurney would have walked or cycled up from his aunt's house at Longford or from Gloucester. From the lane, the walk crosses the meadows to reach the River Severn. As Gurney wrote in a letter to Marion Scott in May 1922, such easy access to the river was 'the chief luck of living out at Longford where the neighbour meadows are matchless – such arrangement of trees, such light, and levelness never known'. The route then follows the Severn Way for 2km northward, before turning away from the river and back into Sandhurst near Gardiner's Farm. Field paths and lanes lead you back to Base Lane and its junction with the Gloucestershire Way. Twigworth lies about 1.5km to the east; however, although you can walk to it along the

Gloucestershire Way and the A38, it may be easier to visit by car.

The walk commentary will be given first and then information about the visits to Longford and Twigworth.

*'Behold me walking' – the riverside walk from Longford to Sandford*

Route Details

DISTANCE/ TIME:
5km (3.1 miles)/ 1.5–2 hours.

MAPS:
OS Explorer 179, 1:25 000, Gloucester, Cheltenham & Stroud
OS Landranger 162, 1:50 000, Gloucester & Forest of Dean

START AND PARKING:
Start on Base Lane, Sandhurst, in the wooded area next to the Gloucestershire Way sign (SO 828218). Single car parking is available here or on the grass verge at the Sandhurst Lane junction. If preferred, there is parking at Point 5 near Gardiner's Farm – then do the walk from that point. Sandhurst Lane is a small turning off the A417 inner ring road (SO 831203) in Gloucester, just before it reaches the A38.

TRACKS AND PATHS:
Lanes and grassy paths. Some sections of the Severn Way may be muddy. There are three stiles.

# LONGFORD: BEHOLD ME WALKING

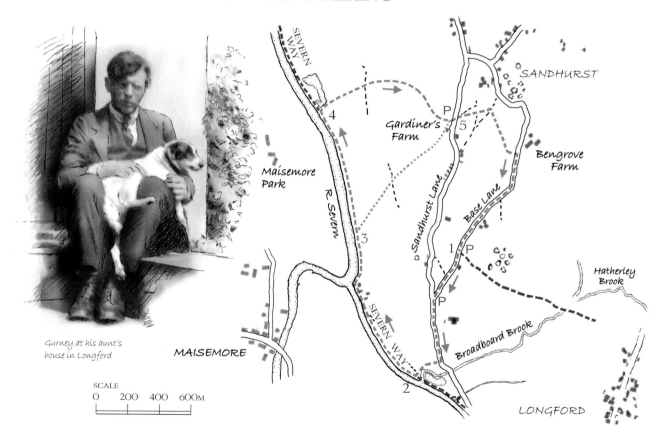

Gurney at his aunt's house in Longford

SCALE

0    200   400   600M

## THE WALK

① Join the Gloucestershire Way in Base Lane and walk down the lane, keeping left at the Sandhurst junction, heading towards Gloucester. Pass a handsome red-brick house, Abloads Court, visible through the willows on your left. Away to your right across the fields runs the River Severn. At a stile and footpath sign just before the sign for Longford, turn right. Walk over a small bridge with gate, across the meadow on an embankment, and join the Severn Way near a pylon.

**NB**: *It should be possible to walk further south into Longford Parish and use the Gloucestershire Way and Severn Way to join the riverbank. However, the path was blocked and virtually unwalkable in Spring 2023.*

Gurney would often have walked out from Gloucester on Sandhurst Lane and joined the river perhaps here or maybe a little further south. Sometimes he walked on up through Sandhurst village to reach Sandhurst Hill and Wainlode (see Walk 18).

② Look around you as you start walking north on the Severn Way. Across the river is Maisemore (Walk 3) and over to the east you should catch glimpses of the Cotswold Edge. As you walk across the meadows, read **February Dawn** written in the 1920–22 period when Gurney was staying with his aunt Marie. The joy and wonder of the first two verses are tempered by the suicidal thoughts revealed in the last verse, and Gurney's recognition that only his Gloucestershire places can save him.

*'The sight of earth and rooks made passions rise' –*
*Severn meadow fields near Longford*

**February Dawn** (*extract*)

Rooks flew across the sky, bright February watched
Their steady course straight on, like an etcher's line
  scratched.
The dark brown or tawny earth breathed incense up,
I guessed there were hidden daisies, hoped the first
  buttercup.

The tunes of all the county, old-fashioned and my own
Wilful, wanton, careless, thronged in my mind, alone,
The sight of earth and rooks made passion rise in my
  blood.
Far gleamed Cotswold. Near ran Severn. A God's mood.

Save that I knew no high things would amaze day-fall
I had prayed heaven to kill me at the most to fulfil
My dreams for ever. But looked on to a west bright at five,
Scarred by rooks in purpose; and the late trees in strife.

(K2004)

• A low industrial-looking building with a tall chimney is ahead at the end of the meadow. This is Ronson Reclaim, seen from the Maisemore Walk (3) and you will have to walk through the grounds past a boat slipway. You are at Upper Parting where the Severn divides into two streams around Alney Island. After leaving the reclamation plant, cross another field. Over to your left is Maisemore, with Spring Hill appearing up behind it, while Sandhurst Hill is visible over to the right. Both hills are remnants of the 35–45m terraces of the River Severn and are climbed in Walks 3 and 18 respectively.

• At the next gate, there are two footpath possibilities – straight on or diagonally right.

③ Go straight ahead on the main Severn Way (note that the right-hand path could be a shortcut back to Sandhurst across fields, if needed). A pleasant riverside walk through two more

*Spring Hill, Maisemore appearing on the opposite bank (where Gurney's grandfather worked as gardener)*

fields provides an open landscape with fine views to Sandhurst Hill and to the Cotswold Edge. Willow trees line the riverbank, and through them you should catch sight of Maisemore Park and House. At a rather derelict-looking gate, a sign survives with 'private elver fishing'. Perhaps this is one of the locations where Gurney found the elver fishermen *stringing their lights 'long Severn like a wet fair* (**Rainy Midnight**, Walk 6).

④ Turn right at the gate to walk alongside a backwater flood pond, with plenty of shrubby vegetation and birdlife. As you walk along the grassy, mossy path alongside the pond and out into a wide field, it is hard to imagine that most years this is all underwater in January/ February. Cross the field in a straight line from the path, walk alongside a ditch and hedge, cross a stile and soon you will pass a low dwelling and a yard with a static caravan.

• The path turns into a wide track which eventually reaches Sandhurst Lane at Gardiner's Farm (parking is possible here).

⑤ Cross the lane and look up the road to the left for footpath signs pointing across the fields. Take the path following the fence across the field, ignoring a cross-path about halfway down. At the end of the fence are two paths – take the one

*'Private Elver Fishing' – sign on the riverside walk*

to the right over a stile and alongside a field boundary, heading for Bengrove Farm on the immediate horizon. Near the end of the field boundary the path turns sharp left and takes you almost immediately out onto the road.

• Ahead of you, notice the Cotswold Edge and Cooper's Hill with its crowning woodland. You are now on Base Lane again and can follow this back to the starting point where the Gloucestershire Way comes in from the east.

• It is possible to walk down the Gloucestershire Way to the main A38 at Longford Bridge and then to walk up the main road for 0.5km to visit Twigworth Church. However, the A38 experience is not recommended and you will have to retrace your steps afterwards.

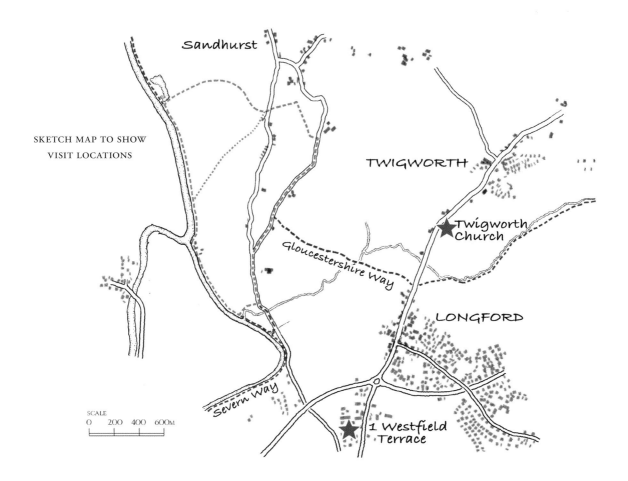

SKETCH MAP TO SHOW
VISIT LOCATIONS

Sandhurst

TWIGWORTH

★ Twigworth
Church

Gloucestershire Way

LONGFORD

Severn Way

★ 1 Westfield
Terrace

SCALE

0   200  400  600M

## Longford and Twigworth

Both villages are on the northern edge of Gloucester and can be reached by bus or, more easily, by car. These visits will help you appreciate the context of Gurney's life in the 1919–22 period.

For Longford, park in Westfield Terrace (SO 836201), a small turning just off the A38 about 1.5km from the centre of Gloucester. Longford is the village where Gurney stayed with his aunt Marie in 1921–22 when he was finding it difficult to deal with his mental instability in the post-war period. Her house, 1 Westfield Terrace, is the first of the Victorian terraced houses on the right, although a newer residential development occupies the corner plot on the A38. The house is still in private ownership, with a blue Ivor Gurney commemorative plaque on the wall. The steps up to the front door are still visible, as seen in a photograph of 1921, which shows Gurney and his aunt's dog.

Aunt Marie was the widow of Gurney's uncle Guy, one of the six brothers of Ivor Gurney's father. She helped Gurney in this post-war period, providing a roof over his head, food, a place to write and apparently long-suffering tolerance: 'My

LEFT: *Aunt Marie's house, 1 Westfield Terrace, Longford*

BELOW: *Archive photo of Gurney sitting on the steps at his aunt's house (© IG Trust)*

aunt who lives here – indeed owns the house – is a dear and spoils me', he told Marion Scott (letter of 26 April 1921). Gurney could not have been an easy lodger. He did not eat at normal hours, he frequently went off walking for a whole day and often the night too, sleeping under hedges or coming back at dawn and raiding the larder like a naughty schoolboy. At other times he would sit up all night composing music and poetry, only to leave the house as dawn rose over the meadows. In a letter written from his aunt's house to Edward Marsh in early 1922, Gurney explains that, 'this morning I have been walking reading the Bohn *Iliad*, shortly after dawn – a good translation and a fitting majestic sunrise. It is the noblest stuff and went with thunder clouds and a streaked east or north-east.'

### Longford Dawns

Of course not all the watchers of the dawn
See Severn mists like forced-march mists withdrawn:
London has darkness changing into light
With just one quarter hour of any weight.

Casual and common is the wonder grown –
Time's duty to lift light's curtain up and down.
But here Time is caught up clear in Eternity,
And draws as breathless life as you or me.

(K2004)

There are several poems Gurney wrote in the 1918–24 period which refer to Severn dawns and may reflect his stay in Longford. **Going Out at Dawn** is mentioned at the head of this walk, and there is also **Spring Dawn** and **February Dawn**. In the poem **Longford Dawns**, Gurney compares London dawns unfavourably with those he has experienced walking out from Longford into Severn mists.

After viewing the house, walk on down the road past a new development called Lime Close (off to the left) and some 1960s infilling on Westfield Terrace. At the end of the road, there is a rather scruffy-looking field, usually occupied by horses, and beyond it a run-down farm building, a railway line and eventually the meadows alongside the Severn. It is difficult to imagine that this was the route across the meadows with great elm trees dripping, that Gurney took to reach Sandford

Lane and the river, and that it inspired him to return and write a sonata by candlelight! We cannot walk this way now.

Twigworth Church is also on the A38 and can be visited by continuing along the A38 northwards for about 1.5km beyond the Westfield Terrace turning. There is a layby for parking (SO 812418), just after a garage and opposite the church. Cross over the road to visit the church and graveyard and Gurney's gravestone.

The Church of St Matthew, Twigworth, was built by the architect Thomas Fulljames in 1842–44 (see Walk 19, Ashleworth) and consecrated in 1844. Alfred Cheesman, Gurney's godfather, mentor and friend, was vicar here from 1912 until his death in 1941.

Gurney died in Dartford asylum in December 1937 and his body was brought back to Twigworth to be buried. It must have been a moving occasion as Gurney was finally returned to the soil of the Gloucestershire he loved. Alfred Cheesman took the funeral service and Herbert Howells, his musician colleague and former walking companion, played the music. The mourners included Marion Scott, Will Harvey, John Haines, Emily Hunt and the Chapman family from High

Wycombe. Gurney's mother, Florence, was ill and so, sadly, was denied the chance to be at her son's funeral. Marion Scott commented that 'there is something tranquillising now in the thought of him lying at peace in Twigworth churchyard and I believe that all the details of his funeral were such as he would have approved.' (Letter to Gerald Finzi of 4 January 1938, in the Gloucester Archives).

*Twigworth Church and Rectory*

If you walk on round the churchyard on a sunny day, it is still possible to raise your eyes to Chosen Hill (see Walk 4) and the Cotswold Edge near Cooper's Hill (see Walk 12) above you. However, in the foreground now, you will notice large areas of housing development filling Gurney's Severn Meadows. The plans aroused much concern from the local people and local councils, partly because of the visual changes and increased traffic, and partly because of flooding risk. After an appeal, objections were overruled by the Government in 2017, so the meadows will change character completely here.

In a surprisingly prophetic poem of this 1920–22 period, **The Bargain**, Gurney tells a story of a parcel of riverside land, purchased by a Danish settler for a few grains of wheat. Through the ages that followed, Waltheof's Field was quarried for clay to make bricks, flooded by the river, used as a tip for the town's rubbish and eventually turned into building land for residential villas. Maybe this should have been read at the Planning Appeal!

**The Bargain** (*extract*)
The last island of clay vanished, and lonelier moods
Possessed the pit now, mere and most melancholy.
Town Council had no poetry and decided ceremoniously
That the rubbish there (surely) as elsewhere might be
  voided.
(Five pounds a year and two grains of wheat was cheap,)
Waltheof's Field will become a rubbish heap,
Villas will stand there and look polite – with folk polite
Where sedges stood for the wind's play and poet-delight,
But Severn will be sorry and it can never be right.

(K2004)

The Gloucestershire Way was impassable and blocked with builders' waste in 2021 but is due to be reinstated in a corridor-like swathe of land between new houses.

Walk round the back of the church and you will find the Old Rectory, now a private house but once the home of Alfred Cheesman. Cheesman welcomed Gurney back after his return to Gloucestershire in 1918 and tried to help him

*'villas will stand there' – the advance of housing on the
Severn Meadows at Twigworth*

cope with his many problems in this period. We know that
Gurney visited him at the vicarage and stayed with him on
more than one occasion. **Twigworth Vicarage** was written
in August 1918 when Gurney was at the Middlesex War
Hospital, St Albans. It is dedicated to Alfred Cheesman and
reveals how important the whole of this Severnside area
was to Gurney.

### Twigworth Vicarage

Wakened by birds and sun, laughter of the wind,
A man might see all heart's desire by raising
His pillowed sleepy head (still apt for lazing
And drowsy thought) – but then a green most kind
Waved welcome, and the rifted sky behind
Showed blue, whereon cloud-ships full-sailed went racing
Man to delight and set his heart on praising
The maker of all things, bountiful-hearted, kind.

May Hill, the half-revealéd tree-clad thing,
Maisemore's delightful ridge, where Severn flowing
Nourished a wealth of lovely wild things blowing
Sweet as the air – Wainlodes and Ashleworth
To northward showed, a land where a great king
Might sit to receive homage from the whole earth.

(S&S/ WE)

The church was closed in 2019, has been deconsecrated,
and in 2022 it was up for sale. The churchyard remains open
and is maintained by the Seven Towers Benefice of a group

of local churches. You can still enter the garden of remembrance and visit the gravestone. It can be a moving experience to stand quietly by the grave next to the empty church (with iron fencing round it in 2022) and read the epithet –'Ivor Gurney, Composer and Poet of Severn and Somme'. *Severn and Somme* was the title Gurney gave to his first published book of poetry (1917), the preface to which explained that, 'Most of the book is concerned with a person named Myself, and the rest with my county, Gloucester, that whether I die or live stays always with me – being in itself so beautiful, so full of memories; whose people are so good to be friends with, so easy-going and frank.'

## Poem for End (*extract*)

So the last poem is laid flat in its place,
And Crickley with Crucifix Corner leaves from my face
Elizabethans and night-working thoughts – of such grace.

And all the dawns that set my thoughts new to making:
Or Crickley dusk that the beech leaves stirred to shaking
Are put aside – there is a book ended; heart aching.

This is an extract from **Poem for End**, the final piece in a book of poems prepared by Gurney in the asylum in 1924, and called by him *Rewards of Wonder*. Despite Marion Scott's attempts during Gurney's lifetime, *Rewards of Wonder* wasn't published until 2000.

～

# REFERENCES & SOURCES

The bulk of Ivor Gurney's music and literary manuscripts, including letters, notebooks and photographs are held at the Gloucestershire Archives as the Ivor Gurney Collection. The Trustees of The Ivor Gurney Estate (also known as The Ivor Gurney Trust) are the owners of the 'Ivor Gurney Collection' and are the copyright holder of all the material (www.ivorgurneytrust.org/copyright/). Thanks to the IG Trust for use of material in this book.

## THE GLOUCESTERSHIRE ARCHIVES

Clarence Row, Alvin Street, Gloucester, GL1 3DW
Tel: 01452 425295  Email: archives@gloucestershire.gov.uk
Website: www.gloucestershire.gov.uk/archives/article/107385/Our-collections

## SOURCES AND LOCATIONS OF POEMS

The poems found in this book are used by permission of The Ivor Gurney Trust. Many of the poems selected have also been published in collections of Ivor Gurney's poetry, and these are listed below with identifying initials for the most accessible publications. A list of poems used in this book is provided and the identifying initials used to show where readers can find each one.

*Severn and Somme*, Sidgwick and Jackson, 1917

*War's Embers*, Sidgwick and Jackson, 1919

*Poems by Ivor Gurney; Principally selected from unpublished manuscripts,* with a memoir by Edmund Blunden, Hutchinson, 1954

*Poems of Ivor Gurney, 1890–1937,* with an introduction by Edmund Blunden and a Bibliographic Note by Leonard Clark, Chatto & Windus, 1973

*Collected Poems of Ivor Gurney*, chosen, edited and with an Introduction by P.J. Kavanagh, Oxford University Press, 1982

*Ivor Gurney: Severn and Somme and War's Embers*, Critical Edition, ed. R.K.R. Thornton, Carcanet Press, 1987  [**S&S/ WE**]

*Ivor Gurney: Selected Poems*, selected and introduced by P.J. Kavanagh, Oxford University Press, 1990

*Ivor Gurney: Best Poems and The Book of Five Makings*, ed. R.K.R. Thornton and George Walter, Carcanet Press, 1997

*Ivor Gurney: 80 Poems or So*, eds. George Walter and R.K.R. Thornton, Carcanet, 1997  [**80P**]

*Ivor Gurney: Rewards of Wonder*, George Walter, Carcanet Press, 2000  [**RW**]

*Ivor Gurney: Collected Poems*, ed. P.J. Kavanagh, Carcanet Press, 2004 [K2004]

*Ivor Gurney; The Complete Poetical Works, Volume 1 March 1907–December 1918*, ed. P. Lancaster and T. Kendall, Oxford University Press, 2020 [CPW]

Some of the poems used have not been published yet (2023) and may be found in the Ivor Gurney Collection, at Gloucester Archives (abbreviation GA used). These are: **Culpeper, Llanthony, Ship Over Meadows, Petersburg, The Salt Box, First Framilode, March, Wilderness, Crickley Cliffs, The Little Way, Harper's Ferry, The Abbey, Quietude** [Quietitude], **Dawn.**

TABLE OF IVOR GURNEY'S POEMS FOUND IN THIS BOOK (102) (K2004 is given as the reference even if the poem also appears elsewhere)

| Name of Poem | Page | Where found |
|---|---|---|
| Above Ashleworth | 251 | K2004 |
| Above the Villa | 158 | GA |
| After-Glow | 76 | K2004 |
| April – Dull Afternoon | 42 | K2004 |
| April Mist | 87 | 80P |
| Ashleworth | 244, 255 | 80P |
| Brave Carpets | 41 | 80P |
| Brimscombe | 125, 134 | K2004 |

| | | |
|---|---|---|
| By Severn | 233, 238 | K2004 |
| Changes | 47 | K2004 |
| Cotswold | 195, 200 | RW |
| Cotswold Slopes | 113, 118 | RW |
| Cotswold Ways | 130 | K2004 |
| Crickley Cliffs | 173 | GA |
| Crickley Hill | 165 | K2004 |
| Crucifix Corner | 231 | K2004 |
| Culpeper | xvii | GA |
| Dawn | 138, 146 | GA |
| Dayboys and Choristers | 21 | S&S/ WE |
| Deerhurst Church | 226 | RW |
| Down Commercial Road | 24, 29 | S&S/ WE |
| Dream | 24 | K2004 |
| East Wind | 172 | K2004 |
| February Dawn | 260 | K2004 |
| First Framilode | 89 | GA |
| Framilode the Queen | 92 | CPW |
| Friendly are Meadows | 228 | RW |
| Gloucester | 71 | K2004 |
| Going Out at Dawn | 256 | K2004 |
| Harper's Ferry | 248 | GA |
| Heights | 150 | CPW |

| | | |
|---|---|---|
| Hell's Prayer | 181 | K2004 |
| *How strange it was to hear under the guns* (untitled) | 108 | CPW |
| June-to-Come | 66, 69 | S&S/ WE |
| Late September | 203 | 80P |
| Leckhampton Chimney has Fallen Down | 185 | K2004 |
| Llanthony | 35 | GA |
| Longford Dawns | 264 | K2004 |
| Longney | 82 | 80P |
| Maisemore | 48 | S&S/ WE |
| March | 79, 84 | GA |
| Midnight | 175 | 80P |
| Near Midsummer | 94 | S&S/ WE |
| October | 123 | RW |
| Old Tavern Folk | 32 | K2004 |
| Old Times | 129 | K2004 |
| Old Thought | 188 | K2004 |
| On Foscombe Hill | 254 | K2004 |
| Pain | 29 | K2004 |
| Passionate Earth | 102 | CPW |
| Petersburg | 36, 39 | GA |
| Pilgrimage | 217 | CPW |

| | | |
|---|---|---|
| Poem for End | 269 | K2004 |
| Possessions | 157 | RW |
| Queen of Cotswold | 142 | RW |
| Quietitude | 170 | GA |
| Rainy Midnight | 83 | K2004 |
| Requiem | 28 | K2004 |
| Riez Bailleul | 253 | K2004 |
| Roads | 106 | K2004 |
| Saturday's Comings | 12 | K2004 |
| Ship Over Meadows | 18 | GA |
| Sheer Falls of Green Slope | 101 | RW |
| Strange Service | 219 | K2004 |
| That Centre of Old | vii, 152 | K2004 |
| The Abbey | 162 | RW |
| The Bargain | 266 | K2004 |
| The Bridge | 23 | K2004 |
| The Change | 60 | K2004 |
| The Coppice | 179 | K2004 |
| The County's Bastion | 206, 209 | K2004 |
| The Dursley Schoolmaster | 108 | 80P |
| The Estaminet | 46 | S&S/ WE |
| The First Violets | 11 | BP |
| The High Hills | 137 | K2004 |

| | | |
|---|---|---|
| The Little Way | 182, 189 | GA |
| The Lock Keeper | 99 | S&S/ WE |
| The Nightingales | 96 | K2004 |
| The Not-Returning | 216 | K2004 |
| The Old City | 3, 4 | K2004 |
| The Poet Walking | 1 | K2004 |
| The Poplar | 133 | K2004 |
| There was Such Beauty | 50, 56 | K2004 |
| The Salt Box | 45 | GA |
| The Soaking | 201 | RW |
| The Touchstone – watching Malvern | 213 | K2004 |
| The Unfamiliar Camp | 111 | BP |
| Time and the Soldier | 120 | K2004 |
| Time to Come | 13 | K2004 |
| To His Love | 77 | K2004 |
| Trees | 163 | S&S/ WE |
| Twigworth Vicarage | 267 | S&S/ WE |
| Up There | 176 | K2004 |
| Walking Song | 144 | K2004 |
| Water Colours | 231 | K2004 |
| When from the Curve | 58 | K2004 |
| When the Body Might Free | 186 | K2004 |

| | | |
|---|---|---|
| While I Write | xiv | K2004 |
| Wilderness | 161 | GA |
| Yesterday Lost | 242 | K2004 |
| Ypres-Minsterworth | 73 | K2004 |

**IVOR GURNEY'S ESSAYS**

Short extracts from three essays, all found in the Gloucestershuire Archives, are used in this book and are also available in the following published versions:

In Introduction: *On Earth* – also published in the *Ivor Gurney Society Journal*, No. 15, 158–160, 2009 (*see p. xix*)
In Part 2: *On Sailing* – also published in *Archipelago 3*, Clutag Press, 2009 (*see pp. 63 & 65*)
In Part 3: *The Springs of Music* – also published in *Musical Quarterly*, Vol. 8 No. 3, pp. 319–22, 1922 (*see p. 122*)

**IVOR GURNEY'S LETTERS**

Extracts from Ivor Gurney's letters have been used to illuminate many walks, with permission from the Ivor Gurney Trust. A good place to read Gurney's letters is in: *Ivor Gurney; Collected Letters*, ed. R.K.R. Thornton, Carcanet Press, 1991

# FURTHER READING

Barnes, A.F. (ed.), *The Story of the 2/5 Battalion, Gloucestershire Regiment 1914–18 Gloucester*, Crypt House Press, 1930

Beckinsale, R.P., *Companion into Gloucestershire*, Methuen, 1948

Bick, D., *Old Leckhampton – Quarries, Railways, Riots, Devil's Chimney*, Runpast Publishing, 1993

Bingham, J., *The Cotswolds: a Cultural History*, Signal Books, 2009

Blevins, P., 'New Perspectives on Ivor Gurney's Illness', *The Ivor Gurney Society Journal*, Vol. 6, 29–58, 2000

—, *Ivor Gurney and Marion Scott*, Boydell Press, 2008

Boden, A., *F.W. Harvey: Soldier, Poet*, Alan Sutton Publishing, 1988

Boden, A. and Thornton, R.K.R., *F.W. Harvey: Selected Poems*, Douglas McLean, 1983

Burrow, E.J., *The Ancient Entrenchments and Camps of Gloucestershire*, Ed J. Burrow and Co Ltd., 1924

Coppin, J., *Forest Vale and High Blue Hill*, Cassell, 1991

Cranham Local Historical Society, *Cranham: The History of a Cotswold Village*, The MPG Book Group, 2005

Darvill, T., *Prehistoric Gloucestershire*, Amberley Publishing, 1987

Dixon, P.W., 'A Neolithic and Iron Age site on a hilltop in southern England, Crickley Hill, Gloucestershire', *Scientific American*, Vol. 241(5), pp. 142–50, 1979

Dreghorn, W., *Geology Explained in the Severn Vale and Cotswolds*, David and Charles, 1967 (republished by Fineleaf Editions, 2005)

Gloucester Cathedral, *Stained Glass Windows by Tom Denny* (Paperback), Dean & Chapter of Gloucester Cathedral, 2016

Harding, G., 'High Brotheridge', *Glevensis*, Issue 11, 1978

Harvey, F.W., *A Gloucestershire Lad at Home and Abroad*, Sidgewick and Jackson, 1916

Hayman, R., *Severn*, Logaston Press, 2012

Hodgson, A., *The Poetry of Clare, Hopkins, Thomas, and Gurney*, Palgrave Macmillan, 2019

Hurd, M., *The Ordeal of Ivor Gurney 1890–1937*, Oxford University Press, 1978

—, *Letters of Gerald Finzi and Howard Ferguson*, Boydell & Brewer, 2001

Kennedy, K., *Dweller in Shadows; a life of Ivor Gurney*, Princeton University Press, 2021

Kirby, D., *The Story of Gloucester*, Sutton Publishing, 2007

Lucas, J., *Ivor Gurney (Writers and their Work)*, Northcote House Publishers, 2001

Massingham, H., *Cotswold Country: the Face of Britain*, Batsford, 1937

Mills, C., *Slow Cotswolds*, Bradt Guides, 2011

Peel, J.H.B., *Portrait of the Severn*, Robert Hale Ltd, 1968

Rawling, E., *Ivor Gurney's Gloucestershire: Exploring Poetry and Place*, The History Press, 2011

—, 'Putting Gurney in his Place', *The Ivor Gurney Society Journal*, Vol. 16, 7–30, 2010

Thornton R.K.R. (ed.), *Ivor Gurney; Collected Letters*, MidNAG/Carcanet, 1991

Verey, D. and Brookes, A., *Gloucestershire 1: The Cotswolds*, Pevsner Architectural Guides: Buildings of England, Yale University Press, 2000


**ALSO:**

BBC Four TV programme, April 4, 2014, 'Ivor Gurney; the poet who loved the war', presented by Professor Tim Kendall, produced by Clive Flowers for the BBC (www.bbc.co.uk/programmes/b03zq4cb)

BBC Radio Gloucestershire programme on World War One at Home: Twigworth, Gloucestershire: Poet Ivor Gurney's Inspiration (www.bbc.co.uk/sounds/play/p01rnyw2)

# INDEX

*Page numbers in **bold Roman** denote main place entries; page numbers in **bold italics** denote images*